CONTENTS

... has a true journalist's instinct for ...rdistani picnickers in the river meadows ...on, pub thugs in the badlands of the lower Thames, other ...ath pilgrims he rubs up against along the way. He also demonstrates ...nose for a juicy tale, from a pre-Raphaelite ménage-à-trois at Kelmscott Manor to the discreet nookie column in the Marlow Free Press. Chesshyre's journey is rich in history and thick with characters, fables and happenstance – a highly readable and entertaining saunter along England's iconic river.'

Christopher Somerville, author of *Britain's Best Walks*

'Chesshyre's book stands out from other accounts of walking the Thames Path in its contemporary (post-Brexit, pre-Trump) immediacy. A portrait of England and the English in our time, it is peppered with fascinating historical and literary markers. It's also a usefully opinionated guide to watering-holes and B&Bs from the sleepy Cotswold villages to the dystopian edgelands of the estuary.'

Christina Hardyment, author of *Writing the Thames*

'Beautifully written and exquisite in observation, Tom Chesshyre's latest book, From Source to Sea *is a fitting tribute to the mighty Thames that flows like a golden thread through the history of Britain.'*

Harry Bucknall, author of *Like a Tramp, Like a Pilgrim*

PRAISE FOR *TICKET TO RIDE*

'Trains, dry wit, evocative descriptions, fascinating people and more trains – what's not to like?'

Christian Wolmar

'This is an engaging, enjoyable and warm-hearted book that will appeal as much to general readers as to lovers of trains'

Simon Bradley

'Like mi... ...s gentle and awesome, ...hn Gimlette

**TOM
CHESSHYRE**

FROM
SOURCE
TO SEA

Notes from a
215-MILE WALK
along the
RIVER THAMES

summersdale

FROM SOURCE TO SEA

An Hachette UK Company
www.hachette.co.uk

Summersdale Publishers Ltd
Part of Octopus Publishing Group Limited
Carmelite House
50 Victoria Embankment
LONDON
EC4Y 0DZ
UK

www.summersdale.com

Printed and bound by CPI Group (UK) Ltd, Croydon, CR0 4YY

ISBN: 978-1-78685-286-1

Substantial discounts on bulk quantities of Summersdale books are available to corporations, professional associations and other organisations. For details contact general enquiries: telephone: +44 (0) 1243 771107 or email: enquiries@summersdale.com.

For Robert and Christine

ABOUT THE AUTHOR

Tom Chesshyre is staff travel writer on *The Times* and the author of *How Low Can You Go?: Round Europe for 1p Each Way (Plus Tax)*, *To Hull and Back: On Holiday in Unsung Britain*, *Tales from the Fast Trains: Europe at 186 Mph*, *Ticket to Ride: Around the World on 49 Unusual Train Journeys*, *A Tourist in the Arab Spring* and *Gatecrashing Paradise: Misadventures in the Real Maldives*. He lives in Mortlake in London.

www.tomchesshyre.co.uk

Sweet Thames, run softly, till I end my song.
Edmund Spenser, 'Prothalamion'

We must build a kind of United States of Europe.
Winston Churchill, 1946

PREFACE

I was born in Hammersmith in west London less than a mile from the Thames. I grew up in East Sheen in south-west London within a mile of its banks. My first flat was in Oval in central London, a few hundred metres from the river. My current home is in Mortlake in south-west London, a minute's stroll from the towpath. I have worked all of my adult life by the river in east and south-east London. One way or another the Thames means a lot to me. I run along it. I walk along it. I take boats on it. I drink with friends by it. I love it. I am drawn to it. I always have been.

Then something happened. One day I noticed a bric-a-brac market at a community centre by my local library, a short distance from the river (naturally). I went inside and the first object that caught my eye, propped against a trestle table as if waiting for me, was a beautiful map of the River Thames. It was a reproduction of an 1834 drawing by the renowned map-maker William Tombleson, showing the river twisting from its source near Cirencester to the North Sea.

I bought this map, and an idea began to form.

This book is the result.

CHAPTER ONE

THAMES HEAD, GLOUCESTERSHIRE

A FIELD WITH NO WATER

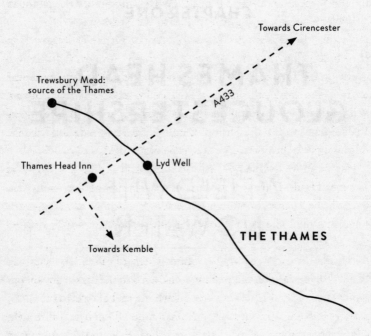

Towards Cirencester

Trewsbury Mead:
source of the Thames

A433

Thames Head Inn

Lyd Well

Towards Kemble

THE THAMES

Beyond a row of oaks in a thistle-strewn field in Gloucestershire stands a stone by an ancient ash. So this is where the Thames begins. I take a look about. There is very little sign of river. To be precise, there is no water whatsoever. I read an inscription on the stone: *The Conservators of the river Thames 1857–1974. This stone was placed here to mark the source of the river Thames.* I would appear to be in the right place. Somewhere beneath my feet, presuming this is not an elaborate hoax, is a spring that trickles to the North Sea.

No one else is around. I have the start of England's longest river (215 miles) all to myself. It is a pleasant sunny July day and there is a gentle breeze. I rest against the stone and sunbathe. I'm in no particular hurry. Wind rustles in the leaves. Dandelion pollen swirls in the air. A bumblebee lands on my hand (but does not sting). A bird makes a whooping sound. The horn of a train echoes and a distant metallic shimmer passes behind trees at the edge of the field.

This meadow is called Trewsbury Mead and is also referred to as 'Thames Head'. During wetter periods water rises at this spot, I am assured: the Thames bubbles up. It is too dry for that now; hence the somewhat unusual sensation of being at the source of a river with no river to see.

I inspect the trunk of the ash to check whether I can locate the initials 'T. H.', Thames Head, said to have been carved in the bark many moons ago (I can't). Then I retrace my steps down the trail of oaks to the A433, part of the Fosse Way, the ancient Roman route. From here, I turn right and a short distance along, past a dead hedgehog and a scattering of squashed shotgun cartridges, I reach the Thames Head Inn.

This is where I'm spending the night, ahead of taking to the Thames Path proper tomorrow morning. I order a drink and take a seat by a sculpture of Old Father Thames on a mantelpiece. The most famous representation of this mythical figure used to be found at Trewsbury Mead but that version was vandalised so often it was moved for safety to a lock near Lechlade. I'll be going to Lechlade in two days' time.

Meg, the assistant trainee manager at the Thames Head Inn, comes over to chat. She has blonde hair and heavy black eyeliner. She's from Cirencester, about three miles away, and has been working at the pub for a couple of years. 'Some people do the whole thing,' she says. By 'whole thing' she is referring to walking the distance of the Thames to the sea. 'They do it as a hobby; over a few years mostly.'

My intention is to complete this feat in 21 days.

Meg shows me a map on a wall with the route to the stone at Trewsbury Mead. 'People come back and say, "there's no water there", but in the winter you sometimes can't even get to the source because it's so flooded.'

This local map is hung next to another that depicts the full length of the river, a print based on the one by William Tombleson that partly inspired my Thames walk. I take this to be a good omen and run my eyes over the stop-offs to come: Cricklade, Lechlade, Oxford, Abingdon, Wallingford, Reading, Henley, Marlow, Maidenhead, Windsor, Runnymede, Staines, Teddington (where the river turns tidal), Twickenham, Richmond, Kew, Mortlake (my home), Chelsea, Westminster, Southwark, Rotherhithe, Greenwich, Woolwich, Gravesend, Cliffe, Hoo, the Isle of Grain… and then, at last, the sea.

So many places, such a long way.

I am aware, of course, that I am not exactly the first to follow this route. It is possible to fill shelves with illuminating and learned books about the river. On top of all the guides and histories are countless novels and poems as well as famous utterances. The Thames seems to encourage a flow of words, with so many luminaries having mused on what the river means to the land through which it winds. Winston Churchill once said the Thames offers a 'golden thread of our nation's history', while the early-twentieth-century politician John Burns commented especially memorably that the river represents 'liquid history'.

A tremendous amount has happened on and beside the river – from invasions by Romans and Vikings to the signing of the Magna

Carta, the births (and deaths) of kings and queens, the execution of traitors, the import of exotic spices and goods from faraway lands, the embarkation to distant, unknown shores. And, not to forget, London has happened by the River Thames: the world's first metropolis grew up by its banks.

On the terrace of the Thames Head Inn the sense of anticipation is tantalising. I am treating myself to a journey that has long lingered in the back of my mind. I am about to indulge in a dream: to embrace an icon of Englishness in the plum days of July and August, with the sun shining and weather warm (at least I hope so).

I do not, however, intend to describe the trip ahead in a vacuum.

I am setting forth on a very particular summer.

Since I planned this walk, Britain has changed. Brexit, the yet to be implemented outcome of a decision in a referendum to leave the European Union, has become a fact of life. There are to be many spin-off consequences and the result of the referendum, one month old, hangs in the air.

The country has altered. Fears about waves of immigrants, unhappiness with Brussels bureaucrats and a 'metropolitan elite' perceived to be in charge at Westminster, plus a much-repeated desire for 'the people' to 'take back control', have come together. The result? A slender majority (52 per cent) in favour of leaving Europe.

Already, a prime minister has stepped aside. And Britain is coming to terms with a new reality. What will happen to the economy? What will happen to the pound? How quickly will Britain leave the EU? Will immigration stop? Will Scotland want to leave the UK? What happens to the border of Northern Ireland? What about inflation? What about a second referendum? What about trade agreements? What about a rise of the far right? What about an increase in hate crime? What about the security of nations in Europe now that post-war togetherness seems about to unravel? What about… just about everything?

It is into this summer of Brexit that I stride.

I am about to follow a trail that has offered reassurance and pleasure to many before me – writers, poets, politicians, amblers of all descriptions – at a time of great unease. I am looking forward to taking to the eternal Thames, if you like: the river that has seen everything and will always be there, no matter what goes on in the wider world. The turmoil of the early twenty-first century will, I hope, fade away, and the simplicity of putting one foot in front of the other will come to the fore, along a river so full of stories. A river that is so loved.

Meg delivers an enormous, delicious steak-and-kidney pie. I eat this enormous, delicious pie while reading the *Wilts and Gloucestershire Standard*. Fire crews have been called after 'a large number of hay bales being transported by a lorry burst into flames'. No one seems quite sure how the bales were set alight. Meanwhile, a swarm of bees has been removed from a war memorial by a church in Cirencester. A local man is quoted: 'You don't see that every day.' Flaming bales of hay, swarms of bees in war memorials: big matters are happening in the world; small and somewhat peculiar matters too.

I go to my little room by a courtyard at the back of the Thames Head Inn to get an early night.

In the morning a river awaits.

CHAPTER TWO

THAMES HEAD, GLOUCESTERSHIRE, TO CRICKLADE, WILTSHIRE

QUICKSAND AND 'A RASCALLY PLACE'

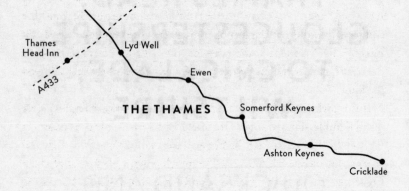

Thames
Head Inn

A433

Lyd Well

Ewen

THE THAMES

Somerford Keynes

Ashton Keynes

Cricklade

When committing to walking 215 miles – 184 of which are on the official Thames Path that runs to the Thames Barrier in east London – there are a few considerations.

The first is quite straightforward: will I be able to walk so far? Earlier in the year I hurt my back and needed to see a physiotherapist. What if that flares up again or I pull a hamstring or twist an ankle? All the overnight stays, spread apart by distances of 8 to 15 miles, would have to be cancelled (and I'm not sure whether refunds would be allowed).

Then there is: the backpack. Apart from three days on a hike in Bosnia, I have never walked a long distance with one before. Ahead of coming, I rooted out the backpack I used in the hills near Sarajevo. It was covered with attic dust and a clip was missing (the one that connects the straps at the top of your chest). The consequence of this missing clip – noticed at the last moment – is that I have to hand-tie the straps, making the bag slope to one side or the other depending on the knot.

This is awkward, as I have already discovered on the mile-long walk from Kemble station to the Thames Head Inn. Another problem is the weight. I have packed the bag with several books, which I intend to read one by one and post back to myself when I have finished them (to reduce the burden). Some might argue that I would have been better off with an electronic reader but I cannot, frankly, stand those things. Anyway one of the books – *Dickens's Dictionary of the Thames, 1887* by Charles Dickens Junior, son of the better-known Charles – is unavailable as an eRead.

The backpack is heavy, containing a few changes of clothes and a tube of 'travel wash' from Superdrug (I am not looking forward to doing the washing). I have also acquired 'travel' tubes of toothpaste, shaving cream and so on. I am wearing light North Face trousers with zips that can convert them into shorts, though I have never used those zips and did not realise they were there when I bought the trousers. I have high-cut boots made by Karrimor that I have worn enough times not to be especially worried about blisters. I have sun cream. I do not have a laptop (too cumbersome and heavy). I do not have a compass. How could I possibly get lost following a river?

Along the way various friends and family members are to join me for short sections; there was surprising interest about walking the Thames among those to whom I mentioned my plan (proof that it's not just me who has a thing for the river). However, for the first few days I am on my own.

Will I be able to make it the whole way?

Answer: I guess I'm about to find out.

The early miles
On the path to Cricklade

In the morning I get ready to go along the A433/Fosse Way, heading towards its cross section with the Thames Path. This is a short distance away and I will be joining the Thames Path at this point to set off in the direction of the small town of Cricklade. The town is 12 miles further on and is where I have another pub room booked.

When I leave at 7.20 a.m. no one else appears to be awake at the Thames Head Inn, including the staff. I put the key through the letter box and tramp off along the road, already busy with a stream of Audis and Land Rovers.

At the cross section of the Fosse Way and the Thames Path, I pause to take another look at Trewsbury Mead, then traverse a field with a ditch on its left-hand side. This ditch is, I presume, 'the Thames', although there is still no sign of water. The sky is a delicate blue decorated with clusters of pearl-grey clouds. The field is nettle strewn, with orange weeds and molehills. A pair of crows flaps in the direction of a copse. I follow the ditch and shortly reach a wood.

This is the first real landmark heading east on the River Thames, if you discount the stone at the start. It is also the first evidence that liquid actually exists, and it is known as Lyd Well.

To see the well you must hop over a wire fence. I do this slightly precariously with my backpack full of books; I'm unwilling to take off the bag, which would require undoing the awkward knot in the straps. The small stone well is mossy and surrounded by beech and oak trees. I reach down and scoop out some water to try a drop or two.

It tastes leafy.

Act of pilgrimage complete, I continue along the ditch, which turns excitingly into a stream not so far away. I am on a wonderfully quiet stretch of the Thames in deep countryside. Yellow and purple wild flowers, thistles and brambles line the way alongside rolling wheat fields (at least, I take the crop to be wheat). A rusty barn stands in one of these, cutting an eerie silhouette and making me think of the American Midwest. Pools of crystal-clear water form at bends where the river seems to be taking a rest while contemplating the journey ahead. The pools are surprisingly big: hot-tub-sized but just a foot or so deep (without a button to press for bubbles). For a moment or two I consider going for a dip. Like a devotee by the Ganges, why not immerse myself in this river I've decided to follow? Plunge in and wallow in the water. Be at one with the Thames. There's no one around to witness such madness. I'm my own boss. I can make up the rules on this walk.

The urge to move on, though, is too strong. I'm less than a mile in with 214 miles to go. Anyway, having left so early forgoing breakfast, I'm feeling hungry. Simple instincts are taking over: I want to find somewhere to eat.

This is when I encounter my first local difficulty, down by the riverside. The Thames around here, close to its source at Trewsbury Mead, is very isolated indeed. I come to the village of Ewen, where there is a sign for the Wild Duck pub, a shortish walk from the path. I amble over but find that the Wild Duck is closed. Of course it's closed! It is nine o'clock in the morning. Pubs are not open at nine o'clock in the morning, although for some reason I seem to be under the illusion that jolly hostelries will magically pop up at all hours and places on long countryside walks. Quite where I picked up this notion I do not know.

I return to the river. It's no big deal. I don't mind: breakfast can wait. The path here follows the Thames through more wheat fields and farmland with cows as the waterway widens almost imperceptibly before arriving at a place called Somerford Keynes. As I enter this village gunshots are echoing across the rooftops; presumably hunters are out in the countryside. Porsches are speeding by along a quite busy road. Dog walkers are walking their dogs.

Yes, other people are walking. So far I've had the river to myself. I ask one of the dog walkers if there is somewhere to eat in Somerford Keynes. He scratches his chin. He is wearing a large green polo shirt and has an air of affluence (the houses round here look pretty well-to-do).

'There's the Baker's Arms,' he says.

'But won't that be closed?' I ask.

'Yes,' he says. 'It will.'

What use is this information to me?

'Is there anywhere else?' I ask, trying not to sound like a typical, pushy DFL (Down From Londoner), a phrase I have heard used in the Cotswolds and West Country.

'Your best bet is the tea room,' he says, waving a hand towards the far end of the village.

I go to find the tea room, passing honey-coloured buildings with names like Jasmine Cottage, Rosemead and Pear Tree Cottage. Quaint... all very quaint, but there is no tea room that I can find. It has gone ten o'clock. I have been walking for a while now without water (lack of breakfast aside). I have not taken anything to drink so as not to add to the ridiculous weight of my library-like bag. I'd been under the impression there must be a shop or two along the way. There has been no shop. I am not used to carrying such a heavy backpack. The straps are cutting into my shoulders. The insole of my right boot seems to have slipped backwards, making my right toes uncomfortable. I have just gone on a half-mile diversion requiring a half-mile return, after a similar detour for the Wild Duck in Ewen.

There is a place called Ashton Keynes ahead, referred to in my guidebook as 'the first village actually on' the River Thames, though I seem to have passed several 'villages' already. Ashton Keynes would appear to be a good two and a half miles away, beyond a series of lakes.

I will, it seems, have to go to Ashton Keynes.

I tell myself to get a grip. The backpack's fine really and I ate a huge meal last night. Silently evaluating the directions given by the man in the green polo shirt – who may well, I admit, have been absolutely right about the tea room – I set off along the river, wondering how I have messed up so quickly. The North Sea is a very long way away, with or without mile-long diversions to seemingly non-existent tea rooms. How have I found myself waylaid so close to the river's source?

Passing a *Thames View* house with a Waitrose delivery van parked outside, I rejoin the river path, which skirts the edge of a high-end housing development. This estate is called the Lower Mill Estate. It is impossible not to gather the name. *PRIVATE LAND: LOWER MILL ESTATE*, says a sign. *NO ACCESS: LOWER MILL ESTATE*, says another. *PRIVATE PROPERTY. NO PUBLIC ACCESS. LOWER MILL ESTATE*, says a third, making the point twice for emphasis, while another says: *PRIVATE LAND. STRICTLY NO TRESPASSING. LOWER MILL ESTATE*. There's a little bridge across the Thames near here – linking to another part of the estate, it would appear. A sign says: *YOU'RE CROSSING THE RIVER THAMES. LOWER MILL ESTATE.*

BOSSY AND ANNOYING. LOWER MILL ESTATE is perhaps more to the point. I pass the entrance of the estate where a security barrier is down to prevent intruders such as Thames walkers, while wondering who can afford to live in a place that contrives to be so exclusive (and has such a penchant for public signs). Hedge-fund managers, lawyers involved in public enquiries, council leaders with six-figure salaries and Jags, retired CEOs of banks, probably in their early fifties and playing rather a lot of golf in between Caribbean cruises?

Maybe (definitely maybe) I'm just being jealous… it's a lovely, peaceful spot.

I stop on one of the estate's bridges. The water in the Thames is still about a foot deep. I read before coming that it was on this stretch that the first beavers to be born in Britain in four centuries were bred in recent times, though I can't see any sign of them. Leaning against the bridge, I look up more information on my smartphone (a good signal to be had here, by the Upper Thames) and discover the Lower Mill Estate's owner was behind this breeding scheme; that the two pairs of beavers he introduced were named Tony and Cherie, and Gordon and Sarah, after the politicians and their wives, and that the estate is in fact the location of various holiday lets.

So much for my hedge-fund managers and retired CEOs rant. Lower Mill Estate is a place where good-hearted people reside, taking care of cute little animals that have been neglected for 400 years.

Beyond a kissing gate the lakes begin and the river winds between them, about six metres wide now. To put this in perspective, where the river meets the North Sea the estuary is 16 kilometres wide. These are very early days for the River Thames. Dappled sunlight filters through reeds by the riverbank. Water ripples in the gentle but steady current. The Thames begins at about 110 metres above sea level, with much of the river's descent in elevation within the first 20 miles, and here the pace of the stream has picked up surprisingly quickly. It's intriguing to see how the river develops and grows so fast – from nothing to something quite substantial, all in a couple of hours' stroll.

I go through a gate and pass an electricity depot with a sign warning: *DANGER OF DEATH*. This marks the outskirts of Ashton Keynes. The first village actually on the River Thames is in Wiltshire; Gloucestershire has been and gone. A house is for sale on the edge of this picturesque village, offered by an estate agent named Bishop Property. How much does an abode in a quiet spot in the first village actually on the River Thames set you back? There's still an internet signal, so I check: £425,000 for a three-bed cottage. You'd hardly get a studio flat for that in some parts of riverside London to come.

I follow the path onwards and come to the stump of an old stone cross destroyed by Oliver Cromwell's army in the Civil War. Here I turn right for another small riverbank detour. Ahead is a pub: the White Hart. Surely now it's eleven o'clock this will be open? No. A message on a blackboard informs me that 'weary walkers' are welcome and that food is served at noon. Beyond, however, is a village shop; the first village shop in a village actually on the River Thames, though it's slightly annoyingly away from the river. I have found a place where money can be exchanged for something that can be eaten or drunk. I buy various rolls, energy bars and pieces of fruit, along with water and a Lucozade Sport, and lean on an old crate next to the wall outside. I consume the lot in rapid succession, watched by an elderly man passing time on a bench. The bench is by the shop window, which features a picture of an Avro Vulcan XH558 nuclear bomber jet dating from the Cold War; Ashton Keynes is close to the former RAF airfield at Kemble.

It is hard to imagine what the elderly man is thinking. Within a few hours of departure, I seem to have gone feral. Bits of brambles have become attached to my trouser-shorts, the back of my polo shirt is soaked in sweat (where the backpack was) and I have just eaten a meal consisting of enough energy bars, rolls and fruit to feed a small family in the time it might take to boil a kettle.

An electric-blue Range Rover with a personalised number plate pulls up. The number plate includes a name, presumably the owner's. I'll call him 'Jez'. Jez gets out, leaving his dog sitting in the passenger seat looking like an extremely regal hound. Jez has well gelled hair and a slouch. The elderly man knows him and they exchange hellos. Jez enters the shop and soon exits with a cigarette packet.

As the electric-blue Range Rover pulls away, the elderly man turns to me and says, 'That dog gets more drive rounds than walk rounds – that ain't no good.'

That is all he says as he almost immediately breaks into a fit of coughs that tapers into silence after a while. He nods at me as though he's well used to such spells. I leave him, hoping he'll be OK, and pass along a lane with cottages and weeping willows. Ashton Keynes really is picturesque, undeniably gorgeous and almost serenely peaceful (if that's not laying it on a bit too heavy). I keep on going. The streets are completely empty. It's as though there's been a terror scare and everyone has been confined to their homes. Where is everyone? It is remarkable how few people seem to walk along the river near its source – this is, after all, the height of summer. It's the tourist season! This is the perfect moment for a stroll along the river! The peak period! Where are all the Thames tourists?

I keep on going, once again. Weeping willows billow in the breeze: wind in the willows indeed. These trees, I know, were introduced to the Thames from China, first planted in Twickenham in 1730. I can also tell you that they consume 1,500 gallons of water a day. Which seems an awful lot. You do risk picking up a large amount of this kind of information (accurate or not) if you read up about the river before setting off.

Beyond the willows, Rolls Royces and Audis occupy the driveways of pleasant-looking cottages. At the end of the village I come to a narrow path lined by nettles and purple loosestrife. This appears to be the way forward. I edge onwards, stepping carefully where somebody has used red spray paint to circle dog mess. A wood pigeon shoots out of a bush. A sign, rather unexpectedly, warns: *DANGER:*

QUICKSAND, KEEP TO PATH. I do as I am told. Who would have thought such perils lurked by the banks of the Thames in Wiltshire?

The scenery opens to farmland. Cows huddle in a field. A peacock-blue dragonfly buzzes past banks of meadowsweet on the edge of Elmlea Meadows, known for its *purple snake's head fritillaries*, says a sign. These are a rare and much-loved type of flower, though it's apparently not the right time of year to see them (April is best).

The Thames turns into a proper-sized river here; previously it might have passed as a stream or a brook. Tall reeds line the banks and lily leaves float on its surface. The reason for the leap in size is that the River Churn has joined the flow. The Churn is the first tributary river and some consider its source, a place called Seven Springs, near Cheltenham, to be the true origin of the Thames. Were this so, the Thames would be 12 miles longer. However, historians have long agreed that Trewsbury Mead is where the river begins. So, apparently, that is that.

Beautiful bucolic scenery continues as far as a weir where old Fanta bottles and sandwich wrappers bob by the barrier. Here 'bucolic' abruptly stops. I cross a bridge and come to a decrepit farmyard with an old, roofless, brick building. A path leads to an estate of modern housing with white vans and Nissan Micras. I pass the elegant tower of St Sampson's Church and find the high street. I have reached my destination: the ancient town of Cricklade.

Two pints of bitter and a Diet Coke
Cricklade

Cricklade has a surprising amount of rather intriguing history. Romans engaged with local tribes here in the period after 54 BC, following Julius Caesar's earlier defeat of forces by the Thames either at Shepperton or Westminster (no one is sure precisely where). Later, during the

Saxon period, around AD 700, it is believed there may have been a university at Cricklade, when the town was known as Greeklade. No one is certain about this either, but if it is indeed true Cricklade would have predated Oxford as the location of Britain's first university by several hundred years. What is known is that St Augustine (AD 354–430) visited the town to spread the word about Christianity. And it has also been established that Alfred the Great (AD 849–899) built a wall around Cricklade to keep out the Danes. It's worth noting here that the Thames (very sketchily) marked the boundary between the Anglo-Saxon kingdoms of Wessex, which Alfred ruled, in the south and Mercia in the north, ruled in Alfred's time by Ceolwulf II. I say 'sketchily' because this boundary was a movable feast.

King Alfred's walls were effective for a while, although King Canute of Denmark eventually broke through. From AD 979 to AD 1100 the town was home to a mint in which 'Cricklade coins' were produced; the location was chosen as defences were by then particularly strong. By the eighteenth century, however, the 'streets had become thick with mud… household garbage mingled with slops and the dung of horses – in summer flies, dust and strong odours took the place of mud'. This is according to a tourist information board by the police station on the high street.

This board goes on to quote the impressions of William Cobbett, a journalist who visited the town in 1821 while researching his book *Rural Rides*: 'I passed through that villainous hole Cricklade, about two hours ago, and certainly a more rascally place I never set my eyes on. The labourers look very poor; dwellings little better than pig beds and their food nearly equal to that of a pig. This Wiltshire is a horrible county.'

'The first town on the river Thames', as the guidebooks say, is a riot of pink and red flowers with hanging baskets along the high street. All sweet and lovely: no odours, dung or flies these days. Cricklade's 'villainous hole' period would appear to be long gone.

I'm staying at the White Hart, a prominent building adorned with a fine array of flowers. The best word to describe my abode for the night is, perhaps, 'unpretentious'. I step inside the seventeenth-century inn to find a solitary drinker at the end of the bar, where a message framed on a wall says: *Beauty is in the eye of the beer holder... buy one pint of beer for the price of two and receive a second pint absolutely free*. Another framed piece of communication says that, at the end of the evening, drinkers who are still not fully refreshed may purchase five cans of Carlsberg to take home for £5. To place this order they should 'ask for cold'; an expression I have never heard before. A pair of men poke buttons on a fruit machine. A map of the River Thames – I'm not surprised to see – hangs near the fruit machine. Techno-style dance music plays.

I do like the White Hart (maybe I'm just easily pleased).

I go upstairs to drop off the backpack in a simple room overlooking a Tesco Express and come straight down to order a ham and tomato sandwich along with a pint of lime and soda. As I do so, two hikers, a man and a teenage boy, enter the bar and ask about a room. There isn't one. They are disconsolate and look utterly worn out. They have truly massive backpacks with coils of bedding dangling, and the man is clutching a large metal object that looks like some kind of canister.

Simon and Jamie are father and son, British, but living in Germany. The large metal canister is a very big tea flask. Simon tells me he calls it 'the King' and that it holds two litres of tea.

'I'm a tea junkie,' he says, soon after we get talking.

Long-distance Thames walkers, I am quickly learning, tend somehow to gravitate towards one another. Even though my backpack is in my room, my trousers and boots mark me out as a walker. A simple look is all it takes to get the conversation going. Casual strollers with dogs are a different breed to us. We are going the whole way. We're in it together. We've got 215 miles to travel – and we've got stories to share.

I soon learn that I am the only other such walker they've met. They set off this morning from a campsite in Somerford Keynes after seeing

Trewsbury Mead the day before. They intend to go as far as Hampton Court or possibly the Thames Barrier, depending on how they do for time. They will camp out most of the way. We fall easily into chatter. Simon is quite a motormouth. He is in his fifties and Jamie is 16. I rapidly learn that Simon married a German woman, Jamie's mother, but they have separated. I also find out that he used to work as an IT director for a US software company but 'had a breakdown'. Now Simon gets by on insurance: 'Like so many Germans I have insurance against being unemployed or unemployable.'

He also tells me that he and Jamie had considered walking the religious pilgrimage route known as the Santiago de Compostela in Spain first but 'in summer one thousand five hundred people a day finish that walk. I worked out that that means that every kilometre there are about seventy-five people. That's a no-go for me. I don't like crowds at all.'

Jamie confirms this: 'He's been known just to walk out of supermarkets or subways.'

Simon shrugs. He doesn't seem to mind opening up about his mild agoraphobia – to a fellow Thames walker, at least.

'You'll probably have no difficulty avoiding crowds if today is anything to go by,' I suggest.

Simon beams a big smile. He knows he's on to a winner: that the Thames Path here will serve up the peace and quiet – and solitude – he craves. He and Jamie have clearly, despite their exhaustion and ongoing accommodation troubles, had a marvellous day.

Their current dilemma is that the campsite they had planned for tonight is still a long way off, they are tired out by their huge backpacks, and a taxi to the campsite would be just as expensive as staying at a hotel in town – or so they have been told.

'I thought that if we ever got stuck there would be hundreds of B & Bs. I thought that round here we'd be in B & B heaven. That's what's thrown me,' Simon says.

He seems genuinely surprised at the lack of B & Bs. Jamie says nothing, but smiles quietly to himself.

'These backpacks, I think we underestimated how much they would hurt,' says Simon, looking at the offending items. Inside, they tell me, are sleeping bags, self-inflating mattresses, a camping gas-stove, changes of shoes for evenings (something I have not bothered with), three pairs of socks each and three pairs of underwear each.

Both Simon and Jamie have long, scraggly hair and are large, hulking figures; like father, like son. Simon wears a red T-shirt and jeans, while Jamie is in a blue T-shirt with tracksuit bottoms. Simon is given to flamboyant pronouncements and seems more than happy to delay worrying about the camping site while having a pint at the White Hart.

I offer to buy a round and go to the bar to fetch two pints of bitter (and a Diet Coke for Jamie). Techno-style dance music is still playing (not loudly, just in the background) and the men by the fruit machine continue to dab the flashing buttons. I return with the drinks and ask what made the duo think of walking so far along the river.

'Jamie has had an interesting time in school recently,' says Simon, choosing his words carefully. 'A drinkee during school hours. That's why he's on the Coke now.'

He is taking his son on an adventure to remove him from bad influences and instil an appreciation for the simpler things in life, it transpires.

They have already had a few run-ins. Near Somerford Keynes they came across 'a couple of unfriendly natives: surly, they were. Not surprising, I suppose – all those idyllic houses on the water and then we come along. I told them that actually we were more civilised than we looked.'

Jamie cuts in: 'They looked quite alarmed.'

In Somerford Keynes itself they had gone to the Baker's Arms pub at 9.15 p.m. the previous night only to be told that 'the kitchen closed at nine o'clock'. So they had eaten only packets of peanuts and crisps.

'A very limited range of snacks,' says Jamie.

They check again how much a cab to their campsite would cost. It is much less than they were told earlier. So they order one.

Simon brings up Brexit: 'It's a disaster. I do not understand it. From the beginning to the end, outright lies. Lies from the Brexiteers. They should be called up on this. My nephews and nieces feel as though their future has been sold. Now France is very far to the right. The right-wing Christian Social Union in Bavaria is putting forward a candidate for chancellor in Germany…'

Simon continues in this vein for several minutes until their taxi arrives. We finish our drinks and agree to meet in Lechlade the following night, though I do wonder whether I'll ever lay eyes on them again.

They disappear down Cricklade high street. It is late afternoon now. I go to Cricklade Bridge, which dates from 1852; there has been a crossing here since the ninth century. Little brown fish swim in the clear water rushing below (my first Thames fish). I poke my nose inside the charmingly old-fashioned Red Lion pub, with its low ceiling, framed pikes, fly-fishing hook collections and microbrewery. I visit St Sampson's Church, which dates from the twelfth century and is notable for having the four suits of playing cards inside its tower. Some believe that this tower was built with the proceeds of a gambling win. I peer up at the playing cards, wondering if there is any other church in the world built thanks to a bet.

Then I return to the high street, passing a man leaning against a wall, with *LOVE* and *HATE* tattooed on his knuckles, and listen to a couple bickering loudly in the street.

Her: 'I wanna walk. I don't wanna go in the ****in' car.'

Him: 'So you wanna go for a walk?'

Her: 'I ****in' do, yeah.'

Him: 'Go on then.' And he indicates that she should walk, infuriating her even further.

A stag group passes.

First lad, wearing a T-shirt with *SLUT* written on it: 'I don't give a **** if you don't like it.'

Second lad: 'You've had too many beers, mate.'

First lad: 'I wasn't slaggin' him off.'

Second lad: 'You're being aggressive.'

First lad: 'Oh shut the **** up. Who's got a ****in' lighter?'

Back in my room, I read a *Swindon Advertiser* article about a 'drug-driving arrest' involving a 43-year-old driver from Cricklade who collided with four parked cars, and another about a drink-driver who 'careered into a hedge' and has been banned from driving for two years.

I go to bed early, but then late at night, I am woken by yet another argument taking place in the high street outside my window.

Woman: 'Tony, **** off!'

Tony: mumbles something.

Woman: 'I ain't joking. **** off.'

A cab arrives.

Woman: 'See ya!'

Silence.

Yes, Cricklade has plenty of pretty hanging baskets these days, but ghosts of the 'rascally place' remain.

CHAPTER THREE

CRICKLADE, WILTSHIRE, TO NEWBRIDGE, OXFORDSHIRE

POEMS, PIES AND A SHEPHERD'S HUT

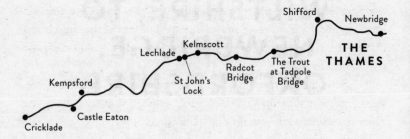

Shifford

Newbridge

Kelmscott

Lechlade

St John's
Lock

Radcot
Bridge

The Trout
at Tadpole
Bridge

THE
THAMES

Kempsford

Castle Eaton

Cricklade

At breakfast I eat scrambled eggs on toast in a room at the White Hart decorated with pictures of butterflies and dragonflies found by the Thames. Asian tourists are munching toast. Tracy Chapman is on the stereo, singing about a fast car. When I express an interest, the cheerful, heavily tattooed waitress shows me a close-up of the swirling patterns on her arms and tells me her ink-art cost 'One hundred pounds an hour. I've done 'em in the last two years.'

It's a Sunday morning and as I head to the river to begin the day's walk, I see that churchgoers are congregating at St Mary's, near the bridge. I go to take a look and am soon being shown round by Monica.

Monica is a church volunteer. She's wearing a flowery dress and a long gold necklace with a ring attached. She informs me that the foundations of a Saxon gate chapel lie in one corner of the church and that 'if the Romans were going to Cirencester, they would cross the river round here'.

She shows me the remains of a Roman pillar at the back. There are, she adds, 'more than one hundred places named "St Mary's" along the Thames. Saxons were keen on that dedication.'

'Why?' I ask.

'Just because they were,' she says. 'There was a legend that England was Mary's dowry in the Saxon period.'

Monica lives on the high street near the White Hart. I mention a dreadful mechanical scraping noise I heard at around six o'clock this morning; I'd half considered going down and asking whoever it was to stop.

Monica knows all about this.

'Someone's burning off paint – and that's not very considerate, is it?'

She gives me her email address and says to write if I have any further questions.

What a very nice Crickladian. (I may just have invented that word.)

A little bit of liquid history
Cricklade to Castle Eaton

It is hot at nine o'clock. I have a medium-length hike ahead: 11 miles to Lechlade, followed by a long day's tramp after that to Newbridge, 17 miles, and then a more modest 14 miles to Oxford. A total of 42 miles, excluding diversions, in three days; I do not think I have walked so far in such a short space of time in my life. During this Upper Thames stretch of the river I'm going to learn a few things. Such as: will these boots start playing up? Will this backpack drive me mad? Will I decide to pack it all in and catch a train home?

Beyond the boundary of Cricklade, Saxon agricultural ridges mark a field as though the landscape has grown a ribcage. Ducks (my first Thames ducks) skip across the shallow water and dip down to explore the contents of the river weed. Tall rushes with purple flowers rise from the banks. I pass beneath a busy road, the A419, and the noise recedes as I follow a tunnel-like path with yellow and white wild flowers and cabbage white butterflies. Swallows swoop and screech above. A breeze rattles the reeds.

The Thames Path begins here on the south side of the river before crossing a bridge into a field with cows. There is no one else in sight. Flies buzz on cowpats. Birds trill. The cows pause to regard my progress. I make my way to a gate where I discover a sign saying, *BULL IN FIELD* written on the other side; good to know, I suppose, even in retrospect. Mellow warmth rises from the soil. The path continues through a crop field. More electric-blue dragonflies dart between clumps of nettles. Clouds billow on the horizon. I cross back to the south side of the water over a wooden bridge. Gunshots echo; another hunt must be in full swing out there somewhere. A pair of swans (my first Thames swans) glides by. On the far bank, a campsite with caravans arises. Was this where Simon and Jamie stayed? Pondering this, I come to a row of pebble-dash houses and the Red Lion pub.

I have reached Castle Eaton.

This is a small village and the Red Lion has a claim to fame: it is the first pub from the source to here to line the banks of the Thames. And it's closed. But I really want to go to the first pub lining the banks of the Thames, so to kill time I decide to take a detour to see a church in the village of Kempsford on the opposite bank, which will require me to cross a little road bridge into Gloucestershire.

Kempsford comes with two Thames-related stories and a (possible) poem.

The first story is from the late thirteenth century and concerns Henry, Earl of Lancaster, who hereabouts murdered his wife Maud as he believed she was having an affair, probably incorrectly. After seeing her meet a stranger, he went into an uncontrollable rage, stabbed her and tossed her body into the Thames. Some claim to have seen a Maud-like apparition by the water, which has become known locally as 'the lady of the mist'.

The second story regards Henry's son, who was so distraught at the death of his own son – who had drowned in the Thames – that he rode from Kempsford, never to return. As he departed, his horse cast a horseshoe. Villagers retrieved this shoe and nailed it to the door of the church. This horseshoe is, apparently, still there.

The Thames poem is the handiwork of none other than Geoffrey Chaucer. John of Gaunt – from the same family as Henry, Earl of Lancaster, and who lived in Kempsford in the fourteenth century – erected the church in memory of his departed wife Blanche. Chaucer was known to both Blanche, who had been his patroness, and to John of Gaunt, who commissioned him to write *The Book of the Duchess* in her honour. From his visits to Kempsford it is believed that Chaucer could have drawn inspiration for his poem *The Parliament of Fowls*:

> A gardyn saw I, ful of blosmy bowes,
> Upon a ryver, in a grene mede,

There as swetnesse everemore inow is,
With floures white, blewe, yelwe, and rede;
And colde welle-stremes, nothyng dede,
That swymmen ful of smale fishes lighte,
With fynnes rede and skales sylver bryghte.

Which translates from Middle English as:

A garden saw I, full of blossomy boughs,
Upon a river, in a green mead,
There as sweetness evermore enough is,
With flowers white, blue, yellow, and red,
And cold well-streams, nothing dead,
That swimming full of small fishes light,
With fins red and scales silver bright.

A village with a 700-year-old horseshoe and an equally ancient poem; a little bit of liquid history to start the day.

It does not look far on the map. Even so, the backpack is not getting any lighter. I see a woman gardening by a house by the bridge (there are indeed white, blue, yellow and red flowers in her garden), who introduces herself as Nicky. She cheerfully agrees to look after my bag while I go to Kempsford, and says, 'I would have lent you my bike but it's got a flat.'

It's a bit of a way to Kempsford along roads with a depressing number of Red Bull cans, McDonald's wrappers and Costa Coffee cups strewn by the side. Further than I thought: about two miles. But there is the horseshoe on the door of the church – another St Mary's, this one with a perpendicular spire and a well-tended graveyard with yew trees and willows.

A member of the choir opens the door as I'm inspecting the horseshoe, which is kept in place by a dozen solid-looking nails. I ask if the tale is true and if the horseshoe is really believed to be the same one.

'Who knows? It's been there a long time,' he says.

The man from the choir does not seem all that big on chat. He departs and I have the place to myself.

I look at the red roses of Lancaster in the ceiling of the tower, requested by John of Gaunt, whose son by Blanche became Henry IV. In this tranquil, contemplative setting, John of Gaunt and Chaucer once mourned the loss of a wife and a benefactress. Blanche was taken by the plague aged 23. John of Gaunt was married twice afterwards but he was buried according to his request, next to Blanche in a tomb at St Paul's Cathedral; effigies showed them holding hands. This tomb was sadly destroyed in the Great Fire of London in 1666.

I return towards Castle Eaton, realising something that may seem rather obvious to the seasoned long-distance Thames walker: set forth two miles from the river and you've soon got to set forth two miles back. And these four miles are on top of a lot of other miles. At least they're without the backpack. I walk along, wondering what kind of people discard Costa Coffee cups and Red Bull cans from their vehicles in the English countryside.

Nicky invites me into her house and makes cups of tea, after initially offering a beer. She has glasses and wears a striped green polo shirt and pink flip-flops. She tells me she's an accountant who has lived by the Thames for 16 years, moving in with her husband, who came here 30 years ago 'coz he wanted to fish, but he hasn't once put a rod in the water'. The weed-filled river is about ten metres across at the end of their garden, which is right next to Castle Eaton Bridge. We sit at a terrace next to a garden shed looking across the infant Thames, joined by a white boxer dog named Hooch.

'What's it like to live on the river?' I ask. It's such a tranquil setting.

'I love it because it's always changing with the seasons – and you never know what's coming down the river next,' says Nicky. 'Once we saw a Venetian gondola, or you might get half a dozen canoes, kayaks, Canadian canoes, inflatable boats. A rowing boat came by a couple of years ago with an imperious Alsatian on board. It saw Hooch and went absolutely mad. The boat rocked all over the place and they almost sank.'

Nicky says she is about to clear out the weeds from the river, an annual task.

'I put on my wellies and wade in. There are crayfish about and they'll nip you: American crayfish.'

'Are you concerned about flooding?' I ask.

'During the bad floods of 2007 the garden was covered with water, but it only came within six feet of the terrace. We're safe. We're more likely to be attacked by Islamic State than have the house flooded.'

Nicky's husband Barry arrives, wearing a pink polo shirt and seeming unsurprised that a Thames walker is drinking tea on his terrace. He joins us and says, 'When I was a young man and looking at people's homes when I was going down the river, I said, "One day I'll have a house like that." Never a day passes when I don't think how lucky I am.'

'It has to start somewhere'
Castle Eaton to Lechlade

The Red Lion has opened and I'm soon ordering a soup and a lime and soda from Melody Lyall, the landlady. Lime and soda, I am discovering, is the perfect drink for walking: providing rehydration, and with sugar thrown in for energy too (there is an ideal balance between the two components, the lime cordial and the soda, and only the very best barman or woman knows how to get it absolutely right). The main saloon leads to a conservatory at the back with a collection of Melody's wooden elephant carvings, while a blue-baize pool table sits in a side room, where pictures of old military planes hang on the walls. Many of these are gifts from plane-spotters who stay at the pub while attending the Royal International Air Tattoo at nearby RAF Fairford.

'We get about three thousand walkers a year,' says Melody, as she hands over my change. 'Some do the whole thing in eight days: serious walkers, distance walkers.'

Which rather puts my 21 days to shame.

'Then there are those doing it in little sections. About one in ten is doing the whole thing. They come from all over the world. A Japanese guidebook writer went up and down six times.'

She pours my lime and soda.

'It's surprising how many people turn up and say, "What's that water out there?" I say, "The Thames." And they say, "No, it can't be." Especially people from London. They've got no idea. But it has to start somewhere.'

With that, I go to a picnic table by a weeping willow by the river's edge and look across the water to a field where battles between the forces of Mercia and Wessex were fought in Saxon times. Alfred the Great would have known this landscape well. I tuck into the tomato soup. It's very good, served with slices of baguette topped with melted cheese.

I raise a glass (of very good lime and soda) to the first pub – of many – lining the River Thames.

Time to move on.

Past yet another St Mary's Church, on the edge of Castle Eaton, a land of combine harvesters and wheat fields opens up. Deep cracks mark the dried-out path, which leaves the riverside for a while, though the presence of dragonflies suggests water nearby. A long series of fields follows, before the Thames Path moves on to the busy A361, well away from the water now. There are no pavements here but there is enough space to walk along.

In the distance, two figures lurk. They look as though they are in the midst of a heated debate.

I have found Simon and Jamie.

Simon's first words to me are: 'I cannot believe how much a 16-year-old can queen it up over a few nettles.'

Both Simon and Jamie are wearing shorts, although Jamie would have been in his tracksuit bottoms had he not covered them in soup last night. They had warmed up cans of Heinz Big Soup on their portable gas stove the previous evening ('really hit the spot,' says Simon), but there had been a spillage. And with nettles overflowing the path in many places, shorts are not a good idea.

The three of us trudge onwards in single file along the A361. Jamie and I stay on the verge, although Simon for some reason walks on the road, causing vehicles to swerve out of the way. This seems simply to be his preferred 'walking style'.

We get to a junction where the official Thames Path veers left to Inglesham. This is a longer route to Lechlade than simply continuing on the A361; Simon and Jamie are worn out so they head straight on, while I return to the river.

If I described every old church I came to along the River Thames... well, I would spend a great deal of time describing an awful lot of old churches. I have, after all, seen three dedicated to St Mary today.

In the village of Inglesham, however, there is a church that would be remiss to ignore.

I will, however, be brief. St John the Baptist Church in Inglesham dates from 1205 and has a thirteenth-century chancel, a Norman nave and Georgian box pews. It is remarkable in that during the Victorian period, when many 'restorations' heavy-handedly swept away the old, thus spoiling the original character of churches, St John the Baptist avoided this fate.

This was due to the interventions of the nineteenth-century textile designer, poet and novelist William Morris, who had a Thames summer house not so far away. He oversaw sympathetic repairs under the auspices of the Society for the Protection of Ancient Buildings (a forerunner of the National Trust). St John the Baptist is now overseen by the Churches Conservation Trust.

The result is simply fantastic, as though time has stood still, with flagstone floors, peeling frescoes, high wooden ceilings, and a smell of varnish and dust. If you ever pass by, stop and take a look. You won't be disappointed.

Outside, afternoon sunshine bathes fields leading to the Thames, where a public information sign on the edge of Lechlade says: *You are standing on the Thames Path. Keep walking downstream and you will reach London in about ten days*. I pause by the sign and wonder if anyone has read this and thought: 'Oh yes, I think I'll drop everything right now and do just that.' I make a few mental calculations. In ten days' time I will be beyond the M25 in Staines, about to go to Hampton Court, on the edge of London. It's strange to consider how far you can travel by foot if you keep steadily plodding away.

Voices rise near the point where the Thames and Severn Canal meets the river. Lads are larking about in the shallow water, swimming beneath an arched pedestrian bridge (my first Thames swimmers). Beyond them are boats (my first Thames boats). An elderly man in a grey cardigan is buzzing about on a little speed launch. In the days when the canal was open (1789–1933) he might have buzzed all the way, eventually, to the Celtic Sea via the Severn River and the Bristol Channel. This would have included a journey through what was then the longest tunnel in England, which runs for just over two miles from a spot not far from Trewsbury Mead.

Lechlade is where the 'navigable Thames' begins, even though some vessels occasionally venture as far as Castle Eaton. Boats and barges are moored here, with names such as *Booz Crooz*, *Alibi*, *Platypus* and *Jess Came Too*. It's almost weird to see them on the water after such a long boat-less stretch. People with picnics, families on strolls and friends casting rods are to be found closer to the elegant grey-stone arch of Halfpenny Bridge. Curious, I ask one of the fishermen what he is hoping to catch.

He looks confused.

'My cousin said we didn't need a licence,' he says.

He thinks I'm some sort of river inspector.

I repeat the question about the fish and he looks at me blankly.

A boy with him says, 'We don't know!'

With this I cross Halfpenny Bridge, admiring the dozen or so swans, and check into the Riverside pub, with its busy terrace overlooking the water.

'You got a car with you?' asks a barman wearing a black T-shirt with *STAFF* written on it. Moments earlier I had said to this barman that I have just walked from Cricklade.

'No,' I reply, trying not to sound sarcastic.

He looks at me sharply.

Another member of staff in a black *STAFF* T-shirt is talking to a third *STAFF* employee. While my paperwork is being dealt with, the first says, 'I'm finishing my shift soon.'

His colleague replies wistfully, 'I wish I was.'

The man with the paperwork returns and says he'll take me to my room. This is across a large car park. I have a ground-floor room facing the car park, with a slither of Halfpenny Bridge within view. The room is bare, with grey and beige two-tone curtains, a brown stained carpet and a laminated set of instructions and rules stuck on one wall: *ALL OUR ROOMS ARE STRICTLY NON-SMIKING* [sic]. The man lingers as if expecting a tip – even though I have carried my backpack. Unimpressed, he departs and I listen through paper-thin walls to a Texan in the next-door room leaving a voicemail message to his girlfriend: 'Just callin' to see how ya doin'. Love ya. Will see ya soon.' This is followed by the sound of a bottle being unscrewed, followed by a long *ahhhh*.

I go for dinner on a patch of artificial grass with sticky picnic tables by the Riverside's bar. Cigarette butts, napkins and bits of food cover the artificial grass and a wind has whipped up, causing some of the sunshades to fly from the tables. I fold mine down. A lukewarm chicken pie with watery mash and almost cold gravy is delivered. The waiter apologises for a lack of napkins; they have run out, he says. The pie is awful but I'm too hungry to complain. I eat it quickly, watching a bevy of swans on the river. There must be about 40. One of the swans is acting aggressively.

'They're getting fruity,' says a neighbour. 'There are a lot of females but I can only see four or five males.'

How on earth she can tell them apart, I don't know.

The Riverside's motto, on the menu, says: *Quality refined through the generations*. Just as I'm wondering what the standard must have been like before it was raised to the current levels of refined quality, Simon and Jamie arrive.

They are both smoking roll-up cigarettes. They join me and I go and get our first round: two pints and a Diet Coke.

'I've never seen anything like this,' says Simon, observing the mess on the artificial grass.

We sip our pints. All drinks are well deserved after a day's walking along the Thames. Simon and Jamie tell me about their cab to the campsite last night and how the driver offers a luggage-to-go service, taking walkers' bags ahead to their next destination. They had been tempted but are doing the walk on a budget. Their campsite was indeed the one I'd spotted and it had 'slightly shabby showers'.

'How little he whinged yesterday surprised me,' says Simon of Jamie. 'Well, he's made up for that today.'

Jamie blows out a plume of smoke and says nothing.

'Several times I left him behind,' Simon continues. He says this in a mock-macho way. 'But my parental instinct would not leave him too far behind.'

Jamie blows more smoke.

'He is my wee boy after all.'

Jamie looks to the heavens.

We decide to ditch the Riverside and go to the New Inn. This is up a short slope by a high street and the tall steeple of St Lawrence Church. The New Inn has attracted many famous guests over the years, but none more so than the foursome of Percy Bysshe Shelley, his wife-to-be Mary Godwin, her stepbrother and the poet Thomas Love Peacock. They had arrived by rowboat from Windsor in September 1815 intending to travel onwards along the Thames and Severn Canal (this itinerary was scuppered as they could not afford the £20 canal fee). At the New Inn they had dined on 'three mutton chops, well peppered'. And Shelley wrote a poem here, about St Lawrence, 'A Summer Evening Churchyard'. Shelley's Walk now passes from the churchyard to the river, and a plaque quotes the verse: 'Here could I hope… that death did hide from human sight / Sweet secrets'.

We find a spot by the big red-brick fireplace. More pints and Diet Cokes are procured (Simon's round) as Simon tells me how he lost his former IT job.

'I'd done so much for those ****ers over so many years. I made them millionaires. I was their scapegoat. A lot of covering your arse goes on in big businesses.' He mentions a multi-million-pound deal in Chicago. 'Twenty years I'd been at the company. I was the technical director for Europe at the end. But then a big meeting went wrong. It was the mainframe prices…'

His voice trails off. Jamie, who has clearly heard it many times before, smiles. Simon does not seem maudlin about his troubles at the IT firm. He's merely telling it how it is in a water-under-the-bridge style. He has a charmingly open character that seems to relish this scenario: making the acquaintance of a new companion (me), having had a shared experience (walking the Thames) during the day.

Simon switches subject abruptly.

'Parachuting, I tried that once,' he says, quite randomly. Simon has a tendency to leap from one thought to another, out of the blue. He and Jamie make good drinking buddies: they don't take anything too seriously. They're just happy to hang out at the end of a long day. Walking has worn us out and Simon and I – if not Jamie – are in that pleasant two-beer zone where talk comes easily. We've earned it. Somehow or other, including the trip to Kempsford, I've covered about 18 miles today. We're just content to be stationary. With a drink. Discussing whatever happens to pop up.

'Parachuting,' Simon repeats. 'I was on my twelfth jump. I'd almost qualified. But on my twelfth jump I made an extra turn to make it a perfect landing. I misjudged and landed at thirty miles an hour on to concrete. My whole right side was torn up.'

He grimaces at the memory of the pain. And we fall into companionable silence for a while. Simon sips his pint and wipes his brow. Jamie taps at his smartphone.

'Gliding!' Simon announces, after a minute or two. Simon tells me he also once tried to gain a gliding qualification, but this came to nothing too. 'I let go of the dragger at the wrong time. The cable was lost and I failed…'

He doesn't seem to have much luck with airborne hobbies.

We discuss this and that – and buy more drinks. It's nine o'clock when we decide (four beers to the good) to call it a day. We are exhausted, almost finding it hard to keep our eyes open. That's the thing about long-distance walking: the physical exertion really does take its toll. And it's very easy, in good company, to while away the hours in a convivial hostelry.

We wish each other luck and agree to keep in touch. The duo heads off to a campsite clutching bags of Lucozade Sport bought from Londis. I return to the Riverside to listen to the Texan snoring in the room next door.

Old Father Thames
Lechlade to Kelmscott

In the morning I go on another pilgrimage. Pale apricot light filters through milky clouds rising to the east. The turf of the river path has a spring. It is 7 a.m. The path is empty. The river is still; the spire of St Lawrence reflects almost perfectly on its olive surface. After a short walk along the River Thames I come to a pillbox on the opposite bank. This is one of a series of such last-ditch defences against Nazi river invasion: a stark reminder on this calm Monday of what might have happened less than a century ago. Not much further on is St John's Lock, the first in this direction of 45 locks on the Thames. It is well maintained with beds of roses and lavender and a curious, trickling water feature. The highlight, however, is right by the path, looking both pensive and grumpy.

Old Father Thames was commissioned in 1854 to be placed in the grounds of Crystal Palace. From 1958 to 1974 the statue stood in the field at Trewsbury Mead, before suffering damage and being brought here to be kept under the watchful eye of the lock-keeper. The mythical figure is shown in recline with a wooden spade propped on his right shoulder; at first, I take this, the spade, to be a prank, but this is how the statue is meant to be. Old Father Thames has a long, flowing beard and his expression suggests: *you'd better not try anything with me.*

I tap him on the shoulder for good luck, before picking up a free copy of *Towpath Talk* from a tourist information booth and adding slightly more weight to the backpack. I'm looking forward to reading *Towpath Talk*.

The next part of the river is one of the loveliest, with a splendid, timeless quality. Hilaire Belloc, the nineteenth- and twentieth-century writer, went as far as to say that a man from the fifteenth century could walk along the river here and 'would hardly know he had passed into a time other than his own'. The course meanders gently, the river wide and mirror-like. A creature, perhaps an otter, pops its head out of the grass ahead and disappears in a flash. Pink wood sage flowers, nettles and dock leaves line the path. A rabbit darts across a field of molehills.

Apart from the occasional pillbox these days (Belloc made his comment in 1907), there is indeed nothing a fifteenth-century man might find untoward. But he would certainly be more than puzzled by these great hexagonal lumps of concrete. I investigate one of the ugly concrete boxes, only just squeezing through with the backpack. Inside the damp, dark space I find an empty bottle of whisky and several crumpled beer cans.

What a spot for a party. Beyond are a few places made for more proper festivities, gin-palace-style riverboats to be rented out for the weekend, moored near Buscot Lock. Not far after this, I veer inland, where I have an appointment.

But I'm early. This is the thing with arranging to meet anyone on a long walk: you look at the map and estimate how long it will take to go from A to B but you can never be quite sure. Having not wanted to be late, I now have half an hour to kill. I go to the only pub in the village of Kelmscott, the Plough Inn, without high hopes so early in the morning. A light is, however, on and I can see a couple eating breakfast. I knock on the door of the old ivy-covered building. A short young woman wearing green trousers and a black top opens the door.

'Not open till twelve, sorry,' she says – it is 9 a.m. – before pausing and looking past me. 'There's just one of you?' She pauses again, looking thoughtful and seeming to change her mind. 'OK.' She widens the door to let me in.

I enter a room with low wooden beams, a flagstone floor and a delightful smell of bacon and eggs mixed with freshly ground coffee. An array of fruit, yoghurts and juices is laid out. I order a coffee. A smart yet unfussy restaurant lies behind the bar; all very 'rustic chic'. It looks like a wonderful place to stay. The couple nods hello. The man is wearing pink trousers, which I tend (usually) to regard as a warning sign for a City banker enjoying downtime or, perhaps, a member of the House of Lords. But they seem friendly enough and I take them to be Down From Londoners enjoying a minibreak.

Outside, I sit at one of the picnic tables in the front garden, facing the main bend in the tiny lane of sleepy Kelmscott. The waitress brings a black Americano.

It's wonderful to do nothing but sip good coffee in a quiet country village on a bright summer's morning after a brisk walk. The backpack is off. The map shows that Newbridge, where I have tonight's room booked, is still a fair distance away. But I feel ready for the hike. As I'm thinking these thoughts, the couple comes out for a breath of fresh air. We get talking.

'Like a museum,' says the man in pink trousers. 'Like visiting a museum. The thing I like is from the architectural point of view: old houses kept like new. It means that you have preserved the charm and character of the countryside. Where we live it is all money and efficiency: make the most space for the cheapest price. We forget the influence this has on the longer term. I think England has made the right choice.'

After this soliloquy, I explain that not everywhere in Britain is quite as well preserved as the Cotswolds, and I learn that the man in pink trousers is named Frank and his wife is named Elsje. They are from Maastricht in the Netherlands. He is the deputy mayor of Brunssum, just outside Maastricht in the southern tip of Holland, and Elsje is a nurse.

Frank tells me that Brunssum is home to both a NATO Allied Joint Force Command base and a British Second World War cemetery.

'On May fourth each year we remember the dead. About three hundred people are buried at the cemetery. Thousands turn up for the memorial. There's a flag parade. Every grave has been adopted locally and at each we place a white rose and a child releases a balloon.'

The conversation turns to Brexit.

'It is a very sad thing,' says Frank, 'but I believe the relationship between Britain and the Netherlands is so close that it will not affect the warm feelings between the countries.'

He pauses and a puzzled expression crosses his features. 'One thing that astonishes me, though, one thing I just can't understand, is that no one I talk to is in favour of Brexit. I ask people what their position is, but I am almost ashamed to ask.'

'Why would you be ashamed?'

'Because they are all very, very nice people,' he says. He appears not to want to offend anyone who voted 'in' by asking a question that implies there could be a chance they voted 'out'.

Both Frank and Elsje seem quite puzzled by it all.

'Heaven on earth'
Kelmscott

Retracing my steps to the river, I stop on the edge of the village at a gateway where I have arranged to meet Gavin Williams, the property manager of Kelmscott Manor, the summer home of William Morris. It is 9.30 a.m. Gavin is bald, bearded and wears a purple shirt and grey jeans, from which a set of keys hangs from a hook. He is new to his job and has rapidly developed a keen interest in the manor's former resident.

'He achieved ten times more than most do in their lives,' Gavin says. 'His membership of the Socialist League, his poems, his writing, his designs, his publishing press, his involvement in the Society for the Protection of Ancient Buildings. When he was dying, his wife Jane asked what he was dying of. One of the doctors replied that his disease was being William Morris, of working eighteen-hour days.'

Gavin has kindly agreed to show me round Kelmscott, which is only open on certain summer days (not today). His enthusiasm is infectious, and we are soon striding into a courtyard with keys being put to use, opening doors to reveal tapestries and curtains with Morris's distinctive strawberry, daisy, poppy and bird patterns. The sixteenth-century house is preserved just as it was during his lifetime (1834–1896). Gavin draws curtains and opens shutters. Shafts of light illuminate flowery armchairs, willow wallpaper, bedcovers depicting lions and leopards, and fireplaces with striking blue floral tiles. The highlight is a four-poster bed that is known as the 'Kelmscott Bed'. A poem written by Morris, 'For the Bed at Kelmscott', has been embroidered into the flamboyant pelmet of this sturdy oak structure. It begins:

> The wind's on the wold,
> and the night is a-cold,
> and Thames runs chill
> 'twixt mead and hill.
> but kind and dear
> is the old house here
> and my heart is warm
> 'midst winter's harm.

'Nice, isn't it,' says Gavin.

He's right: it is.

Morris was not only a mover and shaker in the British Arts and Crafts Movement – he was also a Thames lover. Kelmscott and the river beside it were to him 'heaven on earth'. He cherished the glimpses of the clover meadows by the Thames from the manor. Many of his designs, such as his willow wallpaper, were influenced by nature in the surrounding countryside. However, there is an added story to Morris and Kelmscott: one that feels as though it has somehow become attached to this bend of the river. This story involves a love triangle. Morris's strikingly attractive wife Jane had caught the attention of the poet and artist Dante Gabriel Rossetti, whom Morris had commissioned to paint her portrait.

Gavin takes it up, as we move into a room – right next to the 'Kelmscott Bed' room – that acted as Rossetti's studio and bedroom.

'Morris wanted to move the relationship from the eyes of London,' he says, referring to Rossetti and Jane. The desire to have a country manor was not all about escaping the city in the summer. 'He did not think that people could be other people's property. He felt he couldn't tell Jane what to do. He wasn't au fait with the company of women. He was more au fait with the company of men. He had been to boarding school and then to Oxford.'

His nickname had been Topsy before he met Jane, thanks to his curly hair that reminded friends of the female character with that name from *Uncle Tom's Cabin* by Harriet Beecher Stowe.

'Then he went and married a stunner,' says Gavin. The stunner was Jane, who was regarded by Rossetti as a Pre-Raphaelite beauty.

Morris would leave them together while he went on trips, hoping that Rossetti, whose wife had died in childbirth, would tire of the affair. 'When Jane and their two daughters moved here, he went to Iceland for two months and translated the Nordic sagas into English,' says Gavin, suggesting that this was not perhaps something all husbands would set off to do when a hot-blooded artist was moving in on their wife.

Eventually Rossetti did lose interest. 'After about three years he left. He got bored stiff of it. He practically lived here, rather than using it just as a summer house. He didn't have the right temperament to be in the middle of the country. He called it "the doziest clump of old grey beehives".'

Gavin and I go out into the garden, where there is a hedge cut in the shape of a Nordic dragon; a nod to Morris's Icelandic adventure. It is a couple of minutes' walk from here to the river that Morris so adored, and so enjoyed venturing out upon. On one occasion he hired a rowing vessel and travelled *en famille* from his other home by the river in Hammersmith to Kelmscott, stopping at Sunbury, Windsor, Marlow, Wallingford and Oxford along the way. During this journey, Jane and his daughters would sleep at inns while he stayed on the boat. His daughter May later described this vessel as 'a sort of insane gondola'.

The symmetrical, partially vine-covered facade of Kelmscott Manor is familiar. It features as the frontispiece drawing in Morris's utopian novel *News from Nowhere*, one of the books weighing down my backpack. In this utopia a man awakes in Hammersmith and finds himself in a future that has reverted back to the simpler ways of medieval times. The protagonist travels down the Thames by boat, marvelling at the honest and happy ways of this vision of a socialist future, culminating in a visit to an 'old house by the Thames'.

That house is Kelmscott Manor and it is a highlight of any Thames walk.

Brexiteers and frolicking deer
Kelmscott to Newbridge

Kelmscott was flooded when the river rose in 2007. According to Gavin, the water table is two feet below the surface. Locals joke that during floods they have to 'share the first floor with the chickens'. As I walk from the front gate to the river, I realise the land does seem particularly flat, with quite low banks.

Back on the Thames Path I exchange a few words with a fisherman, who pulls in a small perch as we are speaking. His name is Colin and he's been fishing the river for perch, dace, chub, roach, trout and barbel for 50 years: 'I catch and release; twenty so far today. Not many people fish the river these days. I've been coming since I was a kid.'

I set off at marching pace through meadowland and scrubby fields. I need to make time to reach Newbridge, where I have booked an Airbnb and the owner has arranged to meet me at five o'clock. The sweet smell of a bonfire fills the air. A barge moves serenely downstream. A large military propeller plane buzzes above. I find myself somehow detached from the path and have to roll carefully beneath a 'HOTLINE' electric fence to regain it. By a gate near Grafton Lock, I meet two fellow hikers, who jump a little when I reach them. They are a mother and daughter on a four-day walk to Oxford from Trewsbury Mead.

'To say we've done it' is Beverley's, the mother's, response when I ask them what gave them the idea.

'The family has been roped into taking our bags. My sister's been doing it the last two days,' says Laura, the daughter, whose job is as a headhunter for a pharmaceuticals company. ('I'm a headhunter' is all she initially says when I ask her what she does for a living.)

We part by the next gate and I move on to the Swan Hotel at Radcot. This has a brilliant riverside beer garden, but the pub/hotel is closed on Mondays. There are two bridges at Radcot. The one furthest away from the Swan, now on a side stream due to an eighteenth-century cut being made for the Thames and Severn Canal, is believed to be the oldest on the River Thames. A crossing here is said to date from 958, although the current structure is from 1200.

This place has witnessed horrific violence.

In 1387 it was the scene of the Battle of Radcot Bridge, which involved the son of John of Gaunt and Blanche: Henry of Bolingbroke, the future Henry IV. It was here on the south of the bridge that Henry ambushed forces aligned to Richard II led by Robert de Vere.

De Vere's soldiers were being pursued from the north. As they came to Radcot Bridge, Henry destroyed the central arch, thus cutting them off. Realising big trouble lay ahead, most of de Vere's 800 men fled, as he soon did himself – although unlike many of the others who drowned in the river or were lost in the marshes, de Vere managed to escape to France after hiding in woods and eventually reaching a port.

A sixteenth-century account of the fate of Thomas Molineux, who had been fighting on behalf of Richard II's men but had taken to the river to flee, is spine-chilling. Molineux had become trapped in the water by the bridge and his death by arrows fired from above seemed a certainty. He begged for mercy and climbed out of the river, whereupon: 'The knight caught him by the helmet, plucked it off his head, and straightaways drawing his dagger, stroke him into the brains, and so dispatched him.'

Lovely.

I continue along the river, covering a four-mile series of bends, passing directly through a herd of cattle by a gate by the water's edge. This involves quite a standoff, during which one of the cows proceeds to lick my arm. There's not much I can do about this, as I do not wish to start a stampede. Plus I am unsure whether any bulls make up their number. A little further on, gate-tending cattle herd negotiated, I pause to talk to a couple of members of the Environment Agency. They are, they tell me, in the middle of applying rustproof paint to one of the footbridges.

'We're LTMs,' one of them says.

'What's that?'

'Lead Team Members,' he replies. And he seems satisfied with that.

After four miles, I arrive at the Trout Inn at Tadpole Bridge. This is an eighteenth-century former toll house that's now a gastropub with tan-leather booths, spotlights and copper beer taps.

At the bar I fall in almost immediately with a red-faced man with shiny blue eyes. John is a retired stockbroker analyst who lives nearby and has 'a few acres and a few cattle: usually about six. One of them is always tending to jump in the freezer. I get a few weeks' worth of eating out of that. The problem is: not enough steaks. You get an awful lot of brisket. But I don't like brisket!'

I learn all of this at breakneck speed.

We talk about Europe. Everyone is talking about Europe.

I have met my first Brexiteer.

He leans towards me, as though passing on a stock-market tip: 'Brexit? I'm very much in favour. I read a book by Roger Bootle that said that GDP would go up.'

When he mentions the name of the economist Roger Bootle, his tone suggests: *QED, he's the man… and that's the end of that.*

'I don't like the way the EU considers that everything should be universal throughout the union. Many little things annoy me. One: white asbestos: as far as I know, there is no connection with cancer. Two: the EU Water Framework Directive. The Environment Agency has done very little to dig out the ditches because of this directive.' John seems to be saying that the directive is not strong enough. There is another bone of contention. 'There always used to be dairy farming here but because of the Common Agricultural Policy it became an arable area. It's a policy that encourages farmers to plough the fields: rape alternated with barley, wheat and linseed. But ploughing up the land that was formerly dairy farms has had an effect – it has meant the earth has gone into streams. Then it floods.'

He raises an eyebrow to underline this point. He has somehow, in the midst of all this, managed to order and become a recipient of a fresh pint of Young's Bitter. John tells me about the troubles he had in the 2007 flood. And he joins me – 'hope you don't mind' – when I sit down to rest my legs. 'In 2007, on Sunday morning, it came up through the long room; hardly any damage. We have a wooden floor. Seven floods, I've seen. Usually there's no problem.'

He sips his Young's Bitter. I drink my lime and soda. Then I look at my watch. I'd better push on to Newbridge. As I leave, I ask John if he likes living by the river. It seems to be the source of so many worries.

'Oh yes, I'm quite happy. Perfectly happy,' he says as we part company.

Then it begins to rain.

I put on my pac-a-mac for the first time.

This walk to Newbridge feels like a long way. There are more pillboxes. There are badger setts. There are electricity pylons. My boots get soaked through, even though a label stitched to the side says: *WATERPROOF*. Wild mangrove-like foliage appears on the opposite bank, as though Oxfordshire has temporarily transformed into a jungle. I cross the river near Shifford Lock, passing a field at

Shifford where King Alfred held the first recorded English parliament in 890. So this is one of the birthplaces of British democracy: a damp, clumpy field next to a few forlorn farmhouses and an electricity pylon. A muddy 'beach' covered in goose mess overlooks the spot on my side of the river.

Around here, my guidebook talks of a little bridge where I am supposed to be turning left. This little bridge seems to take a very long time coming; I begin to say bad things about this little bridge and guidebook writers who write about 'little bridges'. Then I find the little bridge and proceed along a path with cracks so big you could lose your mobile phone down them.

Next, a remarkable thing happens. I see two walkers ahead and they are facing a wheat field. In the centre of this wheat field two deer are leaping about playfully, their bodies disappearing beneath the wheat before springing up into the open once again. It's like a ballet performance. The creatures leap and tussle, pirouette and cavort. The other walkers and I are spellbound. We talk while gazing across the field. They have come from Oxford today and are doing the Thames Path walk in stages – this is their sixth – having begun at the Thames Barrier in 2011. They're heading for the Trout Inn and will then get a taxi back to Newbridge in the evening. Karen is a human resources officer for Peterborough City Council and Toni is an NHS doctor's receptionist from Wokingham. Karen loves walking the Thames because of 'the variety, the history, the nature, the beautiful lanes, the parks, the wildlife, the flow'. Toni loves it as it's 'peaceful, it's good for your well-being, and everyone gets a roasting and no one can hear'. By this she seems to mean that she can say what she likes to her close confidante with impunity.

'The children got a roasting today. And my husband asked this morning: "Am I on the agenda?" I said: "Oh, you're always on the agenda."'

We watch as the deer frolic into the distance.

Then we say goodbye and they head off towards Shifford.
I continue onwards, and shortly afterwards reach Newbridge.

Shepherd's hut
Newbridge

This bridge, on a road between Witney and Abingdon, dates from 1250, making it the second oldest bridge over the Thames after the one at Radcot. However, as the one at Radcot is now across a side stream, some argue that Newbridge is technically the oldest on the river. Every good Thames bridge-spotter knows this (or ought to).

My digs for the night are right beside Newbridge. I am sleeping in a 'shepherd's hut' next to the Maybush pub. This is an Airbnb; the first time I have tried this room-sharing online service. The hut is an unprepossessing grey structure on rusty wheels with a corrugated roof; it's not really a shepherd's hut at all, though I knew that from the internet. However, Sean, who took the booking, is on hand to show me the smart but rather cramped interior with a double bed, a retro 1970s-style lamp and a wood-burning heater. There is no bathroom. Instead there is a private shower-room for shepherd-hut dwellers in a barn about ten metres away.

Sean is a ginger-bearded man in his early twenties, and he and his father run the Maybush; they helped build the hut as a sideline business. Apparently a couple spent their wedding night in this hut, which has been on the market for about a year.

'We are superhosts on Airbnb,' says Sean – and that sounds as though it is a very good thing indeed.

Sean leaves. Rain pelts down on the hut's corrugated roof. After a while, I walk to the Rose Revived pub on the other side of the bridge, where I order pasta and chicken and a large glass of white wine.

The Rose Revived and the Maybush were once famous for being in separate counties: Oxfordshire and Berkshire. This meant there could be an extra half-hour's drinking time due to differences in county laws, thus triggering regular stampedes across the bridge. The Maybush is now within Oxfordshire too, and anyway national licensing laws have long been standardised, so this comical booze run is a thing of the past. The Rose Revived gets its name from being where Oliver Cromwell is said to have dropped by once. On his visit he ordered two ales. One of these he drank. Into the other he placed a drooping rose that he had been wearing on his chest. The flower perked up in the beer. Whether this story is historically accurate is a moot point.

Nowadays there is a fruit machine, pop music, tartan armchairs and rows of empty Bombay Sapphire gin bottles placed on windowsills as decoration. My pasta and chicken comes – and it's so small I consider ordering another. My appetite has grown due to so much exercise. I am too exhausted from today's long walk to move much. So I slump in my tartan chair, drinking Chardonnay and listening to my neighbours, who appear to be organising a local charity event.

They are a group of three: a man and two women.

Man: 'That Alex guy is basically saying he can't be team leader but he *can* be in the team.'

First woman: 'I'll tap into him.'

Man: 'I'm quietly confident. We need to get him in the circle of trust.'

Second woman: 'I'm strategising ahead. I asked for two bullet points of what they want.'

Man: 'I'd like a Thursday night meeting. I'm not going to bombard everyone.'

Second woman: 'I'm going to send links to the newspapers.'

All said in conspiratorial whispers; it's as though they're organising some kind of coup d'état.

Talk of the newspapers reminds me of *Towpath Talk*, where the front-page splash is *BROLLY GOOD SHOW!*, about a Canal and River Trust event that took place in the rain. A feature on *ETIQUETTE ON THE INLAND WATERWAYS* advises readers to avoid queue-jumping and to 'be aware of what is going on behind you' while overtaking. I'm disappointed: I'd been expecting all sorts of intriguing shenanigans on the river.

Back in my shepherd's hut I light the fire, resting my damp boots by the side, and quickly fall asleep to the sound of rain on the roof.

CHAPTER FOUR

NEWBRIDGE TO ABINGDON, OXFORDSHIRE

'SEE A BENCH... SIT ON IT'

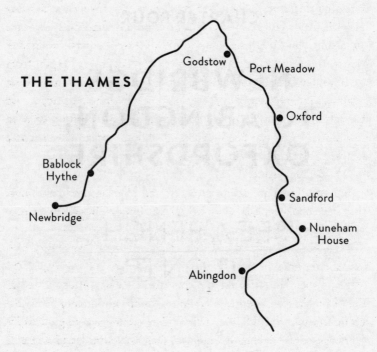

THE THAMES

Godstow

Port Meadow

Oxford

Bablock
Hythe

Newbridge

Sandford

Nuneham
House

Abingdon

Toni and Karen wave me over from the window of the Rose Revived as I walk by in the morning. I've been up for a while in my hut listening to a series of downbeat reports on the BBC's *Today* programme.

As well as the (by now) usual wrangles over Brexit, the US has begun air strikes on Libya, the mosquito-borne Zika virus has broken out in Florida, and in the UK a think tank has unveiled a 'housing crisis' in major cities. This crisis centres on a dramatic fall in home ownership. In 2003 the proportion of homeowners in Greater Manchester was 72 per cent – now it is 58 per cent. An expert from the think tank says, 'House ownership used to be the norm. It is not so now… incomes simply haven't kept pace with house prices… we had access to lots of relatively easy credit and the position we're in now is that credit has been turned off… house prices have become detached from people's earnings.'

All rather depressing.

Toni and Karen are eating breakfast and plotting their day's walk. They have booked a cab back to the Trout Inn and intend to see how far their legs will take them.

'We might not make it to Cricklade,' says Karen. 'We're very laid-back about things.'

This is their final day on the trail during their current time off. They'll be back on another occasion to stomp onwards to finish the job in Trewsbury Mead. They tell me they use luggage-to-go taxis for their bags, or else hole up in one place such as Newbridge for a couple of days at a time.

'We don't like carrying our bags,' says Toni.

Toni shows me an app on her mobile phone that reveals the pair walked a staggering 23.28 miles yesterday, or 47,640 steps. I'm amazed. This seriously outdoes any distance I've covered so far (although they were not carrying a backpack full of books).

Here I must make a declaration.

For this journey I have bought a wristband 'tracking device'. Now, I realise many folk deplore these gadgets, regarding them as yet another manifestation of all that is wrong with modern life: a muppet-like reliance on computer chips and little screens that is the forerunner of the end of human existence. Et cetera. However, on a long walk, I figured one of these would prove quite useful. It is helpful, after all, to know how far you've gone.

So far, I can see that I have steadily upped my game. While messing about around Trewsbury Mead, including a hike into Cirencester and to the Thames and Severn Canal tunnel, I covered precisely 13.70 miles. From Trewsbury Mead to Cricklade, with the various excursions to find somewhere to eat, I went 17.55 miles. From Cricklade to Lechlade, which included the detour to Kempsford, the figure came to 18.51 miles. And Lechlade to Newbridge yesterday broke all previous records, coming in at 19.51 miles.

Don't worry, I'm not going to get obsessive about this.

Toni and Karen's 23.28 miles is pretty impressive, though.

A Hindu ceremony, an altercation and buying a belt
Newbridge to Oxford

I tramp onwards beneath the pub's weeping willow.

The weather is balmy. A heron rests on the bridge, surveying the river. Swallows swoop above giant bamboo-like reeds. Water rushes through the weir by Northmoor Lock. A sign warns fishermen not to cast their rods below an electricity line (I wonder how many anglers have come a cropper that way).

Then I attend a Hindu ceremony.

Expect the unexpected on a Thames river walk.

The Hindu ceremony is being conducted by the edge of a 'private field' next to a static caravan campsite. Tamoden, the groom, and

Shelvina, the bride, are renewing wedding vows after a year's marriage. The ceremony is part of the Aadi festival. The group, from Notting Hill, comprises five people; British, but of Mauritian Tamil Hindu descent. The bride has a golden thread necklace and wears a red and gold sari, while the groom, who works for a paparazzi photography agency, has heavy-rimmed specs and is in a white sarong and white business shirt. He has taken off his shoes and he stands in the shallow water by a grassy bank. Tamoden has spread a banana leaf on the bank, upon which he is placing an orange powder in a cup next to a banana, apple and coconut. The powder – turmeric, apparently – is for the 'purification of the fruits', Tamoden says.

We talk for a while about this and that (Tamoden good-humouredly accusing the newspaper company I work for of being slow in payments). Then, not wanting to intrude any longer than I have, I thank them and continue in the direction of Oxford. What nice people.

This part of the river is at Bablock Hythe, where there has been a ferry crossing for a thousand years, although the service is irregular now and the river here is chiefly known for its mention in Matthew Arnold's poem *The Scholar-Gipsy*. The Thames Path cuts inland here. Fields with sheep open up past a bungalow park. Beyond, a lane leads between bramble-thick hedgerows and back to pasture by the river, where a trick of perspective creates the illusion that a rotund man in a red jumper is gliding god-like above the water. He's skippering a barge, but the vessel below him is out of sight.

A crossing by a lock leads to a boatyard with wrecks. It begins to rain. I put on the pac-a-mac and reach Swinford Bridge. This is one of three toll bridges on the Thames and the current price for a car crossing is five pence, collected by a man in a little booth. I feel sorry for this man collecting five-pence pieces in his little booth; I hope it's just a summer job. Swinford Bridge, I know from my reading up, was built by the Earl of Abingdon after George III fell in the water when taking a ferry at this spot. George III was pleased and granted a tax-free toll in perpetuity.

After the bridge I come to a barge with a sticker saying, *I'M NOT BACKING FRACKING, FOSSIL-FREE CARBON*, and then a shadowy path lined with cow parsley and trees overgrown with ivy. This is Wytham Woods, where bodies from the television series *Inspector Morse* are routinely discovered. I follow long fields through a sustainable farm doing many good sustainable things; a sign explains but it's too wet to hang around. The path continues on a section with a few fallen willows near the noisy A34, where I find the remains of a fire with a scattering of cans of Foster's, melted bottles and broken glass.

The distance from Newbridge to Oxford, where I am staying the night, is 14 miles. This is a long way, but something has got into me – perhaps it's the walking bug – and I have decided to go for lunch at the Perch pub in Binsey on the outskirts of Oxford. The Perch gets a good write-up in one of the guidebooks. This target leaves a mile afterwards to reach my inn for the night.

After the A34 I wander round the remains of Godstow Abbey, suppressed by Henry VIII in 1539 and where Henry II's mistress 'Fair Rosamund' was sent by Queen Eleanor and probably poisoned to death by her in 1176. A sign on a damp wall warns visitors that the use of metal detectors is prohibited. Meanwhile, beneath a Local Historical Society post, heaps of beer and Red Bull cans, vodka bottles and takeaway wrappers have been dumped. A burnt-out disposable barbecue lies close by.

Was it at this very spot or a little further on that Reverend Charles Dodgson, a mathematics tutor at Christ Church College who chose the pen name Lewis Carroll, sat with Alice Liddell and her sisters Lorina and Edith to begin telling the story of *Alice's Adventures in Wonderland* 154 years ago? It must have been close.

Alice was beginning to get very tired of sitting by her sister on the bank, and of having nothing to do: once or twice she had peeped into the book her sister was reading, but it had no pictures or conversations in it, "and what is the use of a book," thought Alice, "without pictures or conversation?" So she was considering in her own mind (as well as she could, for the hot day made her feel very sleepy and stupid), whether the pleasure of making a daisy-chain would be worth the trouble of getting up and picking the daisies, when suddenly a White Rabbit with pink eyes ran close by her.

If not a hot day, it is getting hotter, and it is obvious that the riverbanks here make a perfect place for storytelling in the sunshine (I feel sure, however, that Charles Dodgson and Alice cleared up after their picnics).

The drizzle has stopped and the sun has broken through, with the flat expanse of Port Meadow stretching ahead to the north and a line of distant trees and buildings marking the edge of Oxford proper. Piebald horses have gathered by the shore on Port Meadow. A few of the famous dreaming spires poke above the horizon. I finally reach the Perch pub, feeling as tired as I have so far on the Thames walk. I go down a path into a garden where diners are eating late lunches outside a thatched cottage. Inside, I go to a dimly lit bar with a low-beamed ceiling and a chesterfield sofa facing a blazing fire.

This seems pleasant. The barman hands over a menu. I'm after a sandwich or a baked potato or burger, but the menu is broken down into starters and mains. It looks very fancy – and it is very fancy. Among the starters are 'globe artichoke and pickled carrot, toasted pumpkin seeds, sweetcorn and radish salad' and 'potted kiln-smoked salmon, watercress mousse and toasted soda bread'. The mains include 'grilled sea trout with crushed Jersey Royals, spring onion, parsley and cockle butter' and 'pan-roasted ox cheeks, cauliflower champ and spring cabbage'. All these exotic offerings are quite pricey. A burger is available – a 'chargrilled 8 oz burger' (it couldn't just be a 'burger') – but it costs more than £13. I really don't want to have to mess about with all of this and it's too expensive.

I ask the barman if there is a bar menu.

He raises an eyebrow. I am the only customer in the Perch in possession of a backpack and wearing a pac-a-mac, which I've yet to take off despite the sun coming out. The result of keeping the pac-a-mac on is that I am sweating profusely. I think I must also have a ravenous look in my eye after 13 miles of walking more or less non-stop.

He says there is no bar menu.

I ask him if this is a pub.

He says that it is a pub.

I ask him for a pint of lime and soda. Then I peruse a few bar snacks on the counter. These include sausage rolls and Scotch eggs, or pots of pistachio nuts. Each of these is £3.50. I do not want to pay £3.50 for a Scotch egg. Alternatively, I notice, there is a cigar menu with Cohiba Siglo II cigars available for £24.50. I do not want a £24.50 cigar.

The barman brings the pint of lime and soda.

'That will be £2.95,' he says.

I look at him to see whether he is 'having a laugh'. He is not having one. I tell him that £2.95 for a lime and soda is daylight robbery, or words to that effect. In other pubs so far, the price has ranged from 75p to £1.50. I have always made a mental note of the price as I regard this as a way of measuring a pub (the soda water and cordial cost virtually nothing, after all).

'This is a complete joke,' I say, handing over the money.

'I'll tell the owners it's a complete joke,' replies the barman, straight-faced. He is in his twenties and has a beard.

I return to my seat and drink my lime and soda, muttering to myself as I contemplate the next most likely place to eat. As I do so, the bearded barman comes over. Am I about to be ejected on some grounds about which I am shortly to be made aware? Too much backchat? No muddy boots in the bar (though they're pretty clean)?

Surprisingly, I'm not.

'Listen, I'm just the barman. I agree with you,' he says.

'Oh,' I reply, and mumble thanks of some sort.

Not such a bad place after all.

I quicken my pace to find a late-late lunch.

Beyond a series of ugly student accommodation blocks on the edge of Port Meadow, the river makes a slight right and, despite being so hungry, I stop to watch a couple of kids fishing in the river. They have simple lines, without rods. Each time they drop in a line they pull up small orange crustaceans about a minute later. These are placed in a bucket teeming with the creatures. I ask Daniel, 14, and Charlie, 12, and Simon, the boys' uncle, what they are catching. Crayfish, they tell me, and they are aiming to collect about 150 of them. So far they have captured 80 in an hour. Their method is to put an old sardine head inside a tiny net connected to a line. The crayfish cannot resist the sardine, to such an extent that they cling on as they are being pulled up; their greed leading directly to their doom.

'I'm a fisherman. They're a nightmare,' says Simon, referring to the crayfish. 'They're always stealing your bait.'

The boys tell me that once they have enough they will sell them to a local restaurant. Usually such a catch is worth £30. The boys inform the chefs at whichever restaurant buys them that the crayfish should be kept in a bucket for two days and that the water should be regularly refreshed so as to clean out Thames impurities.

What a marvellous little business.

It's not far from here, via graffiti saying SCUM and ZOMBIE and tourists larking about on a punt, to Folly Bridge and the Head of the River pub.

This is where I'm staying, right by the spot where oxen used to cross a ford; the origin of the city name. I walk across a terrace with red sunshades and enter another bar. This one is cavernous and on two levels, with various black-and-white pictures of boatbuilding days (the pub used to be the headquarters of Salter Brothers boatbuilders) and a mouldy-looking Thames map by Tombleson.

A notice on the top bar says: *All service is from the lower bar.*

So I go to the lower bar, where I am told by a member of staff to return to the top bar for check-in.

I am not having the best of days in Thames riverside pubs.

However, a friendly receptionist surprises me by saying: 'We've given you an upgrade to a superior.'

I am led upstairs to the Lewis Carroll Room, which is on a corner overlooking the river with a Thames-view bed. Lewis Carroll set off from Folly Bridge with Alice on their rowing trips to Godstow, and an iconic photograph of him looking thoughtful in a black leather armchair hangs on one of the walls.

'Everything in the room is complimentary,' says the receptionist, surprising me once more.

I scan the items on offer.

'Including that bottle of London Pride bitter?' I ask, just to be sure.

'Yes, including that,' she says.

Some of the other rooms in the Head of the River pub are named after prominent Oxford figures such as Evelyn Waugh, A. A. Milne, Aldous Huxley and T. S. Eliot. I glance at the pub's terrace menu, which looks good, but I'm too hungry to wait for cooked food. I walk up the road to a Tesco Express next to the Crown and County Court and buy a triple-decker sandwich, pasta salad, banana and an apple. Across the street from the Tesco Express, sitting on a wooden bench by Christ Church Meadow, I consume this hastily assembled picnic with such rapidity that a group of down-and-outs drinking cider on the neighbouring bench pauses from a bout of hectoring one another to gaze my way.

For a moment it feels as though the tramps of Christ Church Meadow are considering whether they have found a new recruit. What exactly is this half-starving man in damp boots and bramble-scraped trouser-shorts doing? Is that a four-pack of Special Brew tucked in that Tesco Express bag?

They turn away. There are important matters at hand, such as discussing their next victims of actual bodily harm.

A twitchy blonde woman is holding court: 'Oh shut up, you ****. She was shaggin' him, so I headbutted 'im. She's skank. You know what I mean. He's not a wide boy. I'll get 'im again. He's got in my 'ead.'

Welcome to the city with the oldest university in the English-speaking world.

Some believe this ancient seat of learning dates back as far as 1096, though the real burst of college-building was during the reign of Henry II when the king, in 1167, banned the English from studying in Paris. Ever since, a town-versus-gown mentality has existed in Oxford. In 1209, relations between students and locals boiled over to such an extent that some scholars fled to Cambridge for safety, setting up a new university.

After my Tesco Express feast, which set me back less than the price of a couple of sausage rolls at the Perch, I rest on my bench.

The twitchy blonde, who I can safely say is 'town', is still going strong: 'Skank, she is. I saw 'em. He was holdin' hands, cuddlin' up to her...'

I try to zone out. Public buses boasting of Wi-Fi and 'electro-hybrid technology' fizz along the busy road. These buses claim to be part of 'Electro-City' and when they draw to a halt their engines cut out immediately. The pavements are rammed with tourists, many of them Asian, possibly Chinese. One of the immediate effects of Brexit has been a collapse in the pound. And while that is awful in many ways, it has a silver lining. The result has been a domestic tourism boom, with the likes of Frank and Elsje from Maastricht jumping in their cars and driving over. Hoteliers across the country have been reporting an increase in business, though it's probably always chock-a-block in Oxford midsummer.

Across the street is a rare and second-hand bookshop, and next to this is Alice's Shop, where 'Alice Liddell bought her barley sweets'. I go to nose around. Inside, a small space is full of shelves packed with Mad Hatter teapots (£38), Mad Hatter teapot stands (£25), Alice costumes (£45), Alice earrings (£55) and Alice mugs (£8). The latter are perhaps the most appropriate gifts for those wishing to buy a gift for themselves.

I have a couple of missions in Oxford. One: to purchase a belt. Unbelievably, after a few days of walking I need one; the olive-coloured trouser-shorts were perfectly OK worn beltless back at Trewsbury Mead, but now they are hanging loose. Anyone wishing to lose weight (something I had neither intended nor wished to achieve) should head straight for the Thames Path: you can eat pies, drink ales and large glasses of Chardonnay, and you will find yourself having to buy new belts. Two: to see Kenneth Grahame's grave. *The Wind in the Willows* is not just one of my favourite Thames books – it's one of my favourite books. The story of the riverside escapades of Mole, Ratty, Mr Toad and Mr Badger captures gentle aspects of the Thames like no other. It's also a wonderful tale about friendship and about seeking pleasure in simple things. It fits my Thames walk like a glove: friendship (in the form of friends and family joining me, as well as the friends I make along the way) and simple pleasures by the water are what I am looking for during this strangest of summers.

First task completed (purchase worn), I find Holywell Cemetery, a short distance north of the high street and the Bodleian Library. Through a little wooden gate and down an ivy-clad passage I enter a graveyard thick with weeds and overgrown grass. An information board helps locate Grahame's crumbling grave. The epitaph, difficult to decipher as the stone is so worn, says: *To the beautiful memory of Kenneth Grahame, husband of Elspeth and father of Alastair, who passed the River on the 6th July 1932, leaving childhood and literature through him the more blest for all time.*

Here lies a former secretary of the Bank of England who wrote children's books as a sideline and who did not, in 1908, have immediate success with *The Wind in the Willows*. However, all this changed when the president of the United States, Theodore Roosevelt, wrote to Grahame the following year to say how much he and his family had enjoyed the story. Then A. A. Milne, creator of Winnie-the-Pooh, made the book into a play, *Toad of Toad Hall*. The Roosevelt–Milne endorsements turned the tide. Sales took off. Milne wrote of the book: 'One does not argue about *The Wind in the Willows*. The young man gives it to the girl with whom he is in love, and if she does not like it, asks her to return his letters. The older man tries it on his nephew, and alters his will accordingly. The book is a test of character. We can't criticise it, because it is criticising us.'

Over the next few days, I will be travelling through quintessential *Wind in the Willows* territory. And I can't wait.

Back in the tourist scrum, I return to the Head of the River pub and sit on the terrace next to an old boatyard crane.

My tracking device says that today's distance was 20.51 miles, the furthest yet; I'm not sure I have ever walked so far in a day. Nearby, two bearded eccentrics huddle in a corner drinking ale and gesticulating. One of them wears a skipper's cap and smokes a pipe. Marxist politics professors considering the policies of Jeremy Corbyn? English literature lecturers discussing *Beowulf*?

Rowers in life jackets arrive and clamber to the terrace. Oars are passed along. I eat an OK chicken burger at an OK-ish price.

Food by the Thames has many quirks, but so far there is one underlying common factor: you pay for the privilege of eating by the water.

I wash my clothes in my room, using a heating rail in the bathroom to dry them overnight. Then I sit at the desk and drink the complimentary bottle of London Pride, looking out beyond the hotel's bright hanging baskets to the ink-black water. My feet feel sore. My back aches. Ducks or possibly swans are squabbling somewhere near Folly Bridge.

Boatyards and karma
Oxford to Abingdon

Folly Bridge was built between 1825 and 1827 in two parts, with an island in the middle. There has been a stone bridge here since 1085, and in the thirteenth century an alchemist named Roger Bacon lived and worked in a folly-like tower that stood across the bridge until 1779. J. M. W. Turner drew the bridge when he was aged 12. It is soul-lifting to wake beside this Oxford landmark and gaze at the tourist boats moored across the way. Soft early sunlight and a clear blue sky suggest a good day's walking ahead.

In the cavernous bar-cum-breakfast-room, I listen to Michael Jackson and Motown hits, eating porridge and watching Sky News.

A screen in a corner shows men in hoods and scarves standing by temporary abodes in the 'Jungle' camp at Calais. A few are being patted down by riot police, while in the background a fire flares from burning tyres. The television's volume is off but subtitles are on and a ticker-tape message says: *Migration crisis: Is the government doing enough?* Some of the day's papers are on a side table. Immigration is the big story of the day. *The Times* front-page headline is: *ONE MILLION MIGRANTS IN UK ILLEGALLY*, with an accompanying article explaining that 'many will not be deported, according to head of the UK Border Agency' and that the Home Office does not know how many illegal migrants are in the UK. *The Daily Telegraph*'s main article is: *CALL FOR NAVY TO PATROL CHANNEL OVER TERROR FEARS*. The Home Affairs Select Committee believes that the Royal Navy should be deployed in the Channel 'to protect the UK against migrant people-smugglers and the heightened terror threat'. Current patrol boats provide insufficient protection against 'the threat to the country from the refugee crisis'. Meanwhile, *The Guardian*'s reporter in the Jungle camp in Calais has interviewed a child who says that police fired tear gas at him and that at night 'rats rustle about' while he sleeps.

Local news is troubled too, but for a different reason. The *Oxford Mail* runs a tragic front-page Thames story: *FRIENDS' HEROIC EFFORTS TO SAVE ELLIS*. The inquest into the death of Ellis Downes, a 16-year-old who drowned in 'freezing water' in the river near Abingdon three months ago, has concluded that it was an accident and that his friends had tried desperately to save him. The coroner said: 'Two of them bravely dived in and swam towards him. He was almost within reach when he sunk underwater. It was impossible for them to retrieve him.' Downes had swum across the river near Culham Bridge on a sunny day but had been seen struggling in the middle and then shaking with fatigue when he reached the bank on the other side. A friend had offered to drive round to collect him, but he declined and dived back into the water. When his friends saw him drifting in the middle, two went in to help. Dean Gunning said: 'As I dived in, I went numb as the water was freezing cold. I couldn't breathe and the current was strong. The water was almost black – you couldn't see your hand in front of your face.' Downes' brother Jack said: 'Just as I got to Ellis, he went under. I used all my strength to go under the water but I needed to get out. It was too cold.'

A chilling story and a reminder that the Thames has moved on a lot by the time it has reached Oxford. A few days ago I was scooping a handful of water from Lyd Well.

Now the river takes lives.

My sister Kate is joining me from her home in Teddington (by the Thames in south-west London) this morning for the ten-mile walk to Abingdon. She's running late, though she's just sent a text: *On the move. My bag is heavy already and I found it tiring walking to the bus stop. Delighted to be going in the opposite direction to commuters.*

While I'm waiting, I take a tour of Christ Church, the grandest of Oxford's colleges, dating from the sixteenth century, with a sweeping cattle-filled meadow leading to the riverfront. Many Asian tourists have had the same idea and we shuffle between the varnished tables of the wood-panelled Great Hall with its fine portraits of Charles Dodgson, William Gladstone and Anthony Eden; the novelist and the two prime ministers are alumni. Parts of one of the *Harry Potter* films were shot at Christ Church, prompting something of a tourist boom, apparently.

Outside the hall is a quad with a perfect lawn and a gate-tower by Sir Christopher Wren. This leads past student digs that feel straight out of Evelyn Waugh's novel *Brideshead Revisited*; Sebastian Flyte, one of the debauched aristocratic protagonists, is a Christ Church undergraduate. I enter the magnificent college chapel, which also acts as the city's cathedral. Here is the tomb of St Frideswide, the patron saint of Oxford, as well as a stained-glass window depicting saints by William Morris, who seems to crop up just about everywhere on the Thames.

Afterwards, by Christ Church Meadow, I eavesdrop on a guide speaking to an American couple. He's talking to them about the tension between students and those who have been raised in Oxford.

'Of course police are aware we have town and gown,' he says. 'There are some Old Etonians who flaunt their wealth. They behave like they are upper-class twits, and they are upper-class twits. Oh yes, Oxford has a dark side.'

The guide with the Americans moves on in the direction of Corpus Christi College, his words tapering off.

I go to find Kate by Folly Bridge.

She's sitting on the terrace by the Head of the River pub and is soon telling me that my two-year-old niece and four-year-old nephew had wanted to come along, going as far as putting on their wellies while still in their pyjamas this morning. Her journey has involved rail-replacement bus services and a confusing walk around various half-constructed retail and housing developments from the station. 'Oxford is a building site,' she mutters.

The sun is out but this may not last according to the forecast.

'I feel as though we're wasting time here – I'm worried about the weather,' Kate says, as though I have been holding her up. 'It's the nice part of the day – we should be getting some miles behind us.'

I say: 'Yes, of course. We'd better get on.'

She says: 'I have got to have at least three hours lying on my bed before dinner.'

We are staying at a B & B in Abingdon.

I say: 'Yes, of course. All of that can be arranged.' Though this had not been mentioned to me before.

We set off down the path. The south bank of the river is empty apart from the odd jogger or cyclist. Smart-looking boathouses belonging to rowing clubs connected to Oxford colleges arise on the opposite bank. The River Cherwell joins the flow. We continue for half a mile and I explain to Kate that I've arranged to meet someone to show me around the boatbuilding yard ahead.

She looks at me.

'A boatbuilding yard?'

'Yes.'

She raises an eyebrow and says nothing as we make a detour over Donnington Bridge to Salter's Steamers boatyard.

Salter's is an Oxford institution, founded in 1858 and still run by the same family. During the golden era of steamboats in the late nineteenth century the company shot to prominence, and its steamboat service between Oxford and Kingston continued till as recently as the 1970s. These days, two old steamers are still in working order and a total fleet of 14 vessels offers tourist trips. The Head of the River pub used to be part of Salter's HQ, which is now a small office facing the hostelry on the other side of Folly Bridge.

We enter a potholed yard on Meadow Lane. At the far end, a couple of long sheds with peeling paint stand next to the river. No one is about. Kate raises an eyebrow once more. She has gone silent. We wait by a warehouse door. It is one o'clock and the day is slipping away, making three-hour afternoon snoozes significantly less likely.

We are waiting for Matt Longford, one of the Salter's managers, who turns up bang on time in a shiny black pick-up truck. He has ruffled grey hair, a black V-neck jumper and the air of a no-nonsense boatman.

We go into the warehouse. 'This is shipping. The oldest working shipping on the non-tidal Thames,' says Matt.

I hadn't realised that the word 'shipping' could be used in this way. We are standing in a cavernous space with a rusting corrugated roof and walls with ivy creeping in from outside. Light filters through skylights, illuminating a riverboat with its hull stripped of paint and rivets exposed. Hoops of wire, metal rods, hoses, buckets, oil cans, planks, lifting machines, cutting machines, wheelbarrows, cardboard boxes, mallets, rakes, bags of sand, cardboard boxes, an old skipper's seat, heaps of plastic sheeting… everywhere you look there are objects that might or might not one day prove useful.

'All of our boats have their winter maintenance here,' says Matt. 'All holes are checked. There's more refurbishment than actual building in this yard now,' he continues, explaining that Salter's might occasionally receive an order for a punt or a rowing skiff.

The shed is silent on our visit, with just a couple of workers about, seemingly on a tea break. Matt says that there are 'fabricators and welders. Four or five guys work full-time for us in the winter from October to April.'

One of these is Bill, who has been an engineer for 60 years. He's wearing oily old boots, olive-green cargo trousers, and a matching T-shirt and sleeveless jacket with lots of pockets for screws, bolts and screwdrivers. He has balding grey hair, glasses and a lopsided cheeky grin.

'What is your role?' I ask Bill.

'Cheese and chutney, please,' he replies.

A funny guy, Bill.

Then Bill explains he's putting new steel plates on the hull of the boat currently in the shed. It's vital work requiring skills possessed by few these days; without such maintenance in old yards like this, the many tourist boats on the non-tidal Thames would be unable to keep going.

'It's brilliant – I love this work,' he says. 'Even if we get quite wet sometimes from the holes in the roof.'

Some of the corrugated roof panels have sprung leaks.

We talk for a while, voices echoing in the shed, then Kate and I thank Matt and Bill, and make our way back across Donnington Bridge.

Despite her doubts, Kate seems to have enjoyed this interlude. She takes a phone call from a friend and I hear her saying: 'Tom's added on all these boatyard visits. It's quite nice being away from the kids for a day.'

I appear to be doing all right.

Downstream of Oxford the river is placid and deep-green. We walk on, investigating an unusual humpbacked stone bridge near Iffley Lock, with its especially picturesque lock-keeper's house and garden. Further on, beneath a rusty railway bridge, someone has spray-painted a hammer and sickle alongside the words *PEACE AND SOCIALISM*, while someone else has inscribed: *GO VEGAN, LOVE IS THE KEY*. All signs of civilisation disappear as the city fizzles out. Countryside opens up. Thistles, nettles and tall grass almost consume the Thames Path. This total greenery does not last long. Millionaires' houses appear – at least, they look very expensive, as though they are quite possibly homes to people with seven figures at their disposal. Some have Roman-villa-style balustrades at the end of stripy lawns facing the river. Others have UFO-like garden 'pods' with mirrored glass by the water's edge; so the millionaires inside can look out, but you cannot see the millionaires.

We stop for a soft drink at the Kings Arms pub in a quiet spot by a lock where there was once a mill in Sandford. Afterwards meadowland returns and at a bend of the river we come to a bench.

'Let's sit on the bench – it would be rude not to,' says Kate. 'See a bench, sit on it.'

This is her new motto, and not a bad one.

'You've been going too fast,' she says.

I think I may have started walking a bit more quickly than usual recently.

'Too much talking,' she adds. We have been talking quite a bit. 'I'm running out of air.'

We sit on the bench.

On a hill across the way is a distinguished sandy-coloured mansion with an unusual yellow and red flag in a rising sun design on its roof. This is Nuneham House, built in 1756 for a local earl who employed Capability Brown to landscape his gardens. Concerned that dwellings in the village of Nuneham Courtenay spoilt the symmetry of his eyeline, the earl ordered that this inconvenient village be demolished. These days, after being given to the RAF during the Second World War, the house is owned by Oxford University and leased to the Brahma Kumaris World Spiritual University.

This, I know from my reading, is a meditation centre run according to the teachings of Brahma Baba, a jeweller from Hyderabad in Pakistan who decided to establish a religion based on 'spirituality'. So, in 1937, after experiencing visions, Brahma Baba began Brahma Kumaris. At Nuneham House students are taught 'the deep collective consciousness of peace and the individual dignity of each soul'. Through yoga and meditation 'a deepening spiritual awareness gradually breaks open the cage of illusions'. Reincarnation, karma and *samsara* (Sanskrit for 'wheel of life') are part and parcel of Brahma Kumaria, which aims to rid the world of 'dark attitudes' and 'unleash the reservoir of positive energy that can be called the soul'.

All by the River Thames in Oxfordshire.

'Maybe you should make this a self-help book for Londoners who need to sort their lives out' is my sister's response when I mention all of this.

We stop sitting on the bench and set off on the last section of Oxford–Abingdon.

This part seems longer than it looks on the map. Diversions shoot off along paths through thickets. We lose sight of the river. Kate questions whether we are going in the right direction, making me wonder the same too. We come to a T-junction and ask a local twenty-something with a goatee the way to Abingdon.

He scratches his chin as though deep in contemplation.

'That's a tough one,' he says. 'I'll need a bit of time with that.'

Kate and I look at each other.

'It's all Abingdon,' he says finally, wafting an arm about. 'This is Abingdon.'

He beams at us.

This is not exactly helpful.

We are surrounded by trees and bushes without a market town dating from the seventh century anywhere in sight.

'Which way is it to Abingdon Bridge?' I ask, trying to pin him down.

He appears startled by this one, and pauses once again to consider the matter.

Kate and I look at each other.

Then he points in both directions.

Perhaps he's got something to do with Brahma Baba (he seems very calm about things).

We say 'thanks' and just as we are about to go right, he points in the opposite direction and says, 'But if you want a nice river walk, go that way.'

This appears to be going backwards but, having no other leads, we turn left. This takes us across a long lock and then along a field with a bridge in the distance. We have found Abingdon.

Thank you, goatee guy.

'They are trying to create fusion to replicate the sun'
Abingdon

Sometimes you just strike lucky with English B & Bs. Not very often, admittedly. There are, as anyone who has travelled about the UK on a budget knows, plenty of shockers: sticky carpets, lumpy mattresses, scratchy nylon linen, functional furniture from the 1970s that could not possibly count as 'retro cool', cheap kettles on side tables with cartons of long-life milk, bathrooms with mouldy showers and body hair. This is why over the past 20 years or so, cheap, mass-market hotel chains such as Travelodge and Premier Inn have done so well: they are affordable, usually pretty clean and come without nasty surprises, even if they are dreadfully dull.

But the Susie Howard B & B is a very good British B & B.

Over the fifteenth-century bridge by Nag's Head Island and beyond Abingdon's imposing seventeenth-century county hall, we turn left into East Saint Helen Street and knock on the door of a fine red-brick townhouse on a Georgian terrace. The door is opened by Susie Howard, owner of Susie Howard B & B. She is in her sixties, smiley and wearing a cucumber-green T-shirt and pearl earrings. Susie is a chatterbox. In the hallway, while we still have our backpacks on, she is soon telling us she has eight rooms, two of which are occupied by long-stay guests, including a parking warden who has been at the B & B for 18 years and a physicist who has been here for six. Many of her guests are physicists as Abingdon is close to the headquarters of JET, Joint European Torus, which is located in Culham and is involved with cutting-edge experiments in nuclear fusion.

'They are trying to create fusion to replicate the sun,' Susie says, as though this is perfectly normal information to impart to two weary Thames riverside walkers. She hands me a pamphlet all about JET.

We talk nuclear fusion for a while, before being shown to our rooms.

'There you are – you've got a physicist between you,' Susie says, inviting us to join her for tea in her garden once we've got settled.

'Oh good, I'd been hoping she'd offer us tea,' says Kate as Susie departs. 'My feet are hurting and my brain is telling me to sit down.'

Our rooms are not en suite – there's a bathroom down the hall – but they are elegantly decorated with ethnic carpets on polished wood floors and antique furniture. We go to the red-brick terrace in a pretty garden with olive trees, roses, geraniums and apple and pear trees. We sit at an iron table as Susie pours tea and tells us about her life.

After leaving school, she had trained to be a midwife, and as she was just starting out she met her husband through an advert for an unfurnished flat that he was offering in *The Times*; she had gone to see the flat and he had asked her on a date. They moved to Abingdon as relations lived nearby and they wanted their son to go to Abingdon School, which has a good reputation. Their elegant Georgian house had cost £75,000 in 1992. After her husband died, she began the B & B.

'I just love to go with the flow,' she says, sipping her Earl Grey. 'Anything I've planned in life hasn't worked. I never thought it would be like that. I thought I'd be a nurse or a teacher.'

Guests at the B & B tonight include two other Thames walkers and two construction workers from Liverpool.

'I overbooked by mistake,' says Susie. 'I'm sleeping on a mattress on the floor of the living room.' The other walkers are getting her bedroom.

There's a delightful throw-it-all-together feel about the Susie Howard B & B.

We finish our tea and pay for the rooms. Then we eat pasta at a place round the corner, and return to the Susie Howard B & B, where we never lay eyes on a nuclear physicist (but hear plenty of nuclear physicists pacing up and down in the halls).

CHAPTER FIVE

ABINGDON, OXFORDSHIRE, TO PANGBOURNE, BERKSHIRE

DREAM HOMES AND A PERFECT CUP OF TEA

Abingdon

Clifton
Hampden

Dorchester

Sutton
Courtenay

THE THAMES

Wallingford

Moulsford

Streatley Goring

Pangbourne

Abingdon has three traditional Turkish barbers within about 50 metres of its main market square. There is also a tattoo and piercing parlour where customers aged over 14 may request piercings as long as they have their parents' consent. Those over the age of 18, with photo identification, may opt for tattoos, nipple piercings and 'dermals'. The latter are little metal, bejewelled studs that are stuck into your body just about anywhere you want; the incision takes about two months to heal. Potential customers at this tattoo and piercing parlour are advised that appointments will be cancelled if anyone turns up 'drunk, under the influence of drugs, underage, pregnant, [or] dirty'.

It does not take long to walk around what many consider to be one of Britain's oldest continuously inhabited towns, believed to have been settled in the Iron Age. Susie had told us that pre-Roman remains had been found in a neighbour's cellar. And there is a Benedictine abbey dating from 676, although most of this has been destroyed, with just a rebuilt gatehouse remaining.

Kate has gone on a hybrid-electric bus back to Oxford to catch a train home. The sun is out; soft light bathes the lovely Georgian houses on East Saint Helen Street. In one of these, William III stayed for a night *on his way from Torbay to Liverpool*, says a plaque. After poking my nose in St Ethelwold's House, a meditation, yoga and poetry centre – apparently of some renown in meditation, yoga and poetry circles – I go for a coffee in the square, overlooking the county hall (Abingdon used to be the county town of Berkshire but it passed into Oxfordshire during a boundary alteration in 1974). This imposing honey-stone structure is famous for the time when buns were thrown from windows to the crowd below on the announcement of the coronation of George III. This bun-throwing tradition continues on important royal occasions.

In the cafe I pick up a copy of the *Oxford Times* and read more about the tragic river death of Ellis Downes. No traces of drugs or alcohol were found in his body, and an expert from the Royal Society for the Prevention of Accidents says that 'cold-water shock' is often responsible for such accidents, which result in many deaths each year. The same paper reports on plans to limit the time boat owners can moor by the river in Abingdon; currently this is five days, but Abingdon Town Council officials want a reduction to three to allow more tourists to visit and to curb the number of people living on boats in Abingdon while working in Oxford. A preponderance of such vessels also means less space for families to go fishing, says the council leader, sounding huffy.

Meanwhile – nothing whatsoever to do with the river – the Abingdon edition of *The Herald* covers the curious goings-on of Eamon Kelly, pigeon fancier from the nearby village of Steventon, who entered his pigeon in a mammoth race to the South of France, and won, but was discovered to have advantageously sent another bird, thus breaking competition rules. In a statement Mr Kelly says: 'I apologise sincerely to all my friends and family for my stupid actions.' The chairman of the pigeon fanciers' National Flying Club comments: 'This is a very disappointing episode for the sport.'

I do love local papers.

George Orwell's grave
Abingdon to Clifton Hampden

Today's target is the medieval town of Wallingford, about 14 miles away. I set off at a stomp.

The Thames Path here moves along the north bank of the river. Ancient houses on the south bank, clustered around the tall steeple of St Helen's Church, make way for mid-twentieth-century Lego-like homes, many with great river views. St Helen's, locked when I went by earlier, contains a memorial tablet to a local named W. Lee who *had in his lifetime issue from his loins two hundred lacking but three* – which sounds pretty good going. Beyond the town, the path cuts alongside wheat fields with the cooling towers of Didcot Power Station jutting in the distance.

A dog walker informs me that the bird of prey with forked tail feathers circling above is a red kite. She says that they have been reintroduced to the area and have flourished: 'There are absolutely hundreds of them. They're quite the scavengers. People don't encourage them any more but they used to: they used to put out food for them.' A dead cygnet lies on the narrow path, looking as though it may have been the overnight victim of a fox. Perhaps the red kite is waiting for us to pass before swooping down to investigate.

Beds of tall yellow flowers and weeds with pale-pink bell-shaped petals colour the banks close to the two stone bridges at Culham. Somewhere in the waters around here Ellis Downes sadly drowned.

I cross the bridges and head south on a diversion.

I'm going to find George Orwell's grave.

Eric Arthur Blair, as Orwell was born, is buried in the graveyard of All Saints' Church in the village of Sutton Courtenay. The village is about a mile and a quarter along a road with detached houses; one with a stubborn *VOTE REMAIN* sign attached to a post. A row of Tudor cottages leads to the George and Dragon, next door to which is the church, where a bulletin board shows the whereabouts of Orwell's grave as well as those of David Astor, the twentieth-century newspaper publisher/editor, and of Herbert Henry Asquith, Britain's prime minister from 1908 to 1916.

The grave is easy to locate, at the back of the churchyard close to a weeping willow. His simple stone says: *Here lies Eric Arthur Blair, Born June 25th 1903, Died January 21st 1950*. The grave of David Astor (1912–2001), who lived in Sutton Courtenay, is a couple of steps away. Orwell had requested that he be buried under his birth name in a 'country churchyard', and Astor helped with arrangements. The author of *1984* and *Animal Farm* was 46 when he passed away after contracting tuberculosis in 1938 and battling with the disease for the rest of his life. Red and white roses are planted on his plot.

I take off my backpack and sit on a bench by a back wall. Pigeons are cooing and I can hear the pulsating chords of the church organ across an avenue of yew trees. I close my eyes for a while. I hadn't expected my Thames walk to bring me here. Blair took up the pen name of Orwell so as not to embarrass his parents when he published his tale of working in menial jobs in *Down and Out in Paris and London* (his first book), and he is in the news this summer. A statue of the writer is soon to be unveiled outside the headquarters of the BBC in London. It is to be inscribed with one of his most memorable lines: 'If liberty means anything at all, it means the right to tell people what they do not want to hear.'

I wonder what Orwell would have made of Brexit.

Herbert Henry Asquith's larger and more prominent grave is closer to the church. The Liberal prime minister lived in Sutton Courtenay and it was here that he signed the declaration that formally took Britain into the First World War.

Inside All Saints' there is a memorial tablet to Orwell and information about his life. Through a blue felt inner door I enter the cool church, where I am soon meeting John, the church 'verger, bell-ringer, choir singer, churchyard keeper and organist'. John explains that each year Orwell's adopted son, Richard, reads a passage from his father's works on the nearest Sunday to the author's birthday. On 25 June itself, a group of a dozen or so Orwell fans holds a vigil by his grave. 'It's not known whether Orwell ever actually came to Sutton Courtenay,' says John, who has a very firm handshake, prominent eyebrows and a twinkle in his eye. 'One time someone left a cup of tea by his grave with a copy of his essay *A Nice Cup of Tea* – it was there for three months before we eventually moved it.'

We shake hands once again and I return to the river after taking a look at the Wharf, Asquith's house that is now in the hands of his great granddaughter, the actress Helena Bonham Carter and her ex-partner, the film director Tim Burton. Winston Churchill and the Aga Khan are among the many famous guests who visited the house.

A lot of connections swirl in the air in the sleepy Thames village of Sutton Courtenay.

The sun is still out and crickets are chirping back on the Thames Path. The earth is dry and cracked. Poppies, blackberry bushes, dock leaves, nettles and beds of purple willowherb jostle for space beside a cereal field. A shower comes from nowhere, the sound of the rain pelting on the crop announcing its arrival ahead of time (I'm able to put on the pac-a-mac before the downpour). It soon passes. A gorgeous red-brick bridge comes into view, with the spire of a church beyond. The river here is wide, slow and olive-coloured.

This is Clifton Hampden, one of the most picturesque spots on the River Thames.

The bridge was designed by George Gilbert Scott, the prolific nineteenth-century architect who was known for his Gothic Revival style. It is said that when he was commissioned for this bridge in the 1860s, he drew up the first plan on his shirt cuff over dinner with the local landowner. Gothic touches such as arches and castellated walls are evidence of Scott's hand.

Not far away, a man and a woman with a Labrador are splashing about in the water by a grassy bank. They are wearing wetsuits and tell me that they have come to give the dog relief from its arthritis. I watch for a while. The river is shallow here and they are able to wade out almost into the middle.

Up a path alongside a quite busy road from this riverside meadow, I come to the Barley Mow pub, the target of my lunch stop.

The Barley Mow and Bishop Birinus
Clifton Hampden to Dorchester

With its thatched roof, whitewashed walls, beams and hanging baskets, the best word for the Barley Mow is 'quaint'. And it is this description that will probably always stick with the pub after being captured in Jerome K. Jerome's amusing Thames adventure book, *Three Men in a Boat* (1889), as 'without exception, I should say, the quaintest, most old-world inn up the river... Its low-pitched gables and thatched roof and latticed windows give it quite a story-book appearance'.

A red plaque by the front door draws attention to this literary connection, with 'quaintest, most old-world inn' prominently stated.

This is my first port of call on what might be described as 'the *Three Men* trail' during this section of the Thames, although the three protagonists and their dog Montmorency row as far as Oxford from their starting point of Kingston. The book remains so popular that some follow religiously in its oar-sweeps and footsteps. I'm hoping simply to visit what happens to pass my way. I have already gone to some of the same places as Jerome and his two friends, who took off on their escapist adventure to relieve 'overstrain upon our brains' and to get 'far from the madding crowd... from whence the surging waves of the nineteenth century would sound far-off and faint'.

In *Three Men* the party spends a pleasant couple of days in Oxford, although Jerome is cutting about Abingdon, which he writes off as 'quiet, eminently respectable, clean, and desperately dull'. One point of interest to raise here is that Jerome, in his own words, did 'not intend to write a funny book'. He set out to describe the scenery and tell the history of the Thames. Before doing so, he wrote a 'humorous relief' to get the trio's escapades off his chest. This 'humorous relief' was to become a comic classic.

All of which is very well, but I'm hungry.

I enter the Barley Mow in search of lunch. Inside, a *Deal Or No Deal* fruit machine flashes next to an ATM that charges £1.85 for transactions.

Pop music reverberates off the low ceiling and a few couples are drinking quietly. It is a weekday lunchtime. I feel eyes upon me as I untie the awkward knot on my backpack. I order a lime and soda and a baked potato with beans and chicken. I sit at a wobbly table with high stools and kill time waiting for the food by reading the drinks list, which includes Aperol Spritz (the Italian aperitif seems popular in the Oxfordshire countryside) and double Bombay Sapphire G & Ts.

At moments on these long walking days, as any walker of distance knows, energy levels collapse. This is one of those crashes. I am worn out, sleepy and hungry. The food is taking ages to arrive.

But arrive it does, delivered with a flourish by a woman with a smile plastered across her face as though the much anticipated entrée at a Michelin-star restaurant, the dish that has the critics in raptures, the one you've been waiting to sample to find out what all the fuss is about, has – at last – arrived.

I look at my baked potato with beans and thin shreds of dried-out chicken. Were I bothered to count the beans, I easily could. There cannot be more than, say, 20. The potato is not a big baked potato. It is a small baked potato with a narrow slit across its length into which the 20 or so beans have been placed. The chicken is rubbery and just about tasteless; the thin strips uncomfortably reminiscent of pet food. But I am famished. I dig in, demolishing the dish in a short space of time. Each time I use the knife the table wobbles, though I do not particularly care.

This jacket potato cost £4.99. I know that in this day and age £4.99 is not a fortune. But how much could the ingredients have cost: 50p, less maybe, or perhaps £1? Why not just a little more generosity?

As I am thinking these thoughts, sitting next to the ATM and the blinking *Deal Or No Deal* fruit machine, the woman with the plastered smile comes over and asks, 'Is everything all right there?'

Clearly it isn't. I've finished 'lunch' in a few bites and flashes of cutlery.

But I hear myself responding: 'Yes, that was good, thanks.'

This encounter, I'll explain to any non-English readers who are puzzled by my response, is what being English is all about.

Inside, of course, I am raging.

The woman with the plastered smile wordlessly takes my plate in a manner that suggests 'victory' is hers – which, I suppose, it is.

There is a chance, of course, that I am imagining the ins and outs of this Battle of the Baked Potato.

But she does seem rather pleased.

Back by the bridge I remind myself that there is no point in getting cynical and grumpy on this walk. I cross over to see the centre of the village of Clifton Hampden, deemed by Jerome to be a 'wonderfully pretty village, old-fashioned, peaceful, and dainty with flowers'. The village is indeed picturesque, although the line of cars with running engines waiting to cross the bridge would not have existed in Jerome's time. The imposing church of St Michael and All Angels, much of which was rebuilt in Gothic style by George Gilbert Scott, is on a sandstone bluff overlooking the river and its principal claim to fame is that William Dyke, a sergeant in the Grenadier Guards who fired the first shot (accidentally) at the Battle of Waterloo, is buried in the churchyard. He was a regular worshipper at the church and his grave is near the entrance. In the village beyond St Michael and All Angels, a row of seventeenth-century cottages bends upwards beyond a village shop where I buy some flapjack to supplement my Barley Mow lunch.

On the Thames Path, I try to make time.

Mansions arise on the opposite, northern bank. Great dream pads with sweeping lawns and willow trees and the look of *yes, I've made it*. On the path side of the river, meadows and farming fields roll to a horizon marked by a pair of tree-topped hills known as the Wittenham Clumps.

Pain from the straps of my backpack seems to shift from shoulder to shoulder. It is the first time I've suffered this and I try to straighten my back (which works for a while). More mansions appear, serious dream pads with boathouses. These people are not just on the property ladder – they're on property's stairway to heaven.

One of the reasons I need to speed up is because I know another diversion is soon to come. The village of Dorchester lies ahead beyond meadows and a big river bend. Red kites sail above. A heron on a log considers watery matters below. A flock of crows lifts out of a treetop. I cross the river at Day's Lock and follow the path along a field with dog walkers in tweeds and wellies.

An old boy wearing plus fours and yellow socks genially booms: 'GOOD AFTERNOON!'

For some reason I can't discern – perhaps it is a knee-jerk reaction to fit in – I find myself booming back to the man in plus fours and yellow socks: 'GOOD AFTERNOON!'

The man in plus fours and yellow socks falters momentarily, nods and mutters indecipherable approval.

I nod and mutter indecipherable approval in reply.

The man with the plus fours and yellow socks and I nod and mutter some more. This seems to be the way you do it in the countryside.

The man with plus fours and yellow socks walks on. And I reach the edge of Dorchester.

Much has happened by the river at Dorchester over the years; people have lived here a very long time. Evidence of an Iron Age fort has been found in the Dyke Hills just to the south of the village. When the Romans came they built a major town with an amphitheatre, Dorocina, on the site of the village. Then, in Saxon times, Dorchester was to become the capital of Wessex. And in 634 something truly remarkable happened here in the very waters of the Thames.

In 634 Bishop Birinus was sent to Britain by the Pope to convert to Christianity the king of Wessex (Cynegils) in the presence of the already Christian king of Northumbria (Oswald). Birinus came and he did just this, kneeling in the shallows of the river to baptise Cynegils. This act left just one significant pagan king in Britain: Penda in Mercia. A religious balance in the country had been tipped. On this windswept bend of the River Thames, some say that Christianity was established in England.

There is another aspect of the Thames that I have waited till now to raise. There are many theories about the origin of the name 'Thames'. The most widespread of these involves the ancient reference to the river from its source at Trewsbury Mead to Dorchester as 'the Isis'; as it is still known, somewhat oddly, where it passes through Oxford. The word 'Isis' is a variant of 'Isa', a Celtic name for 'river'.

'Tam' is also a Celtic word used for 'a river'. It was suggested by Tudor scholars that the name Thames came from the confluence of the Isis, flowing from the source, with the tributary River Thame (coming from 'Tam'), at this very point by Dorchester. The Thame and the Isis combined, so the theory goes, to create 'Thameisis', or 'Thames'.

The likelihood, however, is more mundane. It is probable that Celtic people, wherever they may have been, simply called the river either 'Isa' or 'Tam', and 'Thames' merely emerged as an amalgamation of the two. By Saxon and Roman times, this appellation, Thames, had become established.

A final note on the name, and a bit of an aside (but fascinating if true): the Sanskrit word *tamasa*, meaning 'dark' and predating the Celts, was used in India to refer to a river connecting to the Ganges. It could be that this passed into the Celtic language through movements of nomadic people in ancient times. In which case, the name of the River Thames has subcontinental roots.

Britain's best tea room
Dorchester

Whichever way you look at it, Dorchester is an important place on the river. I reach a little bridge by the point where the River Thames is met by the tributary River Thame, which runs in a crystal-clear channel between reeds and trees in the direction of Dorchester. I turn inland through a meadow and half a mile up an incline I come to the sleepy village.

The streets are empty. Cottages and buildings with Tudor beams line a lane up to Dorchester Abbey, where the remains of Birinus are said to be buried. The original devotional structure here, a Saxon cathedral, dates from his arrival in 634. Over the years this became a monastery that managed to survive destruction at the hands of Henry VIII. Stone columns shoot upwards to a high wood-beamed ceiling and great stained-glass windows cast orange-pink light on flagstone floors. A panel in one of the windows shows Birinus being sent to Britain by the Pope.

The highlight for me, though, is the tea room.

I am met at the door of the tea room, next to a little gift shop, by a woman in a lilac jumper.

'Are you a teacher?' she asks.

I tell her I'm not a teacher.

'I don't normally ask that. You look like a teacher,' she says.

Nobody has ever accused me of that before.

The woman in the lilac jumper, who works at the gift shop, is blocking the entrance to the tea room.

'You know, people say it's Dorchester-on-Thames. It was once called Dorchester-on-Thame; now it's called Dorchester-on-Thames. It's actually on the River Thame,' she tells me, unprompted.

I tell her I had heard about this.

The woman in the lilac jumper ignores me.

'Well, it is on the Thame. Thames! Thames! Lies! That's real-estate agents for you.'

She seems satisfied that she has made this point clear and I am allowed through to the tea room.

The tea room at Dorchester Abbey is without doubt the best tea room in which I ever had the good fortune to drink tea and eat cake. An array of cakes – including lemon drizzle, Victoria sponge, coffee cake, chocolate cake, cherry almond cake (gluten free), lemon almond cake and tea bread – is spread out on two tables with a yellow-and-white checked pattern. The tables take up the best part of the small room and various customers are eating cake and drinking tea at chairs squeezed around the tables. Between these tables about half a dozen waitresses – the cake-makers themselves, all volunteers – prowl like wolves, ready to pounce should an order be forthcoming.

I sit at one of the tables and request a cup of tea and a slice of tea bread from Vera, who happens to be nearest. 'Tea! Tea bread! Tea!' she says, somewhat manically. Vera departs.

There is a short pause.

Cathy drops by. 'Did you want tea?' she asks.

Betty cuts in and says with a dismissive flick of a wrist, 'Of course he wants tea.' Cathy and Betty depart.

There is a short pause.

Sue arrives with a cup of coffee. 'Did you ask for coffee?' she asks tentatively.

'No. Tea for me please,' I reply.

Sue looks temporarily devastated. Then she composes herself and tells me that 'one man here once had sixteen cups of tea – it's ten pence cheaper each cup you have'.

I thank her for this tip-off. Sue departs.

There is another short pause.

Betty arrives, with a cup of tea. 'Are you sitting outside?' she asks. 'I'm not pushing you out.'

Cathy cuts in: 'He's not sitting outside. Can't you see he's sitting inside!'

I am indeed sitting inside, at a yellow and white table.

Cathy and Betty look at each other for a moment. Both Cathy and Betty depart.

Time ticks by.

Vera brings a slice of tea bread. It is delicious, perfectly baked and full of sweet currants. Vera departs.

Cathy arrives. I tell her the cake was excellent, the best cake I've eaten for months; I have already finished the cake.

'Which cake did you eat?' she asks pointedly.

I tell her I had the tea bread.

At this, Cathy, Vera, Sue and Betty stop circling the tables and conduct a conference about who made the tea bread. It does not appear to have been one of them.

Betty asks me what I am doing in Dorchester.

I tell them about my walk.

'He's going all the way to Kent!' says Betty.

Cathy, Vera, Sue and Betty say they can't believe I'm going to Kent.

Vera tells me that the tea room raised £17,000 to go towards the upkeep of Dorchester Abbey last year.

I tell them that I'm not surprised given the quality of the cake.

Cathy, Vera, Betty and Sue look very pleased indeed.

I pay my bill (£3) and head down the hill to the river. I can highly recommend the tea room at Dorchester Abbey.

'Let the river have them'
Dorchester to Wallingford

Around the long looping bend of the river by Dorchester, the path leads to a field with farmers collecting hay, a pillbox, a short section of the A4074, and then the hamlet of Shillingford, where a *VOTE REMAIN ON JUNE 23* sign, partially covered by ivy, is fixed to the front of a cottage. Further on is an ugly static caravan park, followed by a marina with privately owned pleasure boats with names such as *Phantom Lady*, *Velvet Rose*, *Facetime* and *Tree Topper*. These are not quite 'gin palaces' of the sort you might see in the Mediterranean, with multi-level decks and leather swivel chairs in the wheelhouse, but I expect a fair few G & Ts may well have been put away on deck over the years.

This is the beginning of the Benson Waterfront Leisure Park. Next to the marina are rows of varnished-wood holiday homes. These look quite stark, though they appear well appointed and reasonably large, with pleasant river terraces. At a bar/restaurant an outdoor play is being performed to a group of mainly elderly tourists. I keep going, cross the massive weir at Benson Lock and head in the direction of a spire, traversing meadows that once ran up to a mighty castle that Oliver Cromwell pulled down during the Civil War. Wallingford Castle was originally built by William the Conqueror, along with two other major castles at Windsor and Oxford. It was much fortified over the years and was the last Royalist stronghold to fall in the Civil War, following its surrender by royal command after a 16-week siege. This was in 1646.

Cromwell had the soldiers in the castle decapitated: 'Let the river have them before they corrupt the land as the king corrupted England.'

A lot of awful things have happened on the River Thames.

Wallingford Bridge is medieval and has 22 arches. Up an incline by the bridge I enter a smart market town with art galleries, cafes serving smoothies, a bookshop, vintage women's fashion boutiques, an organic 'fair trade' shop and a few teenagers lolling on a bench. Beyond the main square is the Coachmakers Arms, my inn for the night. By now, I am almost crawling. Today's distance, according to the tracker, is 20.7 miles; not far off a marathon (and you don't do a marathon carrying a mini library on your back… I have yet to post any of the books back).

I am shown to a large, perfectly comfortable room on the top floor. I do my washing and hang out socks from the windows to dry. I go downstairs to have a pint of beer, suddenly so tired I can hardly talk. Locals are joshing about. A middle-aged blonde woman is flirting with a man in shorts who is about to go to a barbecue.

Blonde woman: 'You don't want to be tossing your sausage about too much.'

Man in shorts: 'Ha, ha, ha. You know me too well.'

Blonde woman, naughtily: 'Oh! Ha, ha, ha.'

Pause.

Man in shorts: 'I'm off on holiday to Kos next week.'

Blonde woman: 'You'll have the women racing after you in your Speedos on the beach.'

Man in shorts, slightly nervously: 'Oh! Ha, ha, ha.'

Blonde woman, naughtily again: 'Racing after you – *racing*! Ha, ha, ha.'

It's as though I've walked in on a *Carry On* set.

I drink my pint in the low-ceilinged bar, overlooked by pictures of the Rolling Stones. These are limited-edition prints of drawings by the group's guitarist Ronnie Wood, says David behind the bar. I go to the brilliant Avanti Italian restaurant for a pizza and a glass of wine; the wine is on the house when Mocciaro, the owner, discovers I'm walking to the North Sea. What a nice guy.

Back at the pub, I read *The Times*, which has a front-page headline screaming: *19-YEAR-OLD ARRESTED AFTER KNIFE RAMPAGE IN CENTRAL LONDON... ARMED POLICE TO PATROL HIGH STREETS AS TERROR FEARS GROW*. And I can't help thinking it's a very good thing to be well away from 19-year-olds rampaging with knives as police patrol streets as terror fears grow, tucked away here in a medieval town by the Thames.

I fall asleep at the Coachmakers Arms in a shot.

'I'm by the river. What is there to worry about?'
Wallingford to Moulsford

One of the things about long-distance Thames walking is that you tend to arrive at places when the museums and attractions are shut. Then, in the morning, feeling keen to get on with the day, you usually leave before museums and attractions are open. Therefore, you do not always see museums and attractions.

This could be regarded as a disappointment, but I see it as the opposite. A great weight seems to have been lifted. There is no pressure to visit the Wallingford Museum, for example – as wonderful as the Wallingford Museum may be – because it is *impossible due to the walking schedule to see the Wallingford Museum*. You arrive at a major historic place and leave the major historic place with a clean conscience. You have done your best to glean what there is to glean under the conditions of your walking schedule. What more could anyone expect of you?

Before breakfast, I do, however, go to see the site of the former Wallingford Castle. Cromwell did a good job. There is not much left at all, just a couple of fragments of crumbling walls on a grassy hillock close to a noticeboard that shows a drawing of the magnificent castle as it would have been in its pomp.

It seems sad that such a prominent structure should have been destroyed, and on the way back to the Coachmakers Arms for breakfast I come across another downbeat tale.

At the George Hotel on the high street, during the time of the Civil War, a royalist named John Robson was stabbed to death in a barroom brawl. His sweetheart, who had retreated to her hotel room, was so upset that she painted teardrops on the walls using a mixture of her own tears and fire soot. The teardrops are still there and the room, number 214 at the George, can be booked (though I'm not sure I'd want to sleep there).

I make my way back to the Coachmakers and set off for the day.

Down by the Thames, the path is quiet.

It's a bright morning and I do not have too much of a trek; the distance to Pangbourne is only 11 miles. This is a length that would have caused consternation, say, a couple of months ago; I'd have been getting prepared for a 'big walk'. Not now. Now 11 miles seems like a stroll in the park after yesterday's epic hike.

Sunlight catches the contours of lilies. Weeping willows reflect perfectly in the water. The Thames Path dips beneath the graffiti-splattered bridge of the A4130. Meadows with purple loosestrife come to an end at a wood, where twigs snap and there is a smell of bark. Birds cackle. Flies buzz. A train thunders across a red-brick bridge built by Isambard Kingdom Brunel.

There is no special hurry, so I stop for a coffee at the riverside Beetle and Wedge pub/restaurant in Moulsford. Jerome K. Jerome is meant to have written parts of *Three Men in a Boat* here, though the management does not make a fuss about the connection and the more solid literary link is that H. G. Wells was a guest while writing *The History of Mr Polly*. The pub is fictionalised in this novel as the Potwell Inn.

I am the only person at the low-beamed bar when I am joined by another obvious Thames walker. Her name is Jan. She is wearing a pink fleece and is a retired music teacher from Cranbourne in Dorset. I buy her a cappuccino. Among long-distance walkers on the Thames Path, as I discovered with Simon and Jamie, a natural comradeship flows that is quite alien to 'outsiders' such as those merely walking their dogs or going for a wander. We are a breed apart... stalwarts of the trail, pioneers marking out the river-scape, the crossers of frontiers (or at least county lines), breakers of conformity, standing aside from the sheep-like crowd, embracing the spirit of discovery in an era of lunatic internet fixation, shunning the mollycoddled conventions of an insipid and lacklustre front-lounge-dwelling, celebrity-obsessed, square-eyed, immobile, corrupt, turmoil-ridden modern world.

This may be overdoing it a bit.

Yet there is something about going on such a long walk – which must be true of any ramble over a serious distance – that creates a feeling of 'otherness'. Even if you've just been hitting the path for a few days.

Jan is doing the river in stages. In June she covered the source to Oxford. On this burst she is walking from Oxford to Henley. We sit at a table by the water's edge.

'I'm surprised there are so few people in August,' she says.

It *is* remarkable how empty the path has been.

I ask her what she enjoyed most about the walk so far.

'Firstly, it's flat,' says Jan.

This is a most practical point, worth making. Aside from one small hill to come, there is no up and down on the Thames Path.

'Doing the walk just fires my imagination,' she says. 'You do get into a rhythm. I like not worrying about anything else: just putting one foot in front of the other, getting to the next place.'

Jan is not a sightseer. 'I had my husband with me for five days. He wanted to see every bloody church. I just want to keep on going. I did stop at the abbey yesterday, though. Beautiful.'

Her husband had had enough and called it a day. 'He doesn't like walks without a purpose – he certainly can't understand walking in a circle, doing a walk in a loop. I don't mind going on my own. Sometimes I start worrying about things, but then I think: *Hang on, I'm by the river. What is there to worry about?*

Her intention is to do the final 84 miles to the Thames Barrier in September. She has a pedometer that shows she has walked 6.1 miles so far today, after starting in Benson. She begins to tell me that her two sons are in a rock band with a Moroccan singer, then her voice trails off as she looks across the river to the far bank.

'The English summer is all about purple and gold: the fields are golden,' she says, after a while. 'The river meanders endlessly.'

Jan has a look in her eye that suggests that walking the Thames is somehow more than a mere walk.

She is staying at the same inn as me tonight, the George. We agree to try and meet up later to compare notes from the day.

Through the Goring Gap
Moulsford to Pangbourne

I head off. Red kites soar above rolling hills. A woman in cut-off jean shorts sings to herself on a barge. More mansions with perfect lawns appear on the opposite bank. The river widens. A sign says: *STOP GORING HYDRO*. This refers to a plan to create a hydroelectricity generator at Goring's weir that could power as many as 300 homes. Some locals believe the turbines will be an eyesore, potentially noisy and will disrupt fish. Controversy and the river never seem far removed.

Mowers and hedge-cutters murmur. A distant train rumbles. A little path-side honesty stall set up on two stumps of wood offers blackberries and mangetout for 50p, with cash going to a meadow conservation project. Customers are asked to put 50p in a donation tin. As I am considering a purchase, an elderly bespectacled woman appears out of nowhere and says the meadow is 1.6 hectares and home to grass snakes, mallards, reed warblers, sedge and willowherb. I drop 50p in the tin and she disappears, spirit-like, through a gate I hadn't noticed in a fence.

I have arrived at the village of Streatley, on the south side of the Thames, with the village of Goring to the north. These villages, linked by a bridge, are all thatched-roof cottages, Georgian red-brick houses, riverside terraces with parasols, pubs with hanging baskets and village halls offering t'ai chi, yoga and Pilates classes. In other words, about as quintessentially English as they come.

Jerome K. Jerome stopped here, declaring Goring 'charming' and delaying moving on to Wallingford: 'The sweet smiling face of the river here lured us to linger for a while, and so [we] left our boat at the bridge, and went up to Streatley, and lunched at the Bull, much to Montmorency's satisfaction.' The sometimes highly agitated dog that accompanies the trio on their river adventures is in fact purely fictional.

The trio spends a few days in Streatley, where J, the narrator, enjoys mocking local fishermen, who seem full of tall tales, although 'I never knew anybody catch anything up the Thames, except minnows and dead cats'. Fish, he pronounces, are impossible to catch, even though many 'come and stand half out of the water with their mouths open for biscuits. And, if you go for a bathe, they crowd round, and get in your way and irritate you. But there are not any to be "had" by a bit of worm on the end of a hook, not anything like it – not they!'

J says that all that is required to be a good fisherman is the 'ability to tell lies easily and without blushing'. Which, now I think about it, sounds a pretty good definition of most 'good' politicians too.

Goring and Streatley are at another key point on the River Thames, though this time the importance has nothing to do with the history of humans. Many millennia ago, the river did not flow on its current route through this part of England. The water was blocked by a ridge of chalk connected to the Chilterns and was diverted northwards into Hertfordshire and onwards to the North Sea, close to Ipswich in Suffolk. Then the ice age came, 2.5 million years ago. When the ice eventually melted, a great store of water accumulated and slowly worked its way through the chalk, establishing the current course of the river through what has become known as the Goring Gap. This may be a rather simple rundown of the geological story, but it will do for me.

I go to the Bull. It's up an incline and has a plain exterior with whitewashed walls, russet-tiled roof, a postbox built into a wall and a sign advertising for staff positions. Inside, I lean on the small bar, peruse the menu and request the soup of the day. The gangly barman appears startled. He goes to the kitchen, and returns shortly afterwards.

'Sorry, the chef hasn't prepared a soup of the day today,' he says.

I ask for a chicken sandwich.

'That, he can do!' the gangly barman exclaims, as though relieved I have not asked for another unprepared dish lurking on the menu.

I slump at a table, listening to Tom Jones and Beatles hits while flicking through the pub's copy of The 'Three Men in a Boat' Companion by Stephen Lambe. In this, Lambe explains that an episode involving a body that Jerome describes discovering in the river by Goring did not actually happen; the event was lifted from reading a story about a dead woman in the river in the *Berkshire Chronicle*. Jerome seems to have been a fan of local papers too.

The chicken sandwich is a delicious chicken sandwich, and not too expensive. The soup-less Bull is well worth the little detour from the Thames Path.

I tramp back to the water, cross the river and continue through meadows, passing Ferry Cottage, where Oscar Wilde wrote *An Ideal Husband* (a Lord Goring features in the play), before starting to climb.

Yes, the ground begins to go up.

I have reached the Thames Path's hill: the chalk ridge that once held back the melted lake of ice age water. Distant gunshots play out as I enter a wood that smells of herbs and pine. The river is obscured below. Someone in a boat shouts: 'Oi!' A train horn blows on the bridge near Ferry Cottage. After about half an hour I reach the 'summit' up a steep path (it's not much of an ascent really and trees obscure any view). From here the path is downhill to the sleepy village of Whitchurch and then across a toll bridge to Pangbourne, a larger village on the south bank, where I am soon at the George Hotel.

'Zero tolerance of drugs' and pizza with Jan
Pangbourne

As I said when I left the Barley Mow in Clifton Hampden, I do not wish to come across as a serial moaner. I really don't want to whinge my way along the riverside. Quite the opposite: I want to celebrate and enjoy a river I love, to let it take my mind off things, to relax and enjoy the journey. However, the George somewhat tests my resolve on this matter.

A receptionist with a ponytail and jeans, who looks as though he might be a biker, hands me a key with a green plastic attachment; the number ten has been written on a piece of torn card and inexpertly taped to the plastic. I ascend a dirty staircase with a threadbare carpet, where I pause to read a sheet of A4 paper attached to a wall. This piece of paper has also been taped, at a slant, to the paintwork. It says: *This company has a zero tolerance of drugs abuse. We will call the police if there is any indication of drugs use in any part of the premises. The toilets are regularly monitored.*

My room has three single beds, plain white walls with a badly faded, small blue-and-white picture of a lake. Brown bedcovers are folded at the ends of the beds. There is a faux-leather black armchair, a kettle, a few teabags and some plastic spoons (perhaps to prevent the theft of real spoons, or their use in the concoction of class A drugs). A pamphlet tells me: 'The George Hotel, Pangbourne: The Right Choice.' The grimy window faces a car park, beyond which is the Peking Garden Chinese restaurant, an Indian restaurant and a WHSmith next to a busy roundabout. From this rises the sound of revving engines and the occasional siren. Above the Peking Garden Chinese restaurant, almost exactly facing my room, is an apartment with a piece of cardboard jammed into a window with a missing pane. It appears as though the cardboard is not a temporary fix; that it has been there for some time.

Everything had looked so nice on the hotel website.

Pangbourne – and maybe I am just unlucky – is a let-down, and not just because of the George.

The streets are noisy with cars. Everyone seems to be in a terrible rush, tearing round corners and accelerating past little shops and estate agents (about two million pounds for a riverside house). I go to look at the pleasant red-brick Church Cottage where Kenneth Grahame lived towards the end of his life, on a quiet corner well away from the main roads. Then I return to the racetrack of the village centre, stopping to look in the windows of a Bentley, Aston Martin and Lamborghini showroom.

There are clearly plenty of extremely well-to-do people living somewhere in Pangbourne. The Lamborghinis stand out, gleaming in bright traffic-light colours in the showroom window: red, green and orange. The brash shades seem to suggest: Yes, *I am vulgar, but I do not care. I am rich enough to have extremely awful taste: ha, ha, ha, see you later. Vrooom!* Through the window I can see that a red Lamborghini Huracán, which looks like a UFO on four wheels, is available for £184,950. *BUY ME?* asks a display.

Let me just highlight here that the average UK salary, as I write, is £26,500. So it would take seven years for the average person to save to purchase one of these Lamborghini Huracáns. This is, of course, ignoring having to pay taxes and other inconvenient matters such as eating, using public transport and paying for a roof over one's head. Those working full-time on the national minimum wage of £13,124 per annum would have to wait 14 years for a Lamborghini Huracán, without eating, going anywhere or shelling out for shelter.

I raise this here for two reasons. One: to highlight that this neck of the Thames must be one of the wealthiest on the river, despite the odd dwelling in the centre of the village that looks pretty down-at-heel. Two: to suggest that Kenneth Grahame, whose Mr Toad so loved the fast life ('Toad the terror, the traffic-queller, the Lord of the lone trail, before whom all must give way or be smitten into nothingness'), might have raised an eyebrow upon seeing these UFOs with wheels for sale around the corner from his cottage. *The Wind in the Willows* is, after all, about the pleasures of the quiet river life.

At the Swan, I find a spot on a fabulous terrace facing the Thames and next to a car park full of BMWs, Mercs, Audis, Porsches and Jags. Canada geese are paddling in the water by a weir. The barmaid looks blankly when I mention *Three Men in a Boat*. Yet it was here, at the Swan, that the heroes decide to 'chuck it in' and get a train back to Paddington at the end of the book. I watch a man in a pink polo shirt and a gold chain entertaining two women in oversized sunglasses, while a husband in a canary-yellow polo shirt tells his bottle-blonde wife in a leopard-print top and tight black jeans with fashionably ripped fabric that she should stop telling 'half stories' that do not lead anywhere.

'There you go: a half story again!' he says.

The bottle-blonde wife in the leopard-print top looks crestfallen.

I meet Jan at an Italian restaurant opposite the George, where my fellow Thames walker and I discuss Pangbourne over pizzas.

'I was lying on my bed and there was an awful racket,' she says, as yet another car passes with a squeal of tyres.

At times it feels as though Pangbourne is all the episodes of *Top Gear* rolled into one.

We say our goodbyes – I'll be leaving early in the morning before her – and I return to the George, where I have to use a code to enter the front door and the bar is closed... at nine o'clock.

CHAPTER SIX

PANGBOURNE, BERKSHIRE, TO MARLOW, BUCKINGHAMSHIRE

'YOU REALLY LIVE BY THE RIVER? WHAT A JOLLY LIFE!'

THE THAMES

Marlow

Medmenham

Hurley

Bisham
Abbey

Henley

Shiplake

Sonning

Mapledurham

Pangbourne

Reading

After a cold shower – there is no hot water, although complimentary Refreshing Shower Gel is provided – I leave early and buy breakfast from a Co-op store across the street. My room at the George was not cheap and I had assumed breakfast was included. Breakfast is not included.

I am slightly flabbergasted by this. But I suppose I should have known better than to presume £81 would cover both the opportunity to sleep in a bleak room with a view of a car park and a noisy roundabout in a hotel with a 'zero tolerance of drugs abuse' policy on a piece of paper stuck to a hallway wall *and* something to eat in the morning. My mistake. How stupid of me. My rate is, I am informed by the breakfast-room waiter, 'room only'.

Room only. When did this slip into our hoteliers' lexicon? Quite recently, in widespread usage, I think. And it doesn't take much to work out that the phrase is little more than a straightforward ploy to increase hotel revenue by: firstly, making prices seem lower by comparison with any competition that has been dumb enough to include breakfast; secondly, hoping that suckers such as myself, in a hurry when booking, might not notice.

Anyway, something deep down tells me I am better off forgoing food at the George. Hence my Co-op fine dining. Having already checked out, I sit on a bench on the corner by the noisy roundabout and watch cars whizz by as I eat my sandwich. This is not, I reflect, how the glamorous folk in the glossy pages of *Condé Nast Traveller* do it.

'One does not linger in the neighbourhood of Reading'
Pangbourne to Sonning

As I am mulling over this, John arrives. John is one of my best friends going back to secondary-school days. He is wearing a panama hat, a well-ironed pale blue linen shirt, flannel boating shoes, Ray-Ban aviator shades and *Our Man in Havana*-style khaki shorts. A 'manbag' is slung over a shoulder. I have never seen him wear a panama hat before. He looks as though he has just stepped off a yacht in Cannes. I, on the other hand, have not so long ago been given the once-over by the down-and-outs of Christ Church Meadow as a possible newbie for afternoon cider summits opposite Oxford's Crown and County Court.

'Where did you get that hat?' I ask.

'Oh, I've had it a while,' says John evasively. I've only ever seen him in a baseball cap or a flat cap previously. He appears to be going up in the world (or fancies such notions).

'We are walking quite a long way today,' I say, eyeing his flannel boating shoes.

'Yes, yes,' he replies. 'Shall we get going? It's five and a half miles until the first break.'

He seems very certain about this five and a half miles, although this is the first I have heard of it.

'Equidistant,' he says, as though pleased with this word. 'It's logical: equidistant. We have sixteen and a half miles to go so we stop at each third of the way.'

Such military precision has yet to feature in my river days. We are aiming to reach Henley-upon-Thames by around 5 p.m. There is a reason for this timing. Arriving at 5 p.m. will allow the opportunity to drink beer for about an hour at the Angel on the Bridge pub next to Henley Bridge before John has to get the train home to his pregnant Brazilian wife.

'Every time I have driven past it I have always wanted to have a pint in there,' says John. 'You see people on that little terrace having a wine or a beer or whatever. It's one of the most iconic pubs on the Thames. Like going to Caffè Florian in Venice: it's an iconic thing to do. Except you don't have to pay seventy euros for two coffees and two pastries.'

So we have an 'itinerary'. John has it all worked out. We are to stop for lunch – one hour has been set aside for it – at the Bull Inn in Sonning (pronounced 'sunning').

We begin our march along a grass bank with rushes and willows beyond the thin metal curve of Whitchurch Bridge. The river undulates gently as a pleasure boat named *Knights of Windsor* cruises sedately downstream. The far bank is clad with verdant woodland. The sky is cut-out-and-keep blue. It is a Saturday and it is going to be a scorcher.

A couple of shifty teenagers in tracksuits shuffle past, looking furtive and up to no good.

'I suppose every town and village has its undesirable element,' comments John. 'Not exactly the quaint Moley and Ratty image that this part of the Thames evokes.'

He pauses to consider this statement, and further comments: 'Times have changed. People have become more awful.'

The panama hat seems to have transformed him into a cross between the cricket commentator Geoffrey Boycott and a leader writer for *The Daily Telegraph*. This act, however, does not last long. John disappears behind a bush in a field. A short while later he returns: 'Plenty of places for a pit stop. That's a plus side. I had a coffee at home and another at Reading station: a double fillage.'

With this we increase our pace. Somewhere not so far away lies Reading. Our intention is to miss Reading altogether. It is too big and busy. There are too many supposedly idyllic villages such as Sonning and Shiplake to see, and the 5 p.m. Henley deadline does not allow for dilly-dallying.

Dally we do, however, to gaze across the river at Hardwick House, which was sketched by E. H. Shepard, the original illustrator of *The Wind in the Willows*, and was part of the basis of Toad Hall in the book; a rumbustious turn-of-the-twentieth-century local politician and sportsman who lived at Hardwick is said to have been one of the models for Mr Toad. The house is ancient and it was here that Charles I played bowls on day release from captivity during the time of the Civil War. There is another house nearby at Mapledurham that has strong claims to be a model for *The Wind in the Willows'* Toad Hall, but somehow or other, probably due to talking too much, we totally miss this.

We enter a field with black and tan cattle and the Thames Path takes us directly through a herd that has gravitated towards the water's edge. A couple of steps from the path, one of this herd regards us with particular interest.

'That is a bull,' I whisper.

'Yes, you can tell by the balls,' whispers John.

The bull, however, is a placid bull. We increase our pace and, beyond Mapledurham Lock, we are soon turning up a path to a busy road leading to the centre of Reading. We have been following Thames Path signs but this really is the most depressing part of the path so far, passing 'Readings [sic] Largest Used Car Centre' and coming to Tilehurst train station. It is at Tilehurst train station that we realise that we must have made an error of some sort. So we retrace our steps back past 'Readings [sic] Largest Used Car Centre' and discover a sign we had missed to the riverbank.

'We've got to be hawk-eyed looking for signs from now on,' says John. Followed by: 'How did we ****ing miss that!'

It was only a matter of time before the panama hat 'respectability' charade began to unravel completely.

'One does not linger in the neighbourhood of Reading,' wrote Jerome K. Jerome in the 1880s. He considered the town 'dismal and dirty'. We don't hang about either. Down by the river, it feels pleasant to be walking briskly past on a path lined with horse-chestnut trees beneath an escarpment with the railway line. This stretch of the path has an anonymous, hideaway quality. We come to an old barge with American blues music playing and a bankside fold-up table with a cardboard box with the remains of a chicken takeaway next to an empty bottle of rum and a couple of crushed cans of Polish lager. The barge owners appear to have had a party and gone inside for a nap, leaving the doors flung open and music floating out.

Ducks skip across the surface of the river as they come in to land. We follow the path past teams of people putting up fences for Reading's annual music festival. Massive houses arise on the opposite bank.

'I'm so jealous – those houses are probably six million. I suppose it's just the luck of the draw, isn't it,' says John.

'The crimes you must have had to commit to afford one of those,' I reply, completely unreasonably (I admit).

'Or just be born with a silver spoon in your mouth,' John says.

The Daily Telegraph leader writer seems to have morphed into a columnist for the *Daily Mirror*.

Further on, wedding bells toll on the opposite bank in Caversham. The sun blazes down on dragonflies dancing on the gently undulating surface of the river: good wedding weather. We pass beneath busy traffic on Reading Bridge and by a sign for Salter's Steamers Ltd. A boat ride from here back to Wallingford would take three and a quarter hours. Glimpses of the magnificent lawns of the Island Bohemian Bowling Club can be seen through gaps in a perfectly trimmed hedge on a little island, or ait, beyond the bridge. Then round a bend with a field come moorings belonging to a Tesco Extra. This is understood to be the only Tesco Extra with moorings anywhere in the United Kingdom (so say the guidebook writers). A little way past this unique Tesco Extra, a pair of white men with dreadlocks exits a barge carrying art rolled up as though they are heading for a pavement pitch somewhere in town.

Reading, for the record, is the county town of Berkshire with a population of about 160,000, making it the biggest place outside London that the Thames passes. Henry I was buried at Reading Abbey, which he founded in 1121, only for Henry VIII to destroy the abbey during his dissolution of the monasteries. The ruins are somewhere inland from Reading Bridge, not far from Tesco Extra. To complete a connection made back in Kempsford, John of Gaunt was married to his beloved Blanche at the abbey.

On a bridge across a tributary, the River Kennet, someone has scrawled: *TO DARE TO DREAM*. Near here is a higgledy-piggledy cluster of old barges, tied together in an algae-clogged side water. Old suitcases with clothes spilling out and Carlsberg Special Brew cans litter the decks. The windows of the neglected barges are filthy. A group of men, drinking cans of beer, stands around a crackling fire by the path. They are talking animatedly, possibly about their dreams, though there is no time to stop to ask with our Angel on the Bridge deadline. There is something distinctly Pinter-esque about this group of stragglers: wanderers living on the edge who have either fallen on hard times or imagine they have fallen on them. Perhaps times have always been hard. Perhaps times are not really so hard at all.

Beyond, a man and a woman are smoking marijuana with their legs dangling over the riverbank. The woman has stripped to her bra to sunbathe, as though she is wearing a bikini top. There is a freewheeling feel to this odd stretch of the river between the Kennet and Sonning Lock.

We reach the picture-postcard lock-keeper's house, with its roses, hanging baskets and ivy-clad walls. John begins to wax lyrical: 'It does you good just to be by the water. It relaxes your mind. You just relax. It's important to preserve this. If people don't have an outlet to relax and unwind, it's not good for their mental health.'

We continue for a few steps.

'To be honest, Thomas, I'm gasping for a pint.'

The panama hat 'persona' has long ago been discarded.

'Let's find the Bull. It's around here somewhere.'

'A veritable picture of an old country inn'
Sonning

The Bull Inn at Sonning is up a road and down a lane and it is packed. All outside tables are taken, so we go inside to a cool room with exposed beams, red-brick walls and a collection of miniature bottles of liquor. This pub is 630 years old and is yet another Jerome K. Jerome recommendation: 'If you stop at Sonning, put up at the Bull, behind the church. It is a veritable picture of an old country inn, with green, square courtyard in front, where, on seats beneath the trees, the old men group of an evening to drink their ale and gossip over village politics; with low, quaint rooms and latticed windows, and awkward stairs and winding passages.'

John hangs his panama on the edge of a leather armchair. We order and drink pints of Peroni.

'I'm in heaven,' says John. 'The first pint tastes great, doesn't it?'

It does indeed taste great.

We polish off our pints of Peroni.

We order and begin to drink further pints of Peroni.

Great piles of food arrive, sausages and pies with mash and veg.

We devour the great piles of food.

John has a thing for Sonning: 'When we were house-hunting, Sonning was one of the places I thought: *This is ****ing beautiful*. I absolutely love it. If I had my way and had enough money I'd live here or in Oxford or Marlow or Henley or somewhere like that. That's why I jumped at the chance to go along the river today.'

I check the 'tracking device' (usually I try not to during the day as I don't want to become obsessive about the thing). In our hurry we have skipped the 'five-and-a-half mile break'. The Bull is 11 miles from Pangbourne. When we depart it's about 2.30 p.m.; we've made good time.

To the Angel on the Bridge
Sonning to Henley

We leave the Bull and Sonning's rows of picturesque cottages, and cross a stone bridge to the north bank, stopping to witness the spectacle of a large, sprawling white house across the river. This is the home of Uri Geller, the Israeli spoon-bending magician. Cue John launching into an unprintable assault on anyone making a fortune from bending spoons and this particular spoon-bender's taste in riverside dwelling. With its pyramid-shaped conservatory in the garden and high walls with prominent security signs, the place does stick out a bit. It's strange to think of the late Michael Jackson, a friend of Geller's, coming here and gazing from his spoon-bending companion's patio upon one of the loveliest, sleepiest meandering sections of the River Thames.

We surge onwards; two pints of beer at lunchtime, my first walk-time drinking, have provided a boost. Beyond a peaceful section with meadows, we are soon ascending a lane into the village of Shiplake. The houses and cottages here are tucked behind hedgerows. We stop on Station Road to take a look at Roselawn, a mock-Tudor house behind a wooden gate where George Orwell grew up from the age of 9 to 12. It must have been an impressionable time in such affluent surroundings; Blair once confided in one of his playground friends here, the poet-to-be Jacintha Buddicom, that he intended to write a book about the future similar to H. G. Wells' *A Modern Utopia*. So the roots of *1984*, you might say, can be traced to the quiet little lanes of this sleepy Oxfordshire village: newspeak and doublethink came from here. Now that doublethink – fake news or alternative truth (call it what you will) – might seem to be on the brink of becoming mainstream reality, not just in the imagined totalitarian states of novelists brought up in Shiplake by the Thames, it merits a moment's pause for thought.

Visiting Roselawn feels like completing a mini homage to Orwell along the river. The Thames must have meant a lot to him. After all, Orwell later attended Eton College, also by the Thames, though his pen name is believed to have been inspired by a different waterway: the River Orwell in East Anglia.

John and I regain the Thames Path proper, which passes rather oddly between hedgerows and large houses, one of which does not mess about with its security notice: *BEWARE OF FIERCE DOGS*. Another has a large model railway complete with a 'station' in its garden. Cue various unprintable mutterings from John about the nature of millionaires.

On the edge of Henley, we take a long pedestrian bridge past a boat, the *New Orleans*, made to look like a steamboat on the Mississippi River. It is offering short rides and appears popular. Madonna tracks are blaring from its stereo. The Thames Path here is packed with day trippers dropping by at ice-cream stalls. We march through the crowds in the direction of a church tower with, we notice, a bridge at its base. Next to this bridge is a white building dating from 1728 with a terrace overlooking the water... the Angel on the Bridge pub.

We cover this distance in surprisingly quick time and I check – for John's benefit, as we wait at the bar – to find we have covered, with our meanderings, precisely 18.45 miles after leaving at 9 a.m. and arriving at 4.30 p.m. We commandeer a picnic table beneath a blue Brakspear sunshade on the fabled terrace of the Angel on the Bridge. Golden sunlight illuminates the bridge upon which is carved a figurehead depicting Tamesis, a mythical river god. Our beers, despite not being the first, taste great. John tells me how his late father Len, a black-taxi driver in London, was once invited to the Henley Royal Regatta as a guest of a brewery that supplied his social club: 'Even though it was thirty degrees the day he went, officials told him to do up the top button on his shirt.'

He chuckles at the thought of his father in a polyester suit sweltering amid the Henley Regatta crowd.

We drink our beers.

We order more beers.

'A good day, definitely,' says John.

'A very good day,' I reply.

'Yes, excellent. We went a long way,' says John.

'A very long way,' I reply.

For a while this is about as much as we can muster. It's been a tiring day on the trail.

We drink our beers.

We order more beers.

But even though it's been exhausting, today was just right. Pangbourne to Henley, with a stop at the Bull at Sonning for lunch, is a great choice for a decent length Thames day-walk, with convenient stations at both ends.

I show John the entry for Henley from *Dickens's Dictionary of the Thames, 1887.* Its first line explains that Henley's station is a five-minute walk from the bridge.

'One hundred and twenty years on and it's still helpful – unless they've moved the bridge or the station,' says John.

Which they haven't.

We fit in one more pint (we've earned it) and walk to the station. John catches his train, and I head up a long hill to my Airbnb on a quiet, late-twentieth-century residential street on the outskirts of town, where the landlady is charming, the room is spotless and I have an early night.

Rowers, quality downtime, big fish and a Kurdistani barbecue
Henley to Marlow

I am still becoming accustomed to Airbnb. Before booking the shepherd's hut back in Newbridge, I had been vaguely aware of this 'sharing website'. I knew that rather in the same way Uber drivers 'share' rides in their Toyota hybrid cars (in return for cash), people on Airbnb 'share' rooms (in return for cash). The word 'sharing' used in these circumstances had seemed a quaint way of saying 'selling', I had thought. I had also thought: *Airbnb is for other people: millennials.*

Let millennials worry about Airbnb. Anyway it's probably a flash in the pan, a digital bubble that's bound to burst. I'll wait until people 'get over' Airbnb.

As is so often the case with such computer-related mainstream trends of the day, I have been proven completely wrong. Airbnb was, and is, no passing fad. It has turned out to be no less than a worldwide phenomenon, adding thousands of rooms to those offered by traditional hotels, many of which have felt the heat of the extra competition. When the shepherd's hut in Newbridge caught my eye I was required to register on the Airbnb website. Then before coming to Henley I discovered there were no rooms in any hotels, B & Bs or inns. The entire town was booked up on Saturday night. What was I to do?

Airbnb came to the rescue, and Nicola's B & B stood out.

For £30 less than my depressing room at the George, I have a comfortable bedroom with a plush grey carpet, an iron-framed bed with good-quality linen, a dressing table with an octagonal mirror, and a side table in the form of an oriental traveller's chest carved with dragons. On top of this chest there is a tray with a kettle with tea, Costa Rican coffee and real (yes, real, not plastic) spoons. A spotless bathroom with a bathtub leads off to one side. The road outside is quiet and when I wake I am sorely tempted to lie in.

But if you are really going to make it all the way to the North Sea from the source of the Thames, you need to stick to a daily routine. So I force myself up, feeling a little groggy from yesterday's Angel on the Bridge escapades. Today should not be so tough. It's just eight and a half miles to the next stopover in Marlow.

The second 'B' in Nicola's B & B turns out to be excellent too. Nicola has blonde hair, frameless glasses, a kindly smile and an inquisitive nature. She's wearing a white blouse with a gold chain and black slacks, looking as though she is well used to being an Airbnb hostess, despite only having offered rooms for a few months. Nicola used to work in the accounts department of the National Symphony Orchestra. 'My job disappeared. A computer took my job,' she says, after bringing excellent coffee. We are in a room overlooking the countryside (this really is on the edge of Henley). The dining room contains a large table, a grandfather clock and a couple of Dick Francis books on a shelf. In the connecting hall, a framed map of the Thames from the source to Greenwich hangs by the staircase.

Nicola delivers an enormous bowl of porridge along with blueberries, a banana, an apple and raisins; I could have asked for a cooked English breakfast but porridge, I have read somewhere, is good for energy on long walks. When I mention visiting Sonning yesterday, she tells me that the actor George Clooney lives in the village (this is big local news as he and his barrister wife have just moved in). She also tells me that former guests have included a man from Chicago who came to scatter his sister's ashes as well as a woman who only went out once in a couple of days: 'I think she just wanted respite'. Airbnb has worked for her as she can take time off from it whenever she likes, simply by blocking out bookings when she feels like having a holiday. Nicola does not live alone, so she feels safe as an Airbnb host. It was, however, an odd scenario to her when she started offering rooms: 'When I first handed over a key to a complete stranger I found it very unusual. But everyone seems so nice.'

Just like Nicola.

I highly recommend Nicola's Airbnb.

I go down the hill to the riverfront, reaching Henley's River and Rowing Museum. This opens at 10 a.m. As the time is 9.15 a.m. and as Henley is all about rowing, I decide to break my previous museum diktat. I wait, reading the Sunday papers on a public bench near a row of barges moored by the waterfront. I seem to be spending quite a bit of time on public benches one way or another.

The news in *The Sunday Times* is a mixture of the downright bewildering (*MI5'S MIND READERS HELP FOIL SEVEN*

TERRORIST ATTACKS), depressing (*RIO OLYMPICS ROCKED BY NEW DOPING SCANDAL*) and potentially devastating (*ALL SYSTEMS STOP: HOW TO PREVENT A ROGUE PRESIDENT FROM PRESSING THE NUCLEAR BUTTON*). The latter headline refers to the American presidential candidate Donald Trump, who is causing almost as big a stir as the fallout over Brexit this summer. He seems to have just about everyone, bar a hard core of supporters in the US Deep South, on edge with pledges to build a wall between Mexico and America, proposals to ban Muslims from entering the United States, vitriolic personal attacks on his opponent Hillary Clinton ('If Hillary Clinton cannot satisfy her husband what makes her think she can satisfy America?'), claims that Barack Obama's birth certificate is fake and that by this logic he may not be American, a foreign policy objective to 'bomb the **** out of 'em' (the Islamic State, wherever they may be), and a series of simmering sex scandals combined with an unhealthy objectification of women: 'You know, it really doesn't matter what [the media] write as long as you've got a young and beautiful piece of ass.'

I gaze across the river, trying not to think about what might happen if Trump wins this two-horse race for the most powerful job in the world.

The museum opens and I am the first in the warehouse-like building. Steps lead to long rooms with pictures of Olympic rowing champions Sir Steve Redgrave and Sir Matthew Pinsent, as well as the actual boats that carried them to victory. Vintage Olympic posters decorate the walls. A lovely old steamboat sits in a corner. Colourful rowing club blazers fill a cabinet next to a display explaining the intricacies of the River Thames' rainfall catchment area (perhaps a specialist interest). Another focuses on *The Wind in the Willows*, with a first edition in a glass cabinet and a quote printed in large letters on the wall above. Mr Mole is speaking to the Water Rat: 'And you really live by the river? What a jolly life!'

In a far back room, gorgeous oil paintings by the Dutch artist Jan Siberechts (1627–1703) are reason enough to pay the admission fee to the Henley River and Rowing Museum. His depictions of Henley and other Thames scenes are redolent of an age when horses with carts rolled alongside banks, little wooden vessels with tiny sails plied the river, cattle came down to the water's edge (as a few still do) and the countryside swept in from all sides, seeming to confine Henley to a slither of houses by the bridge. Standing here for a while, alone on this quiet Sunday, I feel a sense of centuries sliding away. Good art can do that.

I do not go for a coffee at the museum's Quince Tree Cafe, nor do I buy a museum tea towel (£9.95) or one of its G&T-scented bars of soap (£5). Instead I hit the Thames Path at 11 a.m. (the latest start I've had to any day).

It is overcast and not many people are about. I explore Henley's high street with its estate agents, Thai restaurants, fashion boutiques, second-hand bookshops, and wealth management bureaux promising to 'maximise the wealth you created'. I pop into the landmark fourteenth-century St Mary's Church to see the memorial to the musician Dusty Springfield (1939–1999), who lived in Henley and whose ashes were spread here. Then I cross the bridge and take the path skirting the boathouse belonging to the Leander rowing club. A sign at the front of the boathouse boasts of 111 Olympic medals having been won by club members, although that total is likely to shoot up during the Olympic Games just starting in Rio de Janeiro.

The river at Henley is the longest straight section of the Thames, which is why it has attracted so many boat races over the years, including, of course, the famous summer regatta that has been running since 1839. Past Leander's HQ the path follows the water's edge, and on the river an extraordinary vessel painted red, gold and green is hurtling along, clearly in training for an event. Oars flash, spray flies and a wake rises. This is a Chinese dragon boat and the Sunday morning crew is going hell for leather. It's as though the fashion boutiques, cafes, estate agents and financial management advisors of genteel Henley-upon-Thames are under some kind of mad attack.

A cox stands at one end bellowing at the oarsmen and women. 'Back six! Back six! OK, two, one, go! Head up, guys! Watching your strokes! Watching your strokes!' he yells. 'That's the stuff! It's all about technique! Go, go, go!'

A haughty swan with two cygnets glides in the foreground, ignoring the racket. A bald man, seemingly oblivious to the charging Chinese dragon, lounges on a bench with one shoe on and one shoe off, drinking cider while listening to headphones and watching the swans. Dog walkers are out in force – so many that the polite, almost obligatory Thames Path 'good morning' is no longer required; everyone would go insane if they went through that routine each time. A river-swimming race took place earlier. 'Henley Swim' signs are up; more than 100 swimmers splashed off in the direction of Marlow at the crack of dawn, rather putting my effort today to shame. The course is eight and a half miles.

On this swim, they will have had to negotiate Temple Island fairly early on; named after the classical stone folly from the eighteenth century that was once Britain's fanciest fishing lodge and is now owned by the people behind Henley Regatta. This island was the starting point of the very first Oxford–Cambridge Boat Race in 1829. Across the river here, a large ivy-clad white mansion arises, grander and much more tasteful than Uri Geller's – as far as mansions by the River Thames go (in my opinion). This is Greenbanks, once the home of William Henry Smith, the newsagent.

Most of the dog walkers veer off to a car park as the Thames Path heads on across a lumpy field. I am soon alone again, feeling contemplative as I make my way along this empty stretch. There is of course plenty of time for thinking about the future and shifting through matters weighing on your mind when you're walking on your own by the River Thames. Yes, I have enjoyed the company of my sister, John, Simon and Jamie, but I'm spending many hours on the Thames Path by myself. Quality downtime, you could call it. Some might say: *escaping reality*. Whatever. I have already, on this walk, come to terms with a difficulty I had earlier in the year and decided, just like Jan: *Hang on, I'm by the river. What is there to worry about?* Exactly: what's the point? My minor difficulties mean nothing in the grand scheme of things: just forget it! A good long walk by a river, I am finding, really helps put matters in perspective. It's as though the simple act of stepping forth helps shuffle thoughts. Perhaps it is all this fresh air. Perhaps it is simply seeing the Thames unfold. The river feels like a story, as though I'm walking through an unravelling tale: the histories, the towns, the villages, the ancient inns, the boats, the countryside, the gossip, the people you meet. There is much time for reflection and I am finding that the longer you walk, the closer you seem to get to the river. The river begins to mean more. It becomes a companion (if that's not putting it too strongly). In turn, it provides solace, offers respite, throws up intrigue and, needless to say, brings many and varied delights.

Another one is just coming up. I cross the field enjoying the freedom of the trail – and the path soon bends inland on a detour away from the water and I find myself arriving at the Flower Pot Hotel. *Accommodation for fishing and boating parties*, says an old-fashioned notice plastered across the red-brick facade.

Now, I know I have been to plenty of pubs on this Thames walk. Yes, I am aware of that. But pubs and Thames walks are, as you will have gathered by now, intricately linked. The river leads you to many out-of-the-way places, such as this remote farmland halfway between Henley and Marlow. Fortunately, due to Britain's coach-and-horse era of hostelries and what seems to be a continuing fascination with the Thames, many old pubs are still going. Guidebooks aplenty list the best.

One of these is the Flower Pot. This is a sort of fisherman's dream, and if not ancient, it has been going since 1895. Glass boxes displaying mounted perch, pike and trout fill almost every space on the walls. Collections of fishing hooks and maps of the Thames, including Tombleson's iconic 1834 version, take up the rest. A statue of a famous angler named A. E. Hobbs, author of a seminal (in fishing circles) book entitled *Trout of the Thames*, published in 1920, stands in the beer garden. The landlords are Tony and Pat Thatcher. Tony is sitting in a green leather chair made from an old beer barrel, next to a caged parrot named Paddy. He is a jovial, no-nonsense man with a dry wit, bushy grey moustache and the build of a former rugby player.

'I'm the boss' are Tony's first words to me when I introduce myself; in case I was in any doubt.

I nod in a way that suggests that I appreciate his boss status.

Tony assesses me for a moment.

'This is a near perfect boozer,' continues Tony, who has been running the show for 25 years.

'It's dead man's shoes,' he says, referring to having been landlord here for so long. From this, I gather that he means that anyone would be mad to give up the opportunity to run such a near perfect boozer. 'Everyone's got to walk past. And a lot of 'em come in.'

Tony does not seem to be speaking out of boastfulness, although there is a touch of pride of course. He seems to have a straightforward respect for the inn's location and the way the interior was originally laid out. There is a central serving bar that is sliced in two, with a narrow area for drinking pints and gossiping at the front and a quieter section with tables at the back.

Tony does not like gastropubs; the Flower Pot offers food, but nothing too fancy.

'A gastropub wouldn't survive here five years,' he says. The way he utters the word 'gastro' is suggestive of something deeply rotten at the heart of twenty-first-century Britain. 'A gastropub wouldn't survive coz a gastropub's got themes.'

The way Tony utters the word 'themes' is equally suggestive of terrible, unspeakable matters.

A regular who has been listening to our conversation cuts in: 'Drinking is a good theme. That's the theme in here.'

The regular appears very pleased with this intervention.

Pat, Tony's wife, ushers me to the mantelpiece above a fireplace and shows me pictures of famous guests. 'Tom Jones, the two lads from *EastEnders*, Brigitte Nielsen, Vinnie Jones, Sir Matthew Pinsent,' she says matter-of-factly. Chart-topping singers, former A-lister Hollywood actresses and Olympic champions: not bad. She whispers that Tony may retire in a couple of years 'when he's seventy'.

Then Tony booms over, as though to interrupt my tête-à-tête with his beloved: 'I suppose I'd better get you a drink.' And I am supplied with my best value (free), best tasting pint of lime and soda on the Thames Path so far.

Refreshed, I cross fields with hedgerows, red kites circling above. After a while, the path regains the Thames, where an embankment of fine houses soon appears. Across the way, an imposing white country mansion stands on a hill: the five-star Danesfield House Hotel. This is close to Medmenham, once home to the infamous eighteenth-century Hellfire Club run by Sir Francis Dashwood under the motto *'Fay ce que vouldras'* ('Do what you will'). Its evening meetings were held for a while somewhere over there behind trees on the opposite bank at Medmenham Abbey, which the club leased. Members, who were required to be 'persons of quality', called themselves 'monks', and when gatherings were arranged 'nuns' would be invited to the abbey (women of 'cheerful and lively dispositions', i.e. prostitutes). Among the famous members of the club were the satirical artist William Hogarth and Benjamin Franklin, one of the Founding Fathers of the United States.

Considering this, I arrive at a meadow filled with a large number of people enjoying picnics by the river's edge.

Cars are parked in neat rows along a marked track through the grass. As I walk by, I notice that the vast majority of the picnickers seems to be extended families – mainly, it would appear, of Middle Eastern origin.

Wonderful smells waft from barbecues. Hammocks have been slung between trees. Men sitting on chairs on unfurled Persian rugs smoke hookah pipes, emitting apple and cinnamon aromas. Sophisticated sunshade 'houses' have been erected. Children play on inflatable lilos in the shallows. Many women, more than half, are in headscarves. Kids and dads kick footballs and someone has set up a badminton net. All seems well organised. Everyone is having a great time.

I ask a man what is going on. He is eating corn on the cob while tending to a barbecue. He has a Middle Eastern complexion and is wearing sandals, jean shorts and a T-shirt, looking relaxed and happy in the sunshine. The clouds of earlier have cleared.

'We are from northern Iraq: Kurdistan,' he says, as though this explains everything. He looks to check that I am familiar with Kurdistan.

Satisfied that I am au fait with the troubled region, he continues.

'We kill Isis – now everyone knows us,' he says.

I had not been anticipating meeting anyone involved in the war against Islamic State today, or on any other day on this walk. He asks me where I am going and I explain what I'm doing.

'I walk one thousand miles!' he responds. 'All the people here have.' He waves a hand towards his group. 'One thousand miles into Turkey!'

A mere 215 miles along the Thames, by implication, is nothing. And he's right about that.

I do not get this man's name, although he tells me he is a car salesman and that their family group is from Barking in East London. He turns his attention to the barbecue. His companion Shalwr, in similar Western clothing, says by way of introduction: 'I am Kurdistani.'

We talk about the barbecue; they are cooking lamb and chicken, and the men are in charge of the sizzling grill. 'Women make food at home. Here we help out,' says Shalwr.

The smells are intoxicating; spices, herbs and tomato sauces mixed in with the marinated meat.

'Do you think you will ever return to your homeland?' I ask.

'Hopefully never,' he replies, with a grin.

'What do you like about it here?'

'Everything,' he answers, telling me he has lived in Britain since seeking asylum in 1996. 'More than seventy per cent of my life now is in the UK.'

Shalwr is called over to the barbecue. 'It is not a Kurdistani holiday today,' he says. Word about this Thames riverbank has simply spread among the Kurdistani community in Britain. This is where they choose to gather on summer weekends, and they come from far and wide.

It is a wonderful arrangement in a beautiful spot and I make a mental note to return one day for a picnic of my own. I follow the Thames Path down a lane that veers away from the river, passing a farmyard smelling of country smells and coming to the quiet village of Hurley, where I enter Pub Number Two of the day.

What a lovely-looking pub it is, with its whitewashed facade, slightly crooked walls and old red-tiled roof, tucked down a lane with hedgerows, little cottages, dry-stone walls and rose gardens. This is the English village dream. This is the reason American tourists jump on jumbos when they're heading for these shores: olde England – very olde England. The pub is even called the Olde Bell, serving drinks since 1135, when King Stephen was on the throne and the buildings were a guest house for visitors to a nearby Benedictine abbey. During the Second World War, Dwight Eisenhower and Winston Churchill stayed at the Olde Bell while plans were being made for the Normandy landings. Since then, American actors Cary Grant and Dustin Hoffman have stopped by, as have the British duo Elizabeth

Taylor and Richard Burton. On paper, it's got everything that you could hope for in an old, Grade II listed English pub: serious history, original buildings, a celebrity reputation and a tranquil village setting by a countrified bend of the Thames.

Again, I had better just say here that I really do not want to sound as though I'm looking to pick holes in places. I'm not. I loved today's Pub Number One. I do not, however, love Pub Number Two.

I'll explain why.

In the garden of the Olde Bell, another barbecue is taking place. I join a long queue, keen to order a chicken burger, despite the £12 price tag; the riverside Middle Eastern cooking has made me hungry. I wait about ten minutes and just as I'm getting near the front of the queue, a middle-aged woman in charge of the barbecue yells: 'The chicken's off!' There is, I gather, no more chicken. I had my heart set on a chicken burger and do not particularly like the look of the regular burgers. I keep waiting, though, taking a picture of the general setting in the garden to kill time. As I do, the middle-aged woman who yelled 'The chicken's off!' glares at me. I feel obliged to say: 'I'm not taking a picture of you.' The woman who yelled 'The chicken's off!' seems only partially happy with this, making me feel uneasy. So I think better of trying one of the burgers I do not like the look of. Life is too short for such burgers, especially when they are served by people who do not seem to like you.

I go back into the oldest part of the Olde Bell, the low-ceilinged bar in the front of the building. Black-and-white pictures on the walls depict olde English scenes. No one is in this olde bar, apart from two bar staff. I ask for another lime and soda (yes, I do really like lime and sodas), but only a half-pint as I'm not that thirsty. I'm ordering as much to allow me to sit and rest as for the drink itself. The young woman in black serving me has a glint in her eye.

'That will be £3.20,' she says deadpan, though the glint is still there. She pushes forward a half-pint of lime and soda.

'For a half of lime and soda?' I ask.

'Yes,' she says. Still the glint.

This makes the Perch back in Oxford, scene of my last lime-and-soda altercation, seem a downright bargain.

I point out that according to the Olde Bell's pricing it would appear that a pint of lime and soda would cost £6.40 and that you could get a premium lager in a posh hotel in London for that.

'OK, I'll take off the price of the cordial. It is £2.30 without the cordial,' she says. Deadpan, glint fading.

I say, 'Thanks but no thanks' and leave the olde bar of the Olde Bell and return to the river. As I am almost out of Hurley, I realise I left the £1.50 I had considered enough to cover the drink on the bar. The barmaid may have noticed the change, or perhaps she had not.

Either way, I'm not going back to the Olde Bell in Hurley in a hurry.

It is not that far from Hurley to Marlow, past Hurley weir and beyond Bisham Abbey on the opposite bank. This abbey has a rich past. It was founded in the twelfth century and the house connected to the abbey, long ago pulled down, was given to Anne of Cleves by Henry VIII as part of their divorce settlement; their marriage had been unconsummated as Henry was not keen on his fourth, German, wife. 'I liked her before not well, but now I like her much worse' was his famous, rather blunt assessment.

Later, Princess Elizabeth was detained at this house during her sister Mary Stuart's three-year reign. Later still, the lady of the manor, Lady Hoby, murdered her son, who had been slower at his studies than his siblings, by shutting him up in a room and leaving him to perish. The red-brick and grey-stone house and a church belonging to the house stand by the river's edge. The place feels cursed – and indeed it is. As he was taken away from the abbey, the last abbot, John Cordery, said: 'As God is my witness, this property shall ne're be inherited, for its sons will be hounded by misfortune.' Nowadays the England football team trains on pitches here. I wonder whether, given the recent track record, the country's finest ought to choose a more auspicious meeting spot.

I plod along, enjoying the wild flowers and the peace and quiet of the path, and reach Marlow's elegant metal suspension bridge.

What a wonderful bridge.

As a long-distance Thames walker, one begins to appreciate a good bridge. This is something I had not anticipated when setting off. The heightened pleasure brought by bridges is new to me. Perhaps it is something to do with trudging down the path for long periods bridge-less, as it were, and then having a crossing to focus one's attention.

Marlow's bridge was created by the English engineer William Tierney Clark and opened in 1832. A plaque explains this heritage and that Clark was behind the even more impressive, 375-metre-wide Széchenyi Chain Bridge across the River Danube in Budapest, which linked the Buda and Pest parts of the Hungarian capital in 1849; Marlow's span is a mere 72 metres but the design was the prototype for the one in Budapest. Clark was also responsible for the original suspension bridge at Hammersmith, the first such structure across the Thames, built in 1827.

Such a fine piece of engineering arising after the bucolic scenery of the Thames Path takes me aback. At first sight it's shocking merely for being so unexpected. Yet having taken time to regard the bridge properly, I realise the way the metal chains curve gently across the river, held up by hoop-shaped stone supports that look like mini Marble Arches, does not jar with the surroundings whatsoever. The bridge blends in perfectly, accompanying the spire of All Saints' Church on the northern riverbank, where the town begins.

This is my new favourite bridge (after the one at Clifton Hampden, before which Halfpenny Bridge in Lechlade held my affections). Thames bridge-spotting… it's all the rage. Or perhaps I'm just going nuts in the Thames-side sun.

'A quintessentially English town'
Marlow

I drop the backpack at the charming little Prince of Wales pub (Pub Number Three of the day), and go to Pub Number Four.

Pub Number Four of the day is reached via Marlow's high street. Marlow seems to have more zip and alternative edge than Henley. Burger joints rub shoulders with galleries, vintage clothes shops, cocktail bars, artisan bakeries and boutiques selling Buddhas and scented candles. I turn down Henley Road, passing Albion House, where Percy Bysshe Shelley and Mary Shelley stayed in 1817; Mary put the finishing touches to *Frankenstein* here while her husband was composing the perhaps lesser-known poem *The Revolt of Islam* (much of which was scrawled while on a rowing boat on the Thames).

Then I come to the Hand and Flowers, a place that some traditional pub purists may consider a bit of a monster in its own right.

The Hand and Flowers is run by television celebrity chef Tom Kerridge, who through the skill of his innovative cooking – including dishes such as baked carrot and haggis tart, duck breast *à l'orange* with duck sausages, and stuffed pigs' trotters – has gained not one but two Michelin stars. His pub is the first in the country to have achieved such an accolade, seeming to leap above mere 'gastropub' status into the realms of 'gourmet pub' (or something like that). One wonders what Tony back at the Flower Pot might think of it.

Inside, waiters holding aloft dishes of salt-baked swede with haggis and lamb buzz between tightly packed tables beneath a low ceiling. The Hand and Flowers appears at first to be a restaurant, not a pub. But I walk on and am ushered by a waiter to a back room where I find a small bar with black leather stools, olive sofas, chandeliers and a little fenced-off area for smokers by a car park.

A tall man wearing a flat cap, Ellesse tracksuit bottoms, pristine unlaced Adidas high-top trainers and a Nike T-shirt – he looks like a 1980s

American rap artist – is talking to a motormouthed man with a ponytail and orange Nike trainers sitting at one end of the zinc-topped bar.

The former is Kerridge, Britain's best-known pub landlord. The latter is the controversial comedian Russell Brand, who lives in Henley.

They are talking about football.

I eavesdrop for a while.

'It's going to be very different to Juventus…' says Brand, referring to Chelsea's new manager Antonio Conte. He rattles on about Antonio Conte for a while.

'He's got a contract with West Ham… Amazing, one of the best players in the world, one of the top ten players,' says Kerridge. He rattles on about a West Ham midfielder for a while.

'Guardiola!' says Brand.

A long discourse involving much gesticulation on Manchester City's manager issues forth.

'A big season for Klopp!' says Kerridge.

A long discourse involving much gesticulation on Liverpool's manager begins.

So this is what top chefs and comedians talk about in their spare time.

I order a half of bitter and some 'pork and paprika puffs' from a barman and ask him if he could see if I could have a quick word with Kerridge. He says he'll do his best and adds: 'You are very, very lucky – you have to catch this opportunity.'

The barman says Kerridge is not always in situ at the Hand and Flowers.

While the duo talk football, I drink my half of bitter and eat the pork and paprika puffs (very tasty); I had asked the barman if I could order a main course at the bar, as Brand has, but am told this is not possible. Bookings for meals at the Hand and Flowers must be made many weeks in advance.

Kerridge comes over. He has startlingly blue eyes and a pinkish complexion. His sports clothes seem to hang loose on his frame.

I ask him about Marlow and whether he likes living by the Thames.

'Marlow is a quintessentially English town: the suspension bridge, the rowing club by the water, cricket, the regatta, a fair each year,' he says, admitting that his business benefits from its proximity to the Thames. 'It's the river frontage that draws in English visitors: tourists, people from London.'

He tells me he's a swimmer. 'I swim every day but I don't swim in the river. I like the idea of having a warm shower at the end.'

Kerridge has lost a lot of weight recently due to this swimming regime; hence the loose clothes. The river clearly means a lot to him. Today is the evening summer party for the 100 members of staff at the Hand and Flowers and the Coach, his new, less expensive restaurant/pub down the road. A meal at the Hand and Flowers might set you back £70, although the three-course lunches are a more than reasonable £19.50. At the less formal Coach, a burger is £10. 'Usually we have a boat party to Henley or Boulter's Lock, but this is the first year we're not having a river trip,' says Kerridge. Instead they will be holding their summer party at the Coach.

I ask if the Hand and Flowers is a proper pub or merely a fancy restaurant with a bar on the side.

He is ready for this. 'I would argue: what is a real pub? Moaning about the price of the beer and not being able to smoke, frosted windows, and drinking four pints every night?'

He pauses for me to respond as though I'm a fan of such places. To be honest, I do like an 'old boozer', though the Hand and Flowers has a joyously upbeat style and Kerridge, with his cheap set menus and down-to-earth demeanour is someone who more than understands what pub-goers like.

'Pubs are seen as hubs of the community, but "community" is changing,' he says. 'It's about the experience, not just the alcohol.'

He pauses.

'Will that do?' he asks, as though I've just collected a sound bite for the six o'clock news.

I tell him 'thanks, it will do' in the manner of a correspondent about to file a report to the BBC news desk.

And off he rushes to the kitchen.

I go back to my sofa and watch Russell Brand eating a risotto by the bar in his orange trainers.

It has been a bizarre day.

CHAPTER SEVEN

MARLOW, BUCKINGHAMSHIRE, TO STAINES, SURREY

'£34,000 FULL BOARD'

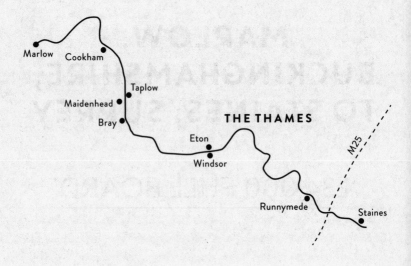

Walkers covering more than a handful of miles each day for several weeks in a row, as I have discovered, inhabit their own world. When embarking on such a long-distance walk, real life is put on hold and baser considerations take over. New rules apply. Put simply, you do not want to be: uncomfortable (too hot, too cold, or with clothes or shoes rubbing), hungry (and therefore short on energy) or lost. You want to know you have a place to sleep at the end of the day, ready for the next assault on the trail ahead. And that's about it. You do not care greatly how you appear to the outside world. Hence the bulky, fluorescent, zip-obsessed, fleecy, nylon-dominated anti-fashion of the outdoor pursuits industry. Natty panama hats, linen shirts and flannel shoes are for other people: part-timers. Fashion style, such as it is in walking circles, whistles to a different tune.

It is all about getting the right kit. There are many considerations here: the perfect shoes, coupled with the perfect socks, the ideal trousers or shorts (light, rainproof), the easily folding pac-a-mac, the correct length of walking stick (for those who need one), plentiful pockets for your compass (the latest versions being connected to the Global Positioning System), detailed map and energy snacks, a light snug-fitting backpack.

Given my chances of getting lost are slim I have, as I have said, forgone a compass. I do not need a stick. My old – admittedly slightly uncomfortable and bulky – backpack seems up to the job. My North Face trousers are OK. I am, however, having trouble with my boots.

This is nothing to do with blisters, the usual boot-related complaint. It's to do with their declaration of being 'waterproof' despite all evidence to the contrary. Whenever rain has fallen my feet have soon soaked. The fabric on the boots seems positively designed to absorb liquid.

I have been lucky so far in that there have been only two downpours, but it would be handy to do something about the matter, so in the morning I go to the Mountain Warehouse on Marlow's high street.

Mountain Warehouse has become something of a second home. In the run-up to Trewsbury Mead, I visited on several occasions, buying special walking socks, a spare pair of trousers (left at home for space reasons), my pac-a-mac and a fleece (a completely pointless purchase given I had several already and the weather is too warm for one). Whenever I have happened to walk past a Mountain Warehouse – and you soon notice, once they are on your radar, that there are a surprisingly large number of Mountain Warehouses – I have found my feet leading me in for a perusal of the latest lightweight jacket range. And as a result of giving my email when buying the special walking socks, I now receive almost daily communications on '70 per cent off bestselling zip-off trousers' and other eye-catching offers. Mountain Warehouse has suddenly become, or perhaps it would like to be, an important part of my life.

I go in, with a mission. I want to find a waterproof spray for my boots. As I am looking, a white-shirted assistant named Kyan soon slides my way; perhaps he thinks I'm about to buy a pair of expensive Hurricane IsoGrip Waterproof Boots. Kyan looks disappointed when I tell him I am just after a spray, not Hurricane IsoGrip Waterproof Boots, although I have to say I am tempted.

There is something about 'walking gear' that, once you get into it, feels quite addictive. Kyan, however, quickly hides his disheartenment and is soon telling me, with great enthusiasm, all about the qualities of Mountain Warehouse's boot sprays and fabric boots.

'In the outdoor industry, with boots, you are looking at a certain number of millimetres on the hydrostatic head,' he says, when I tell him about my waterproof boots not being waterproof.

I look at him blankly.

'What you need is a one-thousand-millimetre hydrostatic head, a one-metre column. That's how they test them, when they're new. Water won't go through. That's when they're new and they've been treated with a chemical product. But that can be rubbed and washed off.'

Kyan really does seem to know a lot about waterproof boots.

'So they are only waterproof boots for a while?' I ask.

'Yes,' says Kyan, as though this is perfectly normal.

'But they say they are waterproof,' I venture.

'They are, when they are new,' he replies, before going off on a tangent. 'In the scientific industry you have PVC. Well, PVC, used for fishermen's gear, is totally waterproof. However, it doesn't breathe. When water goes on it, the water bounces off it in beads.'

This is why new fabrics have been created that are not entirely waterproof – so they can breathe, I learn. Kyan produces a can of spray, but it is a very heavy can of spray. Not wanting to add any extra weight – and being willing to take the chance that the weather will hold (forecasts are promising) – I tell Kyan I do not, after all, want the spray. Kyan seems disappointed once more but not particularly surprised. There must be quite a few awkward customers like me and, anyway, he knows I'll probably be back to Mountain Warehouse to buy a pair of extra zip-trousers or another fleece one day pretty soon.

'Dudes and ballet girls' and no strings attached
Marlow to Taplow

At a cafe I check my map. Marlow to Eton, the next stop, is about 15 miles. I have, I work out, already covered about 110 miles along the 215-mile Thames Path… almost exactly halfway to the North Sea. This is the length travelled along the path itself, of course; the actual total distance I have covered is 175 miles, including various excursions to see George Orwell's grave, Dorchester and so on. I am depending on the accuracy of the godly fitness tracker for this stat.

It is a bright sunny day. In the *Marlow Free Press* I read about Environment Agency plans to build a new flood wall in the town and spend a total of eight million pounds on further defences. The work is designed to 'prevent the scenes of devastation caused by the floods in 2014'. The river is clearly both a blessing, in terms of tourism for the likes of Kerridge, and a major local concern. Another story concentrates on the town's 'parking nightmare'. Residents want a solution to the 'long-running saga' that is also described as a 'parking farce' that has 'rumbled on for decades'. Oh, the joys of journalese (I really do like local papers).

The *Marlow Free Press* also runs an old-fashioned lonely hearts column. In these days of dating websites, this feels almost like a throwback to another era, though the language is perhaps fruitier than in bygone days. Kerry, aged 35, is 'married in open relationship, attractive, tall, slim and very presentable; seeks discreet gent any age for casual pleasurable encounters'; Sophia is aged a 'young 40, married but bored, seeks discreet adult fun, any area, all calls answered'; and Katie is aged 35, a 'slender, well-educated brunette [who] seeks no-strings mutual pleasure with gent aged 40 plus; must be discreet, married or single'.

Goodness gracious.

It's all going on in Marlow.

I take to the path, my head spinning at the thought of wanton bookish brunettes seeking no-strings mutual pleasure with married or single 40-plus gents.

The river is olive-green and empty, save for a man on a paddleboard, who looks at first glance as though he is walking on water. Weeping willows rustle by the banks. Beyond the bridge of the A404, the path cuts through riverbanks thick with meadowsweet, willowherbs and nettles. The morning is fresh and sun-drenched. Ruby butterflies flitter. Fish dart in the shallows. Mansions appear on the opposite bank, a few with their own boathouses (such boathouses are, I know by now, the sign of truly top-notch Thames mansions).

These prominent abodes are surrounded by Quarry Wood, the basis of Wild Wood in *The Wind in the Willows*, and it was not far from here, in Cookham Dean, that Kenneth Grahame was brought up and returned in later life when he invented the bedtime stories for his son Alastair that were to become his classic.

It is touching to imagine Grahame whispering the tale of Mr Mole and his misadventures in Wild Wood. So I do so for a while, recalling the passage in which the Wild Wood is first introduced: 'And as he lay there panting and trembling, and listened to the whistlings and the patterings outside, he knew it at last, in all its fullness, that dread thing which other little dwellers in field and hedgerow had encountered here, and known as their darkest moment – that thing which the Rat had vainly tried to shield him from – the Terror of the Wild Wood!'

I fall into something like a trance, pacing through the meadows.

These come to an end at little, picket-fenced houses and the sailing club of the village of Bourne End. Near here, a pleasure boat named *Damn the Expense!* is on sale for £129,950, which seems a bit more of a case of *Damn the Price Tag!* I cross a green railway bridge and, hoping for the best, walk straight through yet another herd of cattle in a field. One or two of these creatures, I cannot help noticing, are of the Longhorn variety that I believe is native to Texas.

The village of Cookham is next. Here I drop into the Stanley Spencer Gallery, which is to be found in a former Wesleyan chapel on the main corner. This is a bijou gallery with a little atrium and stairs to another level displaying the colourful works of Spencer (1891–1951), who lived in Cookham and painted many riverside scenes, some with religious themes such as *Christ Preaching at Cookham Regatta* and *The Angel, Cookham Churchyard*. My favourite though is *View from Cookham Bridge* (1936), which shows just that and somehow manages to capture the gentleness of the river: milky ripples lapping at a congregation of moored rowing boats by a bank with hedgerows, small wooden houses and a path along the river leading to fields. It is a path like many I have followed.

Beyond the short high street of stylish restaurants, pubs and interior design shops at Cookham, which feels pretty well-to-do (a bicycle shop in the village offers a bike that 'oozes class' for £3,800), comes a cool wood with ivy-wrapped trees.

This wood continues for a long way along the river, with more woodland on a hill on the opposite bank. The hill leads to Cliveden House, the fine seventeenth-century country house that is now a five-star hotel with a chequered past. Not only was the house home to Nancy Astor and the upper-class, late-1930s Cliveden Set, who were believed to be sympathetic to Nazi developments in Germany, it was also the scene of the 1960s Profumo Affair in which John Profumo, the secretary of state for war, became romantically involved with Christine Keeler, a 19-year-old model and 'showgirl' who caught his eye when she went swimming topless in Cliveden's pool. Much of the affair was conducted in the tucked-away, mock-Tudor Spring Cottage, at the foot of the hill; easy to spot across the river. Its revelation in the press and the discovery of Keeler's connections to a naval attaché at the Soviet embassy in London eventually led to Profumo's resignation. Harold Macmillan's government fell soon afterwards in 1963.

For a while, this is the River Thames at its sleepiest but also most secretive; away from the madding crowd, but not so far from it either.

Jerome K. Jerome loved this Cliveden Wood section of the Thames. In *Three Men in a Boat*, he wrote: 'In its unbroken loveliness this is, perhaps, the sweetest stretch of all the river, and lingeringly we slowly drew our little boat away from its deep peace.' A little further on, great mock-Tudor edifices soon emerge next to the path; mock Tudor is all the rage on the edge of Maidenhead. Some of these houses have laser security systems. A sign warns: *POLICE WILL BE NOTIFIED AND YOU WILL BE RECORDED ON CONCEALED VIDEO ONCE THE BEAM IS BROKEN*.

I stop to visit Ray Mill Island, next to Boulter's Lock, a late nineteenth-century epicentre of the messing-about-on-boats craze. The island has a little park, an aviary with parakeets and a cafe where I buy a cup of tea and ask a bottle-blonde assistant how big the island is.

'Oh, I've never been round it,' she replies, in a tone that suggests that seeing the island would be akin to exploring a remote jungle in Borneo.

I do go round, and this circumnavigation takes the length of time required to drink a cup of tea. It is a quiet place, with just a couple of fishermen near the weir. In Jerome's time, thanks to newfangled fast trains bringing in Londoners, the island would have been bustling with a fashionable set including artists, members of the aristocracy and cabinet members. This crowd, however, was not to his liking: 'Maidenhead itself is too snobby to be pleasant... It is the town of showy hotels, patronised chiefly by dudes and ballet girls.'

Here the Thames Path crosses Maidenhead Bridge to Taplow.

I prepare to do so, pausing on the Maidenhead side while considering whether to visit Maidenhead Conservative Club.

Maybe Theresa May, the local Member of Parliament and the country's new post-Brexit prime minister, will be in the middle of conducting her local surgery, wearing her famous kitten heels. I might just strike lucky and catch the prime minister on her first weekend back after her big news. That would be a Thames Path encounter and a half: a few words from the country's *numero uno* so soon after the momentous referendum. You never know.

But I realise this is fanciful thinking. She's probably busy – she's got a lot on her plate. After all, it's only a fortnight since the new prime minister, who voted 'Remain' in the referendum yet is seeing through the European retreat, promised that 'as we leave the EU we will forge a bold new positive role for ourselves in the world and we will make Britain a country that works not for a privileged few but for every one of us'. She's probably busy working on the country's bold new positive role and developing policies for everybody. Besides, she more than probably won't have time for appointment-less Thames backpackers with questions. And anyway, it's a long way down a dual carriageway to the club and security might just be perturbed by a dishevelled unknown man arriving unannounced with a backpack stuffed with books about the Thames. That might set a few alarm bells ringing.

Halfway across the eighteenth-century stone bridge, I stop to take in the Thames Riviera Hotel, on the Maidenhead side. The name makes me chuckle. In the past, maybe the Thames Riviera was a 'showy hotel', but now a dull yellow sign advertises 50 per cent off meals on Monday to Wednesday. Algae and litter has collected by an old concrete jetty. Purple weeds grow in clumps by a terrace above a mouldy wall. It has clearly seen better days.

£2 million houses and £650 meals
Taplow to Bray

On the opposite bank, in Buckinghamshire now, there is a big half-built housing development on the site of what was formerly the Skindles Hotel, once famous as a place for illicit liaisons and for its music venue, where the Beatles and the Rolling Stones played. The Prince of Wales, later Edward VII, took his mistress Lillie Langtry here and that set the tone for a place that became notorious for Mr-and-Mrs-Smith-style adventures. This was in the heyday of trains and showy sports cars, before holidays on jet planes took off.

For many years Skindles was derelict and a year ago it was demolished to make way for 'luxury new homes' from the Berkeley construction group. Curious, I drop by the showroom, passing great placards declaring: *UNIQUE RIVERSIDE LIVING, BEAUTIFUL FAMILY HOMES, ENJOY BEAUTIFUL EXPANSES OF GREEN OPEN SPACE WITH NEW COUNTRY PATHS* and *A NUMBER OF PRIVATE MOORINGS AVAILABLE TO SELECTED HOMES.* Mock-up pictures show rows of neat, narrow, red-brick houses with balconies and little strips of garden running to the water's edge. In close-up pictures of some of the houses not facing the water, Lexus and

Audi cars have been drawn in. These houses are partially in the mock-Tudor style I noticed along the river earlier. The development is called Taplow Riverside.

In the showroom an easy-going man with designer stubble and a suit with a tie – he reminds me a little of the characters who apply to be candidates on *The Apprentice* – tells me that the cheapest riverside property costs two million pounds. Houses not on the river can be had for just over one million. There are 42 houses in all, as well as a selection of apartments in a building where a paper mill once stood. 'Crossrail is coming through Taplow in 2019 – you'll be able to get to Canary Wharf in fifty-two minutes and Paddington in thirty-nine,' he says, gauging my reaction just in case I turn out to be an eccentric potential customer. He offers me an espresso. The sales pitch is smooth and the model of the future neighbourhood looks enticing.

But it does seem sad that scandalous Skindles has gone.

Beyond Maidenhead Bridge comes a series of elegant homes and then a brilliant red-brick railway bridge built by Isambard Kingdom Brunel in 1838 with the 'widest and flattest brick arches in the world', says a plaque. I shall take its word about this. I keep going past many seriously magnificent homes – among the most flamboyantly OTT homes anywhere on the river, I'm guessing – with columns and flagpoles and verandas and perfectly mown lawns and boathouses; some with fabulous well-polished wooden speedboats of the sort you imagine in the South of France. Theresa May's backyard is clearly a very wealthy backyard, with more than its fair share of the 'privileged few'.

Further on is a quiet stretch, which seems to act as a buffer zone before the M4, where I ascend steps and cross the noisiest Thames bridge so far, walking fast to put the screech of lorries behind me as I backtrack for a mile along the south bank to a picturesque village: Bray.

This Thames-side village could claim to be the most famous village for food in the world. It is home to a pair of restaurants with the highest score possible of three Michelin stars: the Waterside Inn (head chef: Michel Roux) and the Fat Duck (head chef: Heston Blumenthal). There are only four such restaurants in the whole of the UK, with two of them in this place with a population of about 4,600. Blumenthal also owns two pubs in the village: the Hinds Head, which has a single Michelin star, and the Crown. In all, a total of seven Michelin stars are to be had within a five-minute walk of one another.

The Fat Duck is closed, although I have neither four hours to spare for a 16-course meal featuring liquid-nitrogen-treated mincemeat ice cream, sashimi eaten while listening to crashing waves on headphones provided by waiters, snail porridge and chocolate-coated carrot lollies, nor do I have £255 set aside (nor a reservation). For the accompanying wines, as chosen by the sommelier, add about another £150.

A writer for *The Guardian*, Tony Naylor, recently estimated that with a bottle of wine, pre-dinner G & Ts and the discretionary service charge, you might expect to pay around £650 for two people at the Fat Duck. He had been to the restaurant in 2008, loving the food but paying about half of this. Since then, however, there had been renovations and a new menu with reset prices. Of the £650 meal for two, he commented: 'No meal is worth that, no matter how sensational.'

Not far from the plain whitewashed exterior of the famous Fat Duck is the Hinds Head, with its many fine hanging baskets; it is easy to see why Bray does so well in the Britain in Bloom awards. I step inside, where a lugubrious barman, upon questioning, tells me that the Hinds Head is 'a building of the 1600s' and eyes me dubiously when I enquire whether there is a table free for lunch; reservations, it seems, are the done thing. As he checks, I take in the polished wood panels, parquet floor, row of pewter mugs above a fireplace and the low ceiling beams. Despite the row of ale pumps and simple bar stools there is a rarefied air. No fruit machines or Sky Sports in here.

A table is, remarkably, found, and the head waiter's eyes nearly pop out of his head when I enter with my backpack. This may be a Hinds Head first. The head waiter retreats and a shaven-headed pub manager,

David Hyde, is soon on hand, seemingly to assess the new boot-clad, zip-trouser-wearing, traveller-style customer at his Michelin-star restaurant. Gathering that I may actually be able to foot my bill, he recommends the Scotch eggs as a 'pre-starter'. 'The best in the country,' he says nonchalantly.

I ask a couple of questions about the pub and David, in return, asks if I want to see some historical pictures in the room upstairs. We go up to a room for large dining parties with a few yellowing clippings on the walls. The most prominent is from the *Daily Mail* of 24 April 1963 and is headlined: *THE QUEEN OF ENGLAND, WITH 28 FOREIGN ROYALS, CALLS IN FOR LUNCH AT AN ENGLISH PUB.* The report, which has pictures by two *Daily Mail* readers – including a couple showing the royal party arriving and departing in what looks like a school bus – explains that the women drank squash, cider and Pimm's while the men drank beer at 'Prince Philip's local'. The Hinds Head is not far from Windsor Castle. As well as the Queen, the Prince of Wales, Princess Anne, the King of Norway, the Queens of Denmark, Sweden, Spain and Romania, and various princesses and barons were in attendance.

'Crazy, huh?' says David.

As a long-time local, David is amazed by Bray's culinary revolution. 'All these Michelin stars a short walk from each other,' he says, as though still getting over it himself. 'It's a hub of gastronomy, but you can't buy a loaf of bread or a pint of milk.'

We stop to look at another clipping, from the *Daily Mirror* of 14 April 1938, showing King George VI walking through Bray in the funeral procession of a friend. And then David tells me about the sixteenth-century Vicar of Bray, who famously had a pragmatic approach to his religious leanings, switching his affiliation three times between Papism and Protestantism as affairs of state dictated. A quote of a ballad about the canny vicar posted on the wall sums up the ultimate aim of his theologically slippery approach:

And this is law I will maintain
Until my dying day, sir,
That whatsoever King may reign,
I'll be the Vicar of Bray, sir.

There may just be a few politicians about today signed up to the Vicar of Bray's method of survival.

My meal is splendid, pricey (£42) but worth it for the sheer unusualness of the Hinds Head. Warm yolk explodes from the crunchy, salty Scotch egg. The pea soup tastes of the very freshest peas straight from the pod and comes with a wispy texture plus little slices of flavoursome ham and good sourdough bread. The main course of chicken, ham and leek pie with wholegrain mustard and Jersey Royals is by far the best pie of the journey so far. I drink iced tap water delivered by the bulging-eyed head waiter, who appears to blow a few blood vessels in his forehead when I say I will not be having wine and would just like tap water. An espresso at the end is thrown in for free, maybe because he has decided, eventually, that I am a lost cause as far as margins are concerned.

There is no sign of Blumenthal. Nor is there any of Michel Roux when I go to see the Waterside Inn, down by the willows by the riverfront. All the three-star Michelin chefs of Bray seem to be in hiding.

'Wasn't it nice before Slough was here?'
Bray to Windsor

I walk back across the M4 and return to the path, which runs for a considerable distance here on a strip of land between the Thames and Dorney Lake, used by the rowers of Eton College. Windsor Racecourse appears on the other side of the river, as does the Queen's castle, looking rather majestic with a Union Jack fluttering from the top of the main circular tower. It's a sight that stops me in my tracks: the turrets and arrow slits and high stone walls peering down on the river. So splendid and regal – and so much grander than anything so far on the River Thames. I keep going and arrive in Eton, where I check into the Crown and Cushion on the high street near the bridge (a small room facing the street on the second floor).

The Crown and Cushion is halfway between Britain's most famous school and perhaps best-known castle. They are separated by a narrow pedestrian bridge dating from 1822, though this is a much more ancient place of crossing. Archaeologists have discovered wooden posts in the water here dating from 1400 BC, during the Bronze Age.

I walk over to Windsor.

Having never looked round Windsor Castle before, I behave like a good, dutiful tourist and head up a street with a vaping lounge selling hazelnut and mandarin vaping liquids, a Lebanese restaurant with 'two belly dancers every Friday and Saturday night, one belly dancer every Wednesday and Thursday', the Yangtze Chinese restaurant, a Wetherspoon's pub, a McDonald's, a Thai restaurant, a pizzeria, a Nando's, the Theatre Royal (showing *The Pirates of Penzance*), and the Duchess of Cambridge pub, cannily renamed to coincide with the royal wedding of 2011.

Her Majesty and Prince Philip are not short of dining options, colourful local entertainment for nights out or refills of smokeless ciggies.

I turn left at a statue of Queen Victoria, depicted pointing a stick towards a junction as though directing traffic, and enter Windsor Castle. Here a woman selling tickets tells me I'm too late to see St George's Chapel, the resting place of a dozen kings of England, as it closes at four o'clock. Oh well. The state apartments and a doll's house collection are available up a hill beyond the main fortified tower, she says. My ticket costs £20.

Gulping slightly at such reckless expenditure today, I proceed amid Chinese and American tourists to battlements overlooking the Thames.

From these it is possible, beyond Eton College, to make out the cooling towers of the power station at Slough Trading Estate. Planes from Heathrow soar above this estate, home to a Mars bar factory, hydraulic hose specialist and an asbestos removal company. Queen Elizabeth, the Queen Mother, among those at rest in St George's Chapel, once said of the view: 'Wasn't it nice before Slough was here?'

It's not quite that bad: the trees may have grown up a bit since her time and there is still a slither of river down there. Anyway, at least the estate is a sign of some form of homespun industry: the making of chocolate bars and hydraulic hoses across the river all quietly helping to keep the economy ticking over in these new go-it-alone Brexit days.

The queue for the dolls' houses is long and I realise I have neither the patience nor a sufficient interest in dolls' houses to wait. A sympathetic attendant, who seems to appreciate my position, lets me through a cord into the state apartments section. Which is nice of her.

The first room I come to after the doll's-house queue is dedicated to William Shakespeare and includes among its initial displays a well-known 1685 portrait in which the playwright looks owl-like and pensive, with protuberant eyes, stubble, pursed lips, the hint of a double chin, and hair that has receded to the point of baldness except for strands over his ears. In a cabinet near this portrait is an original copy of the 1623 *First Folio* containing his works; Shakespeare lived from 1564 to 1616, and a few months ago it was the 400th anniversary of his death. This exhibition room is connected to the occasion. Shakespeare is said to have written *The Merry Wives of Windsor* in 1597 while staying at an inn just outside the castle gates; the play was first performed here for Queen Elizabeth. He would have known the Thames well. In a corner of this room there is a panoramic 1647 etching of London by the Czech artist Wenceslaus Hollar, taken from the perspective of the tower of Southwark Cathedral, in which the Globe Theatre features in the foreground. Shakespeare lived somewhere near the Globe and later in Blackfriars. He would regularly have travelled on the river. Shakespeare, you could say, was a Thames man.

I proceed to the state apartments proper, beginning with a collection of porcelain, where I am surprised to find a small kiosk selling china plates and cups commemorating the Queen's 90th birthday this year.

The small kiosk has no customers and I feign interest in the most expensive item on sale, although I am pretty sure, from the look in her eye, that the woman in the small kiosk is in little doubt I am a time-waster.

'How much is this cup?' I ask, pretending not to have seen the price tag.

'£1,195,' she replies.

'Hmmm,' I say, looking at the gold edge on the cup. 'Is that real gold?'

'Yes, it's real gold,' she replies, studying me. 'It's twenty-two-carat gold and it's all hand-painted.'

The cup has two handles. 'It's an unusual-looking cup,' I comment.

'It's known as a loving cup,' she says.

'A loving cup has two handles,' she tells me.

'How many of these do you shift a day?' I ask.

The attendant looks at me askance.

'I mean, what's your best day ever?' I continue. 'Five or ten of them?'

'Oh yes, sir,' she says, now certain that I am a time-waster. 'Money-wise we're doing very nicely, *thank you.*'

When she says 'thank you' her voice rises a tone or two in pitch.

Her eyes are cast beyond me: end of discussion.

The rooms to come, via a sweeping red-carpet staircase, are full of the trappings of royalty: ornate marble sculptures, sinuous red-silk walls, extravagant dressing rooms, walls covered in priceless paintings (including many that define our knowledge of the appearance of historical figures such as Richard III). Dining rooms dripping with gold lead to ballrooms with fancy oriental vases. Shiny suits of armour stand sentinel in hallways. Cabinets are stuffed with pistols and swords. Echoing banquet halls larger than tennis courts emerge with flowing tapestries, vaulted ceilings and thrones.

All of which is interesting enough – and the 1,000-year history of the castle's Norman origins is intriguing, along with the thought that this one survived while the castle by the river in Wallingford was totally wiped out.

Twenty pounds does seem a bit steep though.

Outside I find what I take to be Ye Olde King's Head pub, where Shakespeare is said to have written some of *The Merry Wives of Windsor* (though there is debate about this). The former pub is now a fish and chip shop. And I return past the belly-dancing Lebanese restaurants and vaping emporiums across the bridge to Eton, upon which a group of drunks has gathered to berate one another on the most prominent benches overlooking the water. I wonder whether the Queen has ever walked this way undercover to see what Windsor is really like. Somehow I doubt it.

'Let me show you Shelley'
Eton

My room at the Crown and Cushion is almost entirely filled with a double bed and comes with a wardrobe shaped like an upright coffin and a tiny television with a remote control that requires you to rub the almost-flat batteries before it works. I sleep well enough, and in the breakfast room the next morning, the Canadian waitress tells me I'm 'nuts' to be walking all the way along the Thames, before regaling me about her father's work as a Canadian truck driver and recommending that I visit Newfoundland where the people are the 'salt of the earth'.

I eat a large bowl of porridge (which I'm now trying to have every day) while taking in a Winston Churchill quote on the wall: 'My wife and I tried two or three times in the last forty years to have breakfast together but it was so disagreeable we had to stop.' A few couples silently poke at English breakfasts with this quote looming large.

I read the *Ascot, Windsor & Eton Express*. It has snippets on a Starbucks opening in Windsor, a budget hotel gaining planning permission in Slough and a version of the set of the television show *Great British Bake Off* being recreated at Legoland theme park. There is one piece of Thames news under the headline *BOAT BROKEN INTO*. It says that a boat moored on the river at Datchet was 'broken into and slept in' after a window was smashed to gain entry. However, 'the man fled before he was caught'. This is just about the day's biggest reported criminal act in the Ascot, Windsor and Eton area.

Eton's high street is home to antiquarian bookshops, cafes and many gentlemen's clothes shops. All sorts of coloured corduroy trousers, loafers with tassels, striped boxer shorts, silk hankies, tweed suits and Eton College three-piece outfits, including jackets with tails, are sold. At Tom Brown Tailors, right next to the college, I get talking to David Coulthard, the master tailor and owner. I ask if he ever made clothes for Prince William or Harry. He replies: 'Oh yes, we helped them out – I remember making William a waistcoat.' Many actors and Members of Parliament return to Tom Brown later in life.

'Old Etonians tend to come back when they're about thirty-five, when they're financially secure,' says David, who has worked here since the 1970s. A suit costs £1,500.

'Business from the college is not as good as it was – only about forty per cent of what we do. It's because of the internet. A lot of people go online, but then if the sleeves are too long or a coat doesn't fit they come here for alterations.'

Next door, in the wood-panelled visitor waiting room of Eton College, photographs of Prince William and Harry with Princess Diana adorn the walls. A gruff gateman/security guard takes a digital picture and asks my name. 'Did you say John Churchill?' he asks. I repeat and am let through into a courtyard with a statue of Henry VI, who founded Eton in 1440. Here I have arranged to meet Jenny Packham, the college's new communications and digital media officer, who is bright and cheery, tall, and wearing long black beads with a white blouse. She proceeds to whisk me round the 'sights' of Eton College, which she is just getting to know herself; she has brought along 'aide-memoire notes so I remember'.

First we go to the Lower School, where we enter 'the longest continually used classroom in the world', dating from 1440. It smells musty. The walls are covered in scrawls of names of past students who have used quill-sharpening knives to gouge the fifteenth-century wood and pour in ink. Jenny tells me no photography is allowed inside. We continue to the Upper School, where there are more engravings in the wood, including the names of William Gladstone and the Duke of Wellington.

'Let me show you Shelley,' says Jenny.

Sunlight falls in shafts through high leaded windows on the panel with the engraving of Shelley's name, written in capital letters, unlike most of the others.

'It's history, isn't it?' says Jenny, gazing at his name.

Then we move on to the chapel, with its high vaulted ceiling, another statue of Henry VI and an organ with 4,000 pipes. Here Jenny tells me that there are 1,300 pupils at Eton College.

'How much are the current fees?' I ask.

'Roughly £34,000 full board,' she replies.

I don't say anything.

What is there to say, other than to point out the obvious: this is a massive amount of cash, requiring someone paying 40 per cent tax to earn £57,000 a year to cover Eton's fees (excluding extras such as waistcoats from Tom Brown Tailors, ski trips and pocket money). This £57,000 is not, of course, realistic: all £57,000 earners must eat, get about and pay the mortgage or rent as well. Plus £57,000 earners may well be sending more than one child into this world where William Gladstone, the Duke of Wellington and Percy Bysshe Shelley have inscribed their names in the Upper School. An education in a top British public school is a very expensive business.

Looking about the chapel, I try to put things in perspective.

Over five years of study, £57,000 amounts to £285,000. That's enough to buy a Lamborghini Huracán in Pangbourne with plenty of cash to spare, and with the annual average UK salary at £26,500, it would take the 'average UK person' 16 years to gather. And this comparison falls down, once again, as it would mean this 'average person' not spending money on anything else. It would take the 'average person' much longer than that… which is why the 'average person' does not send their kids to Eton.

I raise all this here not to come across as some kind of socialist firebrand. I am merely stating the facts, which startle me the more I think about them.

There is also some relevance here to recent events.

Discontent with a perceived 'metropolitan elite' running the country and living one step removed from the public at large was widely reported as being what swung the referendum in favour of leaving the European Union. This imagined 'elite' is at the heart of the ongoing Brexit debate, partially driving the determination of those in favour of a 'hard' Brexit. Joe Bloggs, as many have said, wanted to stick up two fingers to the 'metropolitan elite', many of whom have joined the 'elite' from public school backgrounds: the toffs at the top, if you like, or Theresa May of Maidenhead's 'privileged few'. Many regard Brexit as a protest against a system that seems designed to protect the interests of the wealthy in confined social circles (not all of whom can afford Eton's fees).

It does not take much head-scratching to work out that there is a link between the high fees of public-school education – seven per cent of

British children are schooled privately – and what many regard as this troublesome elitism. Public schools deliver advantages that continue for a lifetime; you only have to look at the backgrounds of judges, lawyers, politicians, City bigwigs, heads of national institutions, members of the media, and even actors (Damian Lewis, Dominic West, Eddie Redmayne and Tom Hiddleston are the latest crop from Eton) to put two and two together.

End of commentary (some might say: dreadful rant).

Jenny shows me fields by the long red-brick wall running down to the riverside where the Eton wall game, a form of rugby, is played. Lawns beyond the castellated red-brick college buildings lead to a quiet bend of the Thames, with the tower of Windsor Castle rising to the south. I think of some of the famous Old Etonians who have passed this way: Robert Walpole, Britain's first prime minister; the novelist Henry Fielding; William Pitt, Britain's youngest prime minister, aged 24, in the eighteenth century; Thomas Gray, the poet who wrote 'Elegy Written in a Country Churchyard' just outside Slough; Percy Bysshe Shelley; Alfred, Lord Tennyson; the economist John Maynard Keynes; novelist Aldous Huxley; prime minister Harold Macmillan (with his Cliveden scandals involving showgirls); George Orwell; the artist Francis Bacon; Ian 'James Bond' Fleming; explorer and travel writer Wilfred Thesiger; Justin Welby, the current Archbishop of Canterbury; Olympic rowing champion Matthew Pinsent; Boris Johnson, former mayor of London and key Brexiteer; David Cameron, Britain's prime minister before Theresa May and the one who gave the go-ahead to the referendum on Brexit. In total, there have been 19 prime ministers who were taught at boys-only Eton.

'Not too shabby a view,' says Jenny, looking across the river.

She's right – and not too shabby a list of former pupils either.

We say goodbye and I return to the Crown and Cushion.

'Those are probably Prince Charles's cows'
Eton to Runnymede and Staines

Here my brother, Ed, awaits and we are soon hitting the Thames Path, on the twelfth day of this Thames adventure.

As we cross Windsor Bridge, past the same bench-bound drunks as yesterday, Ed launches into his own tirade. It's a bright day and he is wearing shorts, a striped polo shirt and old walking boots; Ed, who works in the field of traveller's cheques, is a veteran hiker. He is tall and has a long stride, making keeping up tricky at times. He is joining me to Staines, nine miles away, where we have a twin room booked at the riverside Swan pub. He is going to see how far he feels like continuing beyond there – possibly as far as Richmond, where he lives.

'I cannot believe it!' Ed says, brandishing a slip of paper like a member of the House of Commons calling a point of order.

This piece of paper is from South West Trains and is a penalty fare notice.

'Not a good start to the day. Not a good start. A twenty-pound fine as you can only use your Oyster card as far as Feltham.'

He pauses – for a split second.

'Feltham! A revenue protection officer got me. I said that it was a genuine, honest mistake and that I touched in my Oyster card at Richmond thinking that would be OK to Windsor. He held me up for fifteen minutes. I stayed calm but I was not amused. He asked me what my job was. I said "unemployed", to make him feel bad about it. He was a tall bald guy, had all the union badges on, the RMT and all of that.'

He pauses – for a split second.

He continues: 'I said: "You should sign it better – explain how far Oyster goes. How could I possibly have got away with it!" I pointed out that Windsor is only two stops past Feltham and that there are ticket barriers here. I thought he was going to give in at one point, but then he said: "I'm going to call up that Oyster and check your name." I said he could do that and that he should concentrate on catching real fare dodgers. He didn't like that. He said: "It's been like this for years." I said: "Well, I haven't been here before." I had to back off. Thing is, you can't get too moody with those people – you don't want to end up in court.'

This outburst takes us to the edge of Windsor.

We are walking through a meadow with tall yellow flowers. The sky is cobalt blue and the way ahead is empty of anyone, including revenue protection officers. I point out that this is one of the joys of walking the river: there tend not to be rules or fines connected to rules. Just after I say this, however, we come to an iron-bar fence with a sign indicating that the way ahead is protected under Section 128 of the Serious Organised Crime and Police Act 2005 and that trespass is a criminal offence; the land must have something to do with Windsor Castle.

'Those are probably Prince Charles's cows,' says Ed, looking through the iron bars. We back up along a side path and cross Victoria Bridge to the north side of the river, passing Datchet with its large houses, quiet riverfront and moored boats. Then we cross back to the south over the rose-stoned Albert Bridge and come to many massive riverside houses.

I remark about how nice the houses look.

'Yes, they're pretty nice for now,' says Ed. 'For the time being: fine. But when the polar caps melt, nothing's stopping the water getting those ones.'

Ed tends to take the point of view that we are all, one way or another, going to hell in a handcart.

He strides on (with his small backpack).

I struggle to keep up (with my large backpack).

We reach Runnymede, the place on the river where the Magna Carta was signed by King John and his barons on 15 June 1215 thus establishing the principle that all citizens, including the monarch, are subject to the rule of law. Everyone knows the story: King John had been setting high taxes to fund unsuccessful foreign campaigns; the barons were disgruntled, wanting a better system of decision-making and a more even balance of power; King John made his reluctant way to Runnymede to enter negotiations. Everyone also knows the outcome: this Thames-side document has become a cornerstone of democracy across the globe, famously having a bearing on the wording of the Constitution of the United States.

The set of beliefs feels as relevant now as ever, perhaps more so this summer. The actual signing on the dotted line either happened on the riverbank or on what is now known as Magna Carta Island. Ed and I enter a car park with tourist coaches and a notice explaining that this area is run by the National Trust. We check out a gazebo-style memorial, sponsored by the American Bar Association, which celebrates this 'birthplace of democracy'. The memorial dates from 1957 and is slightly away from the river across a field, as is another memorial in honour of John F. Kennedy. The latter is Britain's tribute to the 35th president of the United States and was completed in 1965.

Ed has itchy feet. He believes that the nine miles set aside for today are insufficient for a walker of his calibre, experience and stamina. So he suggests we take a half-hour detour up the hill in front of us to visit the Air Forces Memorial. I agree and Ed (with his small backpack) and I (with my large, heavy backpack) head up the slope.

The Air Forces Memorial commemorates 20,000 airmen who were lost during the Second World War while fighting in the ranks of the Royal Air Force and have no known graves. It is the most poignant spot on the 100-plus miles of my walk so far.

The simplicity of the grey-stone memorial on the top of Cooper's Hill, with the names of each airman inscribed, confers dignity upon the respectful setting.

We are the only visitors and walk around quietly, seeking out the names of two friends' grandfathers. Below, the vista opens up and the river twists onwards to London beyond the flat fields of Runnymede.

Sir John Denham's poem, 'Cooper's Hill' (1642), written looking down on Runnymede, captures the setting:

> My eye descending from the hill, surveys
> Where Thames among the wanton valleys strays.
> Thames, the most lov'd of all the ocean's sons,
> By his old sire to his embraces runs,
> Hasting to pay his tribute to the sea,
> Like mortal life to meet eternity…
> Here was that Charter sealed wherein the crown
> All marks of arbitrary power lays down.
> Tyrant and slave, those names of hate and fear,
> The happier style of king and subject bear.

Cooper's Hill is a detour every Thames Path walker should make. Even if it is a fair way up.

Ed and I continue along the river.

The quietude of Cooper's Hill and the fields of Runnymede is soon replaced by a bustling cafe outside the stylish-looking Runnymede-on-Thames Hotel. This is the fanciest Thames hotel yet and comes with a strange HotTug vessel moored out front: a small yellow boat with a hot tub that is towed behind another vessel. The HotTug is not being used and, frankly, who would want to be dragged along the river wearing their swimming costume in a bubbling tub while dog walkers look on? I suppose there must be a (rather niche) market for this.

Not far from this floating hot tub we pass beneath the M25. It's a symbolic moment… the capital is drawing near.

After this the river is isolated and mangrove-like until we reach a waterworks with *FISHING FANATIC!* painted in great pink letters on a wall. The water is still and mossy-green. Houses with charming river terraces and weeping willows in their gardens appear, as do the three stone arches of Staines Bridge and, right by the bridge, the Swan Inn, where we check in and go straight downstairs.

A perfect beer terrace on a perfect summer's evening by the Thames. Life could be worse.

We toast our walk, look across the water towards the centre of Staines – hidden behind housing – and plot tomorrow's walk.

CHAPTER EIGHT

STAINES, SURREY, TO KEW

LONDON CALLING

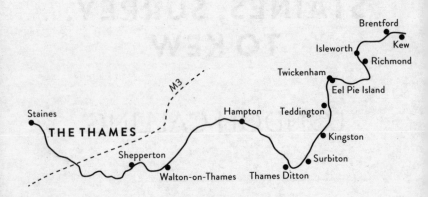

Staines

THE THAMES

M3

Shepperton

Walton-on-Thames

Hampton

Teddington

Thames Ditton

Kingston

Surbiton

Twickenham

Eel Pie Island

Isleworth

Richmond

Brentford

Kew

Staines has two claims to fame that stand out (to me).

The first: this suburban town close to the M25 used to be home to a linoleum factory. Linoleum was invented in Staines in the 1860s by Frederick Walton and his company continued to make the floor covering here until 1969. The factory once spread across 45 acres, covering land where the prominent Two Rivers Shopping Centre with its JD Sports and TK Maxx stores now stands. For years lino production was the town's biggest business. An unusual statue commemorating the former plant, depicting a pair of workers lifting a great roll of the stuff, is to be found in the high street.

The second: the 'Staines Massive'. This name was dreamt up by the comedian Sacha Baron Cohen and used by his alter-ego character Ali G, the tracksuit and gold-chain-wearing wannabe gangster from the late 1990s, who fantasises he is part of a Bronx-style gang, or 'massive', although he lives in a suburb near London's main ring road that once had a linoleum factory.

Understandably perhaps, town officials were not so keen on this gangster image. Ali G smokes cannabis, regards women as either 'fit' (good looking) or 'mingin'' (unattractive), and has a penchant for pornography. The result was drastic action: in 2012 the town was officially renamed Staines-on-Thames.

Many, however, still refer to it as Staines, as I do here, and some regard the name change as a sellout. The club secretary of Staines Town Football Club commented: 'The council have decided they don't want to be linked with the *Ali G Show*. But the one they need to worry about is *Keeping Up Appearances*, where Mrs Bucket changed her name to Bouquet. I think it is as pretentious as that.'

There is, however, another local piece of interest about which most are unaware.

For centuries the town marked the western limit of the City of London's authority over the River Thames. In 1197 Richard the Lionheart sold the river rights to the corporation to fund his swashbuckling crusades to the Middle East, allowing the City to charge tolls and tax fish traps. Just like his younger brother and successor, King John, he was short of cash for his foreign endeavours, although he was not reduced to signing a Magna-Carta-style document with his barons.

Across the river from the Swan pub there is a small monument known as the London Stone, indicating this boundary. There is another such London Stone marking the City's eastern limit of control at the mouth of the Thames by the North Sea in Kent, about 80 miles away.

I intend to visit both.

'Living by the river is lovely – it's social'
Staines

Ed and I have a night out in Staines, crossing the bridge to see the pedestrianised shopping precinct, with its Poundland, Entertainment Exchange and Ann Summers shops, and dropping by at the cavernous George, a Wetherspoon's pub heaving with customers on a Tuesday night. The beer is cheap and good, and the atmosphere is convivial, although Ed takes a different view.

'It's just modern Britain summed up,' he says. 'It's what Tory Britain has brought us to.'

He takes a sip of his pint.

'Give 'em enough bread and beer – everyone's happy,' he says, surveying the crowded space.

I point out that no one here is eating bread and I can't see anything wrong with everyone being happy.

Ed ignores this.

'This must be the busiest place in Staines. Just look at it,' he says.

I do. It seems fine to me, if rather busy for a Tuesday.

Ed takes another sip of his beer. His beer is almost empty.

I ask Ed if he would like another drink.

'Oh, go on then. One more,' he replies.

I go to the long busy bar, return with foaming glasses of John Smith's bitter, and Ed puts aside the state of bread-eating and beer-drinking in modern Britain for a while.

We sip our £1.99 pints.

You cannot really argue about anything with £1.99 pints (which may have been Ed's point in the first place).

In the morning after our knees-up in Staines, I take a stroll outside the Swan to clear my head while Ed goes to the breakfast room.

Next door to the Swan, I somehow fall into conversation with a woman raking her front garden. She is selling her riverside house for just under one million pounds and she tells me, as though I might be a potential customer, that it has three bedrooms and 'one hundred feet of river frontage'. Sarah is a hairdresser and says that 'living by the river is lovely – it's social. There's always something going on; people are always coming by'.

I ask her how much interest she has had in the house.

'Oh, we had quite a few viewings, but then the referendum happened,' she replies. As with elsewhere in Britain, property sales and prices dipped almost immediately after the vote.

'Selling a property by the Thames is difficult enough at the best of times,' she says. 'People are worried about flooding. But we're six feet up and we've got a cellar that's never flooded.'

Sarah was brought up in the house, which dates from 1836 and is next to where an older bridge once crossed the Thames at Staines.

'In a way, I don't want it to sell,' she says, leaning on her rake and sounding whimsical. 'I love it by the river.'

Riverside chatter seems quite normal to Sarah. After we've finished talking, I join Ed in the conservatory-style breakfast room.

He is reading the *Daily Express*, which has a front-page headline announcing: *90 F HEATWAVE TO ROAST BRITAIN*. Ed is eating a full English breakfast with poached eggs and has a couple of papers on the table.

'The *Express* is always doing this,' he says. 'What they really mean is: *it might be 80 F for one day.*'

He hands me the paper, which includes an article about the illegal-immigrant-trafficking gangs. The Conservative Member of Parliament for Dover and Deal, Charlie Elphicke, is calling for a 'war' on the gangs. The article, *SEND MARINES ON PATROL TO HALT THE BOAT IMMIGRANTS*, references the latest immigration figures that show that 1.3 million people claimed asylum in Europe in 2015 compared to a previous high of 700,000 in 1992, not long after the collapse of the Soviet Union. The number of migrants to have reached Europe by sea this year stands at 263,000, while more than 3,000 people have died at sea. There is an undoubted ongoing crisis, but there is also a strong sense that the *Daily Express* is stirring it up. Its editorial talks of putting the military on high alert in the Channel to 'keep the jihadists out' as the Islamic State 'has made no secret of its desire to conduct terror attacks here'.

Elsewhere in the news, the 25-year-old son of the Duke of Westminster has just inherited nine billion pounds.

'I wonder what the family will pay in inheritance tax,' says Ed, polishing off his poached eggs. '*That's* not mentioned here.'

We drink coffee, discussing the son of the Duke of Westminster's likely tax arrangements and the *Daily Express*'s coverage of immigration. The issues of the day that triggered Britain's decision to withdraw from Europe, fear of foreigners combined with frustration with the 'elite', simmer on.

Pulsating crocodile-filled waters (sort of)
Staines to Shepperton

Back on the Thames Path, however, it has the makings of a fine morning.

The temperature is mild, the sun occasionally breaking through to suggest a *Daily Express* heatwave could really be on the way. Today's target for me is Hampton Court, although Ed is stopping in Walton-on-Thames to meet an old friend and stay overnight at a Holiday Inn using 'hotel points' for what will effectively be a free room. He is then going to rejoin me the following morning at Hampton Court.

On the other side of the river from the Swan, our first port of call is the ancient London Stone, erected at this spot in 1285. Staines was selected as the western edge of the City of London's control as it was the old tidal limit of the river before locks were invented. The current stone, we discover from an information board (feeling a little disappointed), is a replica. The original is in a local museum. Ed takes my picture by the authentically-gnarly-but-fake rock. It's another Thames landmark ticked off… one for the Thames Path walking purist, perhaps.

Beyond a railway bridge with a shopping trolley dumped in the olive river water, we continue towards London. Many low-level houses are built along the river here and some of the older ones have been demolished and replaced by modern shoebox-like houses on stilts. The spate of construction must be, despite what Sarah said, because of concerns about flooding. We move on past the Beach at Laleham. This is within a campsite where the attractions are listed on a colourful sign featuring a wide expanse of sand and a turquoise sea. These consist of a 'large sandpit area' (presumably 'the beach'), 'beach food and refreshments, donkey rides (weekends), deckchairs and much more'. Donkey rides and deckchairs! Large sandpit areas! Beach food and refreshments! Much more! If only I'd known about all these attractions so close to home before. Move over, the Med: Laleham by the Thames, next to Staines in Surrey, not far from Two Rivers Shopping Centre and the M25, is the new Ibiza.

Soon afterwards we pass beneath the M3; Laleham is close to that motorway too, the third motorway so far. The thunder of vehicles recedes and the path weaves through a field with a party of fishermen trying their luck. They have found a spot to pitch their tent in Dumsey Meadow near the seven elegant arches of Chertsey Bridge.

Alan, who works in security and lives in Camberwell, is fishing with his son Terry, who is a carer for his wife, also living in Camberwell. They are in hoodies, wellies and jeans. The heatwave has yet to strike Chertsey.

'Carp, perch, roach, barbel, bream, pike, catfish – they're all in there,' says Alan, who has a fisherman's tan and reminds me of the actor Sid James. He tells me he would be happy catching a ten-pound barbel today. His best Thames haul in terms of the weight of the fish was a 31-pound pike reeled in by London's East End docks in the 1980s.

'They've put a Tesco where that is now,' he says, sounding sad about losing a favourite fishing spot.

Terry, who has brought along his young son, is hoping for a barbel as well. He says that the best way to catch a barbel is to use a boilie.

I ask him what a boilie is.

'A boilie is an egg that has been boiled,' he explains. 'They add in shellfish or tutti-frutti or chocolate.'

Variations of mixes of these ingredients are squished together and rolled into little marble-like balls.

Terry shows me a bag of tutti-frutti boilies that have been infused with a tangerine flavour as well as a bag of chocolate boilies. Who would have thought that Thames fish could have such fussy tastes? It was not so long ago, after all, back in the 1950s, when parts of the Thames bubbled with gas from the pollution of raw sewage and there were said to be no fish whatsoever from Gravesend in Kent to Kew. Now, thanks to much improved sewage treatment, more than 115 species survive and some will only grace a fisherman's hook when lured by a tutti-frutti boilie.

That's progress for you.

Ed and I walk on. A few disposable barbecues and beer bottles have been discarded by the path a bit further ahead, where stark apartment blocks rise by Chertsey Bridge, making me wonder: *How did they get planning permission for those?* Then willows line the riverside and we come to a partly rotten barge named the *Caresana*. A piece of laminated paper pinned to a pole says that the *Caresana* was one of the little ships that was used in the evacuation of Dunkirk in 1940. It is being slowly returned to its former glory by the Dunkirk Little Ships Restoration Trust.

We reach Shepperton, where we check the ferry timetable to go across the river to Weybridge on the south bank. Satisfied that we will not be stuck in Shepperton for ever, we head inland to its high street on a diversion of about a mile and a half.

The writer J. G. Ballard, author of so many wry, witty and dark dystopian novels describing the (increasingly relevant now, perhaps) fragility of modern civilisation, lived a shortish walk from the Thames in Shepperton in a nondescript semi-detached house from 1960 until his death in 2009. He is one of my favourite authors, like Orwell, so a little detour to see the semi-detached seems in order (and Ed doesn't seem to mind).

Shepperton is very much in London's suburban belt and Ballard drew inspiration from – and revelled in – what some might regard as its 'normality'. He once described this neighbourhood as being a 'paradigm of nowhere', with a supermarket, shopping centre, a petrol station and not much else (apart from a film studio tucked away by a reservoir not so far from the high street). Ed and I pass a BP garage, an M&S, a beauty salon and a tanning parlour, arriving at a red-brick house with two bamboo plants placed either side of an egg-yolk-yellow door. There is no blue plaque on the wall; as might be expected, Shepperton does not seem to make much of its hermit-like literary recluse. When Ballard lived here, the front garden (not a whole lot better now) was overgrown with weeds, and net curtains yellowed by age hung in the windows.

Ed gives me a look that suggests *And?* So we retrace our steps to the ferry, passing a police roadblock where there has been a car accident in the past ten minutes; an ambulance is already on the scene.

One of Ballard's most popular novels, *Crash*, which was turned into an eerie film by David Cronenberg, was all about the dark fascination many have with car crashes, the phenomenon that explains rubber-necking traffic on the opposite side of motorways to accidents.

I mention this to Ed.

'Yes, I've read the book,' he says, giving me another look suggestive of *And?*

We return to the ferry.

A small vessel with an outside motor awaits – as does Ben, the 16-year-old ferryman, who says he has been working on the boat for three months. He likes the 'social side of things and that it's outdoors'. He seems to be greatly enjoying his unusual summer job. The ferry runs every 15 minutes and is part of the official Thames Path; i.e. you are expected to cross to the other side to continue on the towpath. This particular ferry has been going for 500 years, says Ben – although a Shepperton ferry is listed in the Domesday Book of 1086. Tickets cost £2.

We bob across to the opposite bank – it's a very short journey (just a couple of minutes) – taking the route used by humans fleeing Martian invaders as described by H. G. Wells in *The War of the Worlds* (1898). The literary connections of the River Thames are many and varied. Ballard's take on the Thames was his novel *The Drowned World* (1962) in which he graphically describes southern England flooded by seawater carried in by the river after the polar caps have melted. Temperatures touch 130°F (higher even than a *Daily Express* heatwave), and the protagonist lives in London in a sweltering penthouse on the top floor of the abandoned Ritz Hotel, just above pulsating crocodile-filled waves that have become the lawless domain of scavenging pirates.

All dreamt up in sleepy Shepperton.

Julius Caesar… and a murder
Shepperton to Hampton Court

We say goodbye to Ben, who buzzes off with another passenger in the direction of Staines.

And on the Weybridge side of the river, we gather pace, Ed striding ahead. A heron steps across a mudbank. Moorhens bob in the water. A pair of swans glides past. The path is quiet. The bustle of Shepperton – what bustle there was – is behind us.

A little further on, we pause for breath at a point known as Coway Stakes, about a quarter of a mile upstream of Walton Bridge.

This is where some believe Caesar crossed the Thames in 54 BC, defeating Cassivellaunus and thus beginning the Roman march north of the river. The belief is based on the supposed discovery of broad stakes in the water here, said to have been placed as a defence by the tribe led by Cassivellaunus. Historians from the sixteenth century have written as much, as did the Venerable Bede in the eighth century. However, the stakes have long since disappeared and there is a serious amount of guesswork about the location of this momentous crossing, with other experts suggesting Wallingford, Brentford and Westminster. The latter is historian Peter Ackroyd's pick in his excellent (and heavy, as in physically heavy) book *Thames: Sacred River*. He bases his choice on the river being much shallower then, possibly by more than four metres at Westminster; that the tide would have ended at Westminster in those days; and that the crossing point of one of the main early Roman north–south roads was at the site of the Houses of Parliament. Ackroyd suggests that stakes in the water here may have been from an ancient bridge or perhaps used as underwater lines of a 'swimming way' for cattle.

I have no strong feelings on the exact location, but it is nice to consider such Thames matters on a long river walk. At places such as Coway Stakes, the lure of *liquid history* is strong.

Another heron flaps low across the water as we approach Walton Bridge, a modern structure, opened in 2013, with two low white arches that look like giant coat hangers. Egyptian geese, with their distinctive brown eyepatches, pad about on the Thames Path and a teenager, dressed in an Ali-G-style tracksuit, sits at a bench talking on a mobile.

Beyond an upmarket boat sales office – with pleasure cruisers available for £435,000 – we reach the Anglers pub. We have walked about a dozen miles.

We sit at a picnic table, where Ed has a pint of beer and I have a (reasonably priced) lime and soda.

Some of the wood-framed houses on the opposite bank here look as though they may be second homes; holiday pads with cruisers moored at the end of little lawns. The houses are either bungalows or on two levels, half hidden behind cabbage palm trees and with wooden decks that look perfect for an early evening G & T.

At a table next to us, we listen to two Thames day-walkers discussing their morning. Both are of retirement age.

Walker Number One (Rolex watch, white polo shirt, tanned): 'Those cyclists on the path! Those cyclists: that's what I don't like. They're going too fast. No bells. Kids and dogs: it's dangerous for them.'

Walker Number Two (comfortable 'walking slacks', bald, tanned): 'Hmmm, yes.'

Walker Number One: 'Flooding. You do get flooding here. Two years ago it was up to our wall. You couldn't walk by.' Walker Number One seems to live a few doors down from the Anglers. 'We were well above it, but all those over there...' he gestures to the opposite bank, 'they were flooded.'

Walker Number Two: 'Hmmm, yes.'

They discuss Walker Number Two's imminent knee-replacement operation and then the subject turns to Brexit. Both are in favour of the decision to leave.

Walker Number Two: 'Oh yes, I stayed up all night for the vote count. I knew we were going to win.'

Walker Number Two looks very pleased.

So does Walker Number One. 'Hmmm, yes, yes!' he says.

The subject of the summer is never far from people's lips.

Ed disappears in the direction of his Holiday Inn and I continue for about a mile to the Weir pub.

Here I learn of a murder.

The murder took place on the banks of the Thames not far from the Weir on the day before I set off for Trewsbury Mead. The body of Scott Wilkinson was found in the river near Waterside Drive in Walton and a post-mortem revealed he had died from an 'appalling' head injury. The 48-year-old grandfather had been fishing when he had gone missing; his equipment was discovered abandoned on the riverbank. The police have, according to the *Surrey Comet*, arrested six people. Detective Superintendent Adam Hibbert is quoted as saying that 'the victim sustained significant, and ultimately fatal, head injuries'. Meanwhile, the *Surrey Advertiser* (Runnymede and Spelthorne Edition) has talked to Jim Bates, manager of the Weir pub, who said: 'It is a very popular spot for people to fish. Hearing a body was found over there is shocking and a bit of a strange one.' The main picture on the front page shows a police diver in the shallows under the headline *MURDER PROBE: FISHERMAN'S BODY IN RIVER*.

All of those arrested, the youngest of whom is 16, have been released on bail according to the latest report on the BBC. Inside the mock-Tudor pub, I ask the tight-lipped barman about the murder and he simply says: 'They found the body on the other side of the river.' The way this is spoken suggests that if I have any questions, I should take them over there: across the river. Taking this hint, I read the rest of the local papers over a sandwich on the paved terrace facing the weir. Guys in hoodies and baseball caps sit at a picnic table on the far side of the terrace, seeming to assess whether I am some form of challenge, but they do not seem particularly perturbed and soon lose interest. My backpack and Thames map mark me out as just another pootling passer-by.

Afterwards I come to the point where Scott Wilkinson went missing while fishing. Flowers and cards have been attached to a metal railing by a narrow pedestrian bridge. One message is from his brother: *Tight lines brother, go catch the big one you wanted. Love you. RIP.*

It is unnerving and, frankly, awful to imagine what happened here a fortnight ago. I sit on the bridge for a while, thinking about how many dreadful events have been played out by the River Thames. Death and awful deeds never seem to be all that far away.

The stretch from the Weir to Hampton Court is about four miles. The river winds past Sunbury Lock, a waterworks, some idyllic clapboard riverside houses, some very ugly houseboats and an old boatyard with a rusting corrugated boathouse. Weeping willows rustle and a dog, somewhere nearby, howls. I come to a housing estate. Across the way a half-sunk, abandoned pleasure boat pokes out of the water. Canada geese and swans patrol the milky surface of the water as I pick up pace on a straight stretch in the run-up to Hampton Court. On the far bank I catch a glimpse of the cupola and columns of Garrick's Temple, built in Hampton during the eighteenth century by actor David Garrick as a tribute to William Shakespeare.

Close to Garrick's Temple I experience 'Thames Path rage'.

As I walk along, minding my own business and keeping to the left of the towpath, a cyclist in a tight-fitting Lycra fluorescent top heads straight towards me without seeming to intend to move. He is a middle-aged man wearing red-tinted shades. It is not just these glasses, however, that are causing him to see red. He is angry about something. Me? I suppose so. I am in his way. He is a busy man on a leisure cycling expedition, wearing a tight-fitting Lycra fluorescent top and red-tinted shades. He does not want a backpacker (in his eyes, a tramp?) taking what appears to be his 'racing line'. He stares angrily at me and swerves out of the way at the last moment, brushing my arm. It is an act of outright aggression. And I am afraid, dear reader, that I tell the man in the tight-fitting Lycra fluorescent top and red-tinted shades what I think of him using an unprintable expression.

I do not feel proud of myself for this.

The leisure cyclist in the tight-fitting Lycra fluorescent top and red-tinted shades either hears or does not hear my outburst.

I hope he did, though.

The best house on the river
Hampton Court

I check into the Carlton Mitre Hotel, where I have a room with a four-poster bed facing the river. The rambling brick hotel, made up of a series of buildings and with a circular facade with a restaurant, is bang opposite Hampton Court.

Without further ado, I go to visit Henry VIII's favourite palace.

It is shocking really that so many of us who live on this historic island pay so little attention to the splendid historic sights that clutter the landscape. My home is about a dozen miles from Hampton Court Palace, yet I have not ventured in as an adult (I have hazy recollections of coming as a child). Down a long driveway I come to the orange-brick and grey-stone entrance, where I find three women with little zapper-style machines of the sort used by supermarket workers to check barcodes on groceries.

'Would you like to go in?' one of them asks.

'Yes,' I reply.

'Do you have a ticket?' she asks.

'No,' I reply.

'Tickets are back there.' She points to a building a long way down the drive, not so far from the entrance of the Carlton Mitre Hotel.

'Oh,' I say.

'Sorry,' she says.

I shuffle back on sore feet and return to have my ticket (which cost £21) zapped by one of the three women with zapping machines.

Inside is a cobblestone courtyard surrounded by buildings with tall chimneys and castellated turrets. An audio guide informs me that chimneys were a sign of extravagant wealth at the time of Henry VIII (1491–1547). Henry had had Hampton Court requisitioned from the disgraced Cardinal Wolsey and developed into what is probably the most splendid of all Thames riverside abodes. The audio guide leads me into the tapestry-lined Great Hall, where lavish banquets were once held, and Henry VIII's private chapel, with its ornate ceiling dripped in gold and decorated with cherubs. In this rarefied chamber, Henry VIII learnt of his fifth wife Catherine Howard's supposedly ongoing relations with Thomas Culpeper, with whom she had some kind of romantic attachment before her marriage to the king at the age of 16, or possibly 17; she had once called Culpeper 'my little, sweet fool' in a love letter. The result was, of course, her beheading aged 19, or possibly 20, and Culpeper's beheading too; his skull was stuck on a spike on London Bridge for all to see.

Henry VIII married Catherine Parr, wife number six, in Parr's privy closet at Hampton Court. The chapel at the palace is said still to be haunted by Howard.

A striking and well-known portrait of Henry VIII by the German–Swiss painter Hans Holbein the Younger hangs in a room along a corridor. The picture, dating from 1542, depicts Henry with a broad, square face bearing a narrow nose, thin lips, bags under his eyes, ginger beard and determined brow. His right hand is in a fist holding a glove by his waist, while his left hand is hooked in a belt. Gold rings with red jewels adorn the fingers of both. His chest is barrel-like and his girth substantial. He is wrapped in red and gold fabric studded with woven-in jewels.

You would certainly step to one side if you met such a character coming at you on the Thames Path.

The river was clearly important to Henry. He was born by the Thames in Greenwich, died by it in Whitehall, lived most of his life by it, was married (several times) by it, and had his enemies' heads placed on spikes by it.

His is the presence felt most strongly at Hampton Court. It tickles to think of him prancing about playing a form of tennis known as 'real tennis' at the palace. A court, dating from after his time, is still in use and I look on as two players in white thump a ball about the enclosed space, which has an orange surface, green lines and black walls with golden royal emblems. It is said that Anne Boleyn, Henry's second wife, was watching a game of tennis at Hampton Court when she was rounded up and taken to the Tower of London. A pamphlet explains that she had been gambling on the outcome and 'even complained that she could not collect her winnings' after she had been locked up.

The other presence at Hampton is that of William III (1650–1702), who rebuilt a third of Hampton Court in a baroque style. Of his additions I enjoy his 'privy garden' by the Thames the most. It is a glorious garden with circular box hedges, lawns in the shape of fleur-de-lis, sculptures of classical figures, beds of marigolds and gravel paths leading to a golden fence topped with spikes and crowns overlooking the river. When this sunken garden was first completed, William demanded that it be redug as he could not see the Thames from his orangery. William, it would seem, must have loved the river too.

My legs are tired, so I leave the maze for another time, exiting the palace and crossing Hampton Court Bridge, which was built by Sir Edwin Lutyens in 1933. Back in 1753 there was a Chinese-style bridge at Hampton Court, complete with four pagodas at its centre and a series of humpbacked loops over seven arches. This extraordinary oriental crossing had to be pulled down in 1778 as it proved impractical. It is extremely strange to imagine such a structure now. Only a couple of drawings of this Chinese bridge remain.

At an Italian chain restaurant I order spaghetti bolognese and am delivered what to me, in my permanently famished Thames-walking state, seems such a tiny portion that I send the dish back asking for more. It looks like a children's meal. Luckily, the portly Italian waiter considers my Oliver-Twist-style request both a compliment to the chef and a sign of a good healthy appetite.

Then I return to the Carlton Mitre Hotel, and sit in its little library reading *The Book of Knowledge*, which I find on the shelves. *The Book of Knowledge* tells me that the Thames is 750 feet wide at London Bridge, 2,100 feet wide at Gravesend in Kent and 5.5 miles wide from Shoeburyness in Essex to Sheerness on the Isle of Sheppey at its mouth into the North Sea.

There are many other such facts.

Were anyone to know everything there is to know about the River Thames, I can't help thinking, they would certainly know an awful lot.

All the way to Tide-end-town
Hampton Court to Teddington

It is marvellous to wake to a clear blue sky above a silvery bend of the Thames with a good day's walking ahead.

I draw back the heavy curtains and lean against a sofa with a cup of coffee, contemplating the trek from here to Kew, about 11 miles away. Then I pack my clothes, washed in the sink and then dried on a heated towel-rack overnight, and go downstairs.

In the reception, with its portrait of Anne Boleyn and old photograph of another strange wooden bridge at Walton (long since gone), a lizard-eyed receptionist and I have a disagreement over whether I should pay £25 extra for breakfast. My room is 'room only' and I cannot bring myself to fork out £25 for breakfast so have decided to get a bite to eat along the way.

I explain as much.

The lizard-eyed receptionist replies: 'But did you have breakfast yesterday?'

She asks this in the manner of a current-affairs television host who has an evasive politician on the ropes.

I point out to the lizard-eyed receptionist that I could not have had breakfast yesterday as I checked in during the afternoon.

My tone here might, I admit, be slightly *off*.

The lizard-eyed receptionist does not like this. She registers my response but continues to consider me with suspicion. Maybe it's the backpack. The very fact that I have had to defend myself against the accusation of breakfast-fee-dodging appears to have tainted me with the air of a breakfast-fee dodger. There are now others in the checkout queue and I can sense their impatience; that I am somehow to blame for holding them up. The lizard-eyed receptionist arches an eyebrow. If only she could add £25 for breakfast to my bill. She really seems to want to add £25 for breakfast to my bill. Alas, I am guiltless of the crime of breakfast-fee-dodging.

'I'm new here,' says the lizard-eyed receptionist, eventually, handing me my breakfast-less receipt.

On this, one must admit, somewhat sour note, I step outside.

On the pavement by the bridge, Ed awaits. He has already put in four miles this morning from the Holiday Inn Shepperton, near Walton Bridge. He looks both tired and anxious to move on. His assessment of the Holiday Inn Shepperton is: 'Very good, could be in the middle of nowhere. There's a good grass area at the back and a brook. Very quiet. Swimming pool, hot tub, steam room, the lot. The fire alarm went off when I was in the pool and we all had to get out.'

Apart from that it was fine (and breakfast was included).

We hit the Thames Path beside the red-brick wall of Hampton Palace and make haste. Ed is keen to return home to Richmond so he can put his feet up and watch the cricket, England versus Pakistan. Barges are moored by the palace and across the river chalet-style houses with wooden decks and little lawns in Thames Ditton and Surbiton look like inviting places to live. The river is calm, the surface swirling with gentle eddies.

Joggers jog. Cyclists cycle (and don't try to run us down). The path here has blackberry bushes, thick with berries. Startled wood pigeons shoot out of the branches of riverside trees. All is peaceful and pleasant.

Then we reach Ravens Ait Island. This is not such a wonderful spot. A hulking weather-stained building, now a wedding venue, dominates the ait. On this island in the thirteenth century Henry III (1207–1272), son of King 'Magna Carta' John, and King Louis IX of France arranged a peace treaty. Henry III was nine years old when he took the throne, and in his teenage years agreed to abide by the principles of the Magna Carta. His settlement with King Louis on Ravens Ait, when he was 52, finally put to rest many of his father's territorial disputes in France.

Not far from Ravens Ait, we reach Kingston Bridge. Kingston Bridge is a long grey-stone bridge, its current incarnation dating from the early nineteenth century. Until 1729, when Putney Bridge opened, the bridge was the only one between London Bridge and Staines Bridge. This was where Jerome K. Jerome began his journey upstream in *Three Men in a Boat*.

The southern bank of the river here has seen better days. Great warehouse-like structures of brick and glass arise, housing Waitrose and John Lewis stores. Box-shaped buildings with little architectural merit merge into one another and spread along the bank, fusing into garish apartments.

Ed and I cross the bridge and enter a street with retail outlets. A sign at Bentalls department store says: *WHERE STYLE REIGNS*. Sultry women in cocktail dresses and men with designer stubble and smart-casual shirts who look like David Beckham stare down from billboards. Ed says: 'A bit like an upmarket Staines.' And we continue past mobile-phone shops and a fruit and vegetable market in search of the 'king's stone' that gave birth to Kingston.

We find the stone, known as the Coronation Stone, next to council buildings and a police station. The small block of sandstone is behind a blue metal fence in a little hexagonal enclosure. According to tradition, this stone was part of the ceremony used during the coronation of seven Saxon kings: Edward the Elder (900), Athelstan (925), Edmund (940), Edred (946), Edwy (956), Edward the Martyr (975) and Ethelred II the Unready (979).

We flip a couple of coins on top of the old stone, for luck, and return past the council office, where a young woman in fishnet tights and a miniskirt is yelling into her mobile phone: 'CAN YOU STOP SAYING THAT TO ME COZ I'M GOING TO DO WHAT I WANT, UNDERSTAND!'

At the market I attempt to buy an apple from a stallholder who does not have change for a one-pound coin as he is on the other side of his stall from his till. 'Pay next time you come past, mate,' he says, probably realising from my backpack that that may be never again. What a nice fellow.

Then Ed and I return to the Thames Path.

We arrive at a stretch with a few ramshackle houseboats that look on the point of sinking. Official signs warn: *Construction site. Keep out.* After this, we reach a pedestrian crossing to Teddington. Here Ed keeps along the south bank to his home after saying: 'It's only day three for me, but you've broken me. I'm on my knees.' Which is good to hear after his quick march up Cooper's Hill.

He does look satisfyingly worn out.

Chandleries and Gothic Revivals
Teddington to Twickenham

I cross a blue metal suspension bridge at this key point on the Thames and go to eat breakfast at the Flying Cloud Cafe on the opposite bank.

Teddington marks the end of the tidal Thames. It is the location of the first major lock from here to the sea. Yes, there is a lock further downstream at Richmond, but Richmond Lock is next to a river barrier that can be raised at high tide to allow vessels through. Teddington is where the Thames, you could say, goes wild. Beyond here, fish with enough stamina and determination might swim to the coral of the Pacific Ocean, the sandy palm-fringed shores of the Caribbean or beneath the centuries-old ice of the Antarctic Sea. The world's waters have opened up and anywhere is possible, as the explorers of bygone days in search of riches and fame must once have imagined. This marks a new phase of any Thames walk: the geranium pots and beds of pansies by lock-keepers' houses have been left behind and a rawer, less predictable – but no less lovable – river lies ahead.

Justine, the cheerful blonde owner of the Flying Cloud Cafe, and I discuss locks for a while. If you have been walking along the Thames for a fortnight, such conversations, I am finding, begin to come naturally. She tells me she found the shiny chrome Airstream trailer in which her cafe is based on eBay. She seems happy being by the river (the way some people just are). I eat her excellent granola and yoghurt, drink her well-brewed coffee and hear about how she set up the cafe after renting the space from next-door offices.

Then Justine introduces me to Malcolm Miatt, who owns a chandlery next door and runs the 50 or so moorings at Teddington Lock.

Malcolm is a wizened character with ice-blue eyes, a gravelly voice and hunched shoulders. He is bald and tanned with a neatly trimmed grey beard. He wears jeans, a khaki shirt, a gold TAG watch and leather deck shoes. He brings to mind a character in a Graham Greene novel; a castaway in Panama or West Africa perhaps – except he's in Teddington in south-west London.

There is a theory that the name of Teddington comes from it being the town where the tide ends: tide-end-town. Rudyard Kipling's children's poem 'The River's Tale: Prehistoric' refers to this:

> Twenty bridges from Tower to Kew –
> (Twenty bridges or twenty-two) –

Wanted to know what the River knew,
For they were young, and the Thames was old
And this is the tale that River told: —
'I walk my beat before London Town,
Five hours up and seven down.
Up I go till I end my run
At Tide-end-town, which is Teddington.

I ask Malcolm about this. 'There's a lot of discussion about the name,' he says, after lighting a cigarette. 'Some say it's from Tuddington. That there used to be a King Tudd. You know what? I 'aven't got a ******* clue.'

At least he's honest, although I have never previously heard of this mysterious 'King Tudd'.

Malcolm shows me inside his chandlery. It's a little curiosity shop of ropes and bolts and paints and club-hammers and sail repair kits. Here he holds up a hand with four digits remaining, as though forming some kind of masonic greeting. 'Lost one in an accident using a power press. Two hundred tonnes of pressure. Forty-one years ago that was,' he says. Malcolm seems to enjoy bandying about numbers.

Then Malcolm sits at a little table and talks about his days before being a chandler at Teddington. He draws on his cigarette and rests back in his chair. Many years ago, he says, he was involved in an offshore bank in Anguilla and was paid by the FBI. 'There was really dodgy fraud,' he begins. 'I sent information back to the Feds but they didn't want to take the first player out, the small-time guy – they wanted to take them all out, to go to the top.'

He winks conspiratorially and continues about the Feds in Anguilla for a while, explaining that he's thinking of one day writing an autobiography. 'The Feds, the Feds,' he says, and begins another story. Malcolm, once started – his ice-blue eyes darting and dreaming – has many a tale to tell.

From here, the Thames Path deviates along small suburban roads, about a hundred metres or so from the water. Houses with recycling bins full of champagne bottles appear, as does Strawberry Hill House.

Horace Walpole, son of Robert Walpole, Britain's first prime minister, lived at Strawberry Hill during the eighteenth century. Like his father, Horace attended Eton College. He was a man of letters, a politician and a fan of Gothic architecture and interior design. I enter the driveway, aware that the house is closed to the public today. I do not have an appointment and I'm guessing I'll just be able to take a look at the outside.

The peculiar white building is a strange concoction of castellated towers, pinnacles, and windows shaped like four-leaf clovers known as *quatrefoils*. I learn this, to me, new word after meeting Judith and Bernadette, volunteers from the Strawberry Hill Trust. They are standing by the door to Strawberry Hill, wearing blue print-patterned dresses and waiting for a private bus group that is running late. They kindly agree, impromptu, to show me round. Soon I am being escorted up a cathedral-like staircase leading to room after amazing room on an unexpected tour. Ornate Gothic chimney pieces appear in sitting rooms with tall blue stained-glass windows and striking apple-green wallpaper with *quatrefoil* patterns. OTT gilded paintings depict angels at medieval jousts. Libraries overflow with leather-bound volumes in bookcases decorated with Gothic arches and pinnacles. Bedrooms are painted lavender and wine-red. Side chambers emerge with gold vaulted ceilings. It's as though I've entered a fantasy land.

'Walpole bought a cottage in 1749, Gothicised it and added to it over fifty years,' say Judith and Bernadette, who talk so rapidly and finish each other's sentences so often that what they say seems to merge. 'This is the iconic building of the eighteenth-century Gothic Revival. Most people were interested in neoclassical style then: the Palladian style of country house based on symmetry. Walpole preferred a Chinese lack of symmetry in buildings. He believed that lofty ceilings finished in marble were quite cold and not suited to our climate. He preferred theatre. He liked the use of contrast: dark colours mixed with bright colours. The unusual. The theatrical. He had a collection of art by Holbein in one room and Cardinal Wolsey's hat hanging on a hook by his bed.'

I try to imagine this extraordinary son of Britain's first prime minister as he directed his architects in between embarking on a Grand Tour of Italy (in the company of the poet Thomas Gray), politicking and writing his Gothic novels – in his Gothic house, with Cardinal Wolsey's hat hanging by his bed, a short amble from the Thames. Strawberry Hill really is rather remarkable.

His Excellency Prince Pan
Eel Pie Island

From high Gothic fantasy to high street UK: I walk to Twickenham, with its Starbucks, KFC and Iceland supermarket. Back by the river, I cross a narrow pedestrian bridge to Eel Pie Island, where I go for a cup of tea with my friend Jeannette.

Eel Pie Island is famous in rock music circles as being where the Rolling Stones, David Bowie, Pink Floyd, Eric Clapton and Rod Stewart played early gigs. The Eelpiland dance club, which opened in 1956 but closed many years ago after a fire, attracted the avant-garde seeking to escape the confines of the mainstream. Early gig-goers, before the bridge, had to cross by boat and were given 'passports' rather than tickets to events. The passports bore the words 'We request and require, in the name of His Excellency Prince Pan, all those whom it may concern to give the bearer of this passport any assistance he/she may require in his/her lawful business of jiving and generally cutting a rug.'

Before the days of His Excellency Prince Pan, another Excellency, Henry VIII, is said to have used Eel Pie for courting. Now the island is home to a bohemian community of artists, inventors (including the inventor of the wind-up radio, Trevor Baylis) and those generally one step removed from the common flow.

Jeannette lives in a modernist, minimalist terrace of modernist, minimalist houses with a tiny garden and a tiny pontoon on the Thames. Her home is down a narrow path with the faint sound of drilling, chipping and hammering coming from an old boatyard nearby. Jeannette is a former staff journalist on a national newspaper who has retrained as a nutritionist and has recently written a book entitled *The Gut Makeover*. We sit in her minimalist kitchen, decorated with a giant poster from a Beyoncé concert at the O2 Arena and tall purple flowers in a vase. She is wearing red lipstick, designer tracksuit bottoms and sandals.

I have caught her just before a client is due for a consultation; her customers are often, she says, 'very, very stressed, highly qualified professionals, many of them lawyers, with terrible diets'. I ask Jeannette why she chose to live on Eel Pie Island. 'I'm here because I'm unconventional,' she says. 'We used to live in a 1930s house in a cul-de-sac and I was going nuts. Here everyone knocks on other people's doors to check if they are all right, especially the elderly. It's a community.'

On the private island there are, she says, about a hundred people living in 40 houses. It is a great place to bring up her children. She loves the river, she says. Then she begins to tell me about an apartment she is hoping to buy next to a beach in Ibiza, about classes she's running in the Med for people who want to 'make over' their guts, and about how margarine is very bad for me but how broccoli and brazil nuts are very good. As I'm taking all of this in, her phone rings. Her client is arriving in a moment. It's all go on bohemian Eel Pie Island, even if the Stones and Bowie are long gone. We chat for a bit more beneath the poster of Beyoncé and say goodbye in a hurry.

Then I look around Eel Pie Island, peering into chaotic artists' studios and potteries in little yards. In one of these yards in an old boathouse,

I talk to a man with Buddy Holly glasses named Michael. He's in the middle of making an armchair from reclaimed wood and discarded motorbike jacket leathers, I discover. 'It's pretty creative round here,' he says as he shows me various lamps and deckchairs carved from old wood. His customers tend to be high-earning west Londoners. A single chair made from bits and bobs picked up here and there, taking a week to piece together, costs £1,250 and looks like a work of art you might find in an avant-garde gallery in London's East End.

Eel Pie Island really is rather remarkable, too.

'Oh aye, I like it here. It's a nice spot'
Twickenham to Kew

I recross the footbridge into Twickenham and pass the late-seventeenth-century White Swan pub, with its gorgeous riverside terrace that sometimes becomes an island cut off from the rest of the pub when the tide is high. The path snakes through a park with horse-chestnut trees and I stop for a while to watch a family of Egyptian geese shuffling on a jetty near Hammerton's Ferry across the river to Ham. They are such peculiar creatures with their distinctive brown eyepatches and strange choice of home many thousands of miles from their natural habitat in the Nile Valley and southern Africa.

Near here the poet Alexander Pope (1688–1744), famous for his translation of Homer's *Iliad* and sayings such as 'hope springs eternal in the human breast' and 'damn with faint praise', once lived. His long-since-demolished home had a curious underground grotto that still exists and can be visited by appointment on certain days. This grotto is close to Marble Hill House, a fine white Palladian villa where Henrietta Howard, a mistress of George II and friend of Pope, lived.

The river has a name-dropping quality in these parts – feeling almost haunted by such figures. Alfred, Lord Tennyson lived near here. So did Henry Fielding when writing *Tom Jones*. Thomas Gray, when not eulogising about the river by Eton, said: 'I do not know a more laughing scene than about Twickenham and Richmond.' While renting a nearby summer house, Charles Dickens used to wake at six in the morning and swim in the Thames from meadows on the opposite bank to Richmond Bridge.

Meanwhile at the top of Richmond Hill, which opens up all of a sudden through a clearing in the riverside trees, Mick Jagger of the Rolling Stones once lived (and still owns property). Perhaps he likes to be close to where he began getting noticed on Eel Pie Island.

From that hilltop, J. M. W. Turner many times peered down on this bend of the Thames and painted what he saw. The results are some of the most evocative of any works by a Thames river artist, including the especially alluring *England: Richmond Hill, on the Prince Regent's Birthday* (1819), with impenetrable-looking woodland turning golden in late afternoon light as a slither of milk-blue river snakes to the horizon beneath an ethereal sky.

I pass a ramshackle raft that was once (and perhaps still is) home to a hermit and look up to the hill again. Cranes hang over the imposing red-brick shape of Royal Star and Garter Home, formerly a place of rest for injured servicemen. Now the building is being converted into luxury apartments, with the marketing department, not unsurprisingly perhaps, making much of 'Turner's view'.

Richmond used to have a grand royal palace, built by Henry VII in 1501 and named after Richmond in Yorkshire (instead of the local name of Shene). Long since gone, it was a favourite haunt of Elizabeth I, who died at the palace in 1603. I cross the fine old bridge (London's oldest, dating from 1777) and descend stairs to the waterfront, where there is a cluster of boatyards to the side of the bridge.

Here I happen to meet Mark Edwards MBE, master boatbuilder at the Richmond Bridge Boathouses. Edwards built the *Gloriana*, the 29-metre, elaborately gilded barge requiring 18 oarsmen that was commissioned to carry the Queen along the river during her diamond jubilee celebrations. I do not know that Mark is one of the country's most renowned boatbuilders when I introduce myself. I'm merely hoping for a bit of boat talk – as I said earlier, after a fortnight of walking along the river these are the kinds of conversations that one somehow strangely seeks, perhaps without even quite realising why. Maybe the rhythm of the walk beside the flow of the river has put me in some sort of 'Thames zone'. There is another factor at play, too. As the miles click by, a 'river cred' has built up, simply from having walked all the way from the source. This 'cred' begins to open both doors and mouths. True river dwellers, *river people*, seem more inclined to tell you their secrets if you've paced all the way from Trewsbury Mead.

Mark and I do not, however, get off to the best of starts when I ask how long he has been making boats.

'We don't make 'em – we build 'em,' he says.

Mark is in a striped blue-and-white French onion seller's top and jeans, sitting by a laptop in a chamber full of hooks, glues, vices, planks, ropes, wires, masking tape and pots of paint. He is cherry-cheeked and has a down-to-earth manner. He's only feigning hurt feelings about being accused of 'making' boats.

He tells me he first worked in a boatyard in 1970 when he was aged 14. He has been at it by the river more or less all his life. We inspect a couple of half-built rowing boats and, as we do so, he casually mentions the *Gloriana*, which was built in Isleworth, and his MBE, which he says stands for Mad Boating Enthusiast. Had he not, I would never have known about his part in the magnificent vessel or his Queen's Honour (or how he and others working on the river, who came up with his Mad Boating Enthusiast nickname, like to refer to his medal).

We natter for a bit about this and that. Mark says he has often seen Jerry Hall, Mick Jagger's former wife, by the river; she still lives on Richmond Hill. I tell Mark about meeting Malcolm back in Teddington and he comments cryptically, 'I bet he had a thing or two to say', before going on to praise Malcolm's RNLI work. The river community, I am increasingly discovering on this walk, is tight-knit – and gossipy, too.

We say goodbye. Beyond Richmond's flagstone terrace, past designer clothes shops on King Street and the picnickers and Carlsberg Special Brew drinkers of Richmond Green, I slip beneath an arch that is just about all that is left of Henry VII's Richmond palace. A little stone plaque says that royalty first occupied the banks here as early as 1125, when Henry I selected Richmond for an earlier palace (where Edward III died in 1377).

Then I meet Graham.

Graham is a riverside dweller of no fixed abode. He is leaning against a metal fence, resting on a backpack with a roll of foam bedding attached, and smoking a Chesterfield cigarette. An upturned beanie cap with a couple of coins and a lighter is at his feet. His long, grey hair is brushed back. His blue Nike trainers look as though they may well soon fall apart and his tattered Mountain Warehouse winter jacket (worn despite the warm weather) has clearly seen better days. Amused jade-green eyes twinkle beneath a dark brow. His forehead is noticeably whiter than the rest of his weather-tanned face, perhaps from wearing the beanie pulled down. Cars zoom above on the A316 bridge. His 'spot' is right by the bridge.

I go up to Graham and say 'hello'. He seems pretty mellow, chewing over a few thoughts, weighing up some ideas in the sunshine and watching the world go by.

'Do you enjoy being by the river?' I ask. I have often wondered what attracts wanderers to the riverside.

'Oh aye, I like it here. It's a nice spot and all that,' he says, sounding cool, calm and in no hurry whatsoever.

He pauses and draws on his Chesterfield.

Then he says: 'I could get moved, I suppose. I've been here a couple of years.'

By this, I gather, he means that the police could decide that he is spending too much time on public land, breaking a by-law of some kind, and tell him to get on his way.

I explain that I am walking along the Thames. He lets this sink in, assessing my long-distance walking garb. By now I could not possibly pass as someone taking a stroll, or even someone walking on a weekend excursion with a backpack. Clearly, I am in it for a long haul.

'Oh aye, for twelve years I was walking non-stop, like,' Graham says. 'From the age of thirty-three to forty-five: walking. I'll be fifty in two months. All over, I walked. Aye, I've walked the Thames. Took me two weeks. I ended up on the south coast. In Poole, I was. I'd already been to Cambridge, and to Skegness. Aye, yes – Skegness.' He seems to have especially fond memories of the seaside town in Lincolnshire. 'Then I went down to the estuary, the Thames Estuary, and it was beautiful, like. I decided just to do it. To walk it. Along the river. Along the Thames, aye.'

He pauses and lights another Chesterfield; he has a packet of ten with him. He seems to have walked the length and breadth of the country and is originally from the north of Edinburgh.

'Sherwood Forest: it's beautiful there.' He smiles as he remembers Sherwood Forest, clearly another one of his special places. 'Cornwall's not too bad either,' he adds, happily reminiscing, though the far south-west does not seem to rank as highly in his estimation as Skegness or Sherwood.

I ask him how he gets by.

'Busking, singing. Folk music,' he says.

I put a pound coin in his upturned beanie. He raises his Chesterfield as a 'thank you'. He pauses. And then he shifts tack.

'You know the Queen of England is my mother, like,' he says. 'The Queen, I was born to her, I was – my mother, aye.'

His voice trails off. His jade-green eyes fix on mine for a moment or two. He seems to be assessing whether I believe his story or not.

After this examination, a distant look falls across his features. He appears to want to be alone.

I say, 'Oh well, then, thanks for talking.'

He nods and blows a plume of smoke.

'Oh aye, see you later,' he says quietly. 'Take care.'

And with that I leave Graham and head down the path a short distance and cross the footbridge by Richmond Lock.

On the opposite bank, I pass a half-built upmarket 'riverside development'. Teenage gangs in low-slung jeans and boxer shorts are milling about by a flood protection wall. 'I ****** her up, boo, man,' I hear one lad say to another as I walk on through. The London Apprentice pub in Isleworth comes next, with what looks like a great little riverside beer garden at the back. Then the fields of Syon Park open up and I reach a lane where marijuana wafts over a wall. Beyond Syon Park the path takes me to a narrow bridge by the Grand Union Canal, an MOT garage and a scrapyard of old cars. This section, with the river now completely lost, leads onwards to a furniture warehouse, an apparently people-less council estate, a half-demolished building and a litter-strewn alley. At the end of the alley is Brentford Dock, with its rusty hulks and old corrugated sheds surrounded by stagnant algae-clogged docks next to the River Brent, a tributary. A waterway of some sort has appeared once again, if not the Thames itself.

There had, obviously, been an option of taking the south bank of the Thames past leafy and lovely Kew Gardens as the official path splits to cover both banks on this part of the river. But I have gone for the northern side. This was a random, last-minute choice after talking to Graham – and it is proving to be an eye-opening one.

Enormous ramshackle house-barges emerge with decks cluttered with gas canisters, cables and half-collapsed picnic tables. On one of these a couple of elderly men passes the time of day, perhaps recalling the good old days. The smell of oil and tar mingles with seaweed and mud. I cut through another seemingly people-less estate, the River

Brent falling from sight as I amble onwards beyond a nondescript Premier Inn London Brentford and a colourful, higgledy-piggledy mini-market selling African food.

A road here leads northwards to Brentford Football Club. The Watermans Art Centre emerges (so resembling a car park that a colourful ironic notice reads: *I AM NOT A CAR PARK*). Then comes an 'anywhere' McDonald's and a no-nonsense Irish pub with pewter mugs hanging from beams and regulars who turn to regard an outsider with an air of cautious cool (when I go in to look). A bright yellow-and-blue JET garage has attracted a queue of cars. Close to this garage, modern apartments with rooms available for rent and riverside apartments for sale are to be found in a development of buildings by Kew Bridge. These apartments offer potential residents the possibility of 'a natural balance of living', according to the window displays. Cars thrum towards the M4 and Heathrow at a busy junction. I walk past more 'natural balance' advertisements and come to the Thames once again.

I have reached the river proper after my curious perambulations through the backstreets of Isleworth and Brentford. I cross the Thames at Kew Bridge and find myself on Kew Green.

On the other side, things are very different.

Sunshine bathes picnickers and a game of cricket is in full swing next to a thicket of cricket nets. St Anne's Church, where the artist Thomas Gainsborough is buried, advertises home-made cream teas on Sundays. I circumnavigate the green, finding an entrance to the Royal Botanic Gardens and a couple of charming-looking riverside pubs. A blue plaque on a house on a smart terrace says that another artist, the Danish–French impressionist painter Camille Pissarro (1830–1903) once lived here. Shiny Land Rovers and Audis are parked by Pissarro's house, as they are around much of the green. I pause to examine the window menu of a grill restaurant run by a celebrity chef.

Then I go up the steps of the Coach and Horses pub, where I have a room booked for the night. I drop my bag in a comfortable and sophisticated space decorated in shades of grey, with a digital radio, espresso machine and organic seaweed-extract toiletries. After settling in, I go downstairs and sit at a wooden table looking out across the green from the pub's little terrace while drinking a pint of Young's Bitter. Then I buy a (very good) pork-belly baguette from a jolly man drinking rosé wine while attending a barbecue on the terrace.

This is a restful place to end a long day – that's for sure. The contrast between the north bank that I walked along an hour ago and the south bank of the river here is stark; one minute, stagnant docks with tumbledown vessels that may never take to the water again, desolate scrapyards, litter-strewn alleys and gangs; the next, almost bucolic scenes with picnickers, botanical gardens, historical plaques, the sound of cricket bat on ball, and good-humoured fellows drinking rosé as they flip burgers.

But that's London for you: walk half a mile in almost any direction and whole new worlds emerge. 'The other side of the tracks', to use the American phrase, is always close by. The width of a river can mean a lot.

CHAPTER NINE

KEW TO BERMONDSEY

A DAY IN THE LIFE OF THE THAMES

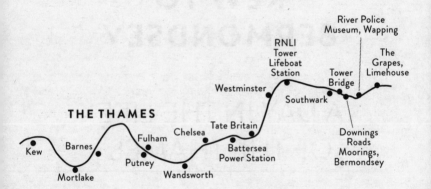

My breakfast wars continue.

Checking out of the Coach and Horses, I ask the receptionist whether the price of breakfast could be taken off my bill. I am leaving before food is served as I need an early start.

The receptionist regards me as though I have lost my mind. Never in her many years as a receptionist, her visage suggests, has such an outlandish request been made. There is a twinkle in her eye. It seems almost delicious to her that a guest – a guest at her very own pub-with-rooms – could have begun even to formulate such a proposition.

'We don't do that, sorry,' she says.

I decide to let the matter slide. Life is just too short for endless breakfast disputes with receptionists.

The receptionist – chipper now – eyes my backpack and asks where I'm going.

I mention Wapping and Bermondsey.

'The most walking I'm doing is to that coffee machine,' she says.

That, the receptionist implies, is a sensible amount of walking for the day, thank you very much.

I depart the Coach and Horses on this fifteenth day of my walk from Trewsbury Mead to the sea.

'When all the liquid world was one extended Thames'
Kew to Mortlake

Sunlight filters through horse-chestnut trees on the Thames Path. A heron shaped like a long thin question mark perches on a branch overhanging the water. It has just gone seven o'clock. The river is high, the water calm and muddy. The sun is out. It's a crisp, hopeful morning. London is already up and at it; traffic is busy on Kew Bridge.

I look back at the grey-stone arches of today's starting point.

Like just about every bridge on the Thames, Kew Bridge has a story. It was shortly after crossing a previous version of this bridge, or possibly on it, in 1760 that the then Prince of Wales is said to have been informed by a messenger that his grandfather had died and he would ascend to the throne as George III. Thus, in effect, began the rule of the king in charge during America's War of Independence (the last king of the United States) and the defeat of Napoleon. When told this news, George, later famously to lose his marbles but in those days a tall strapping man who inspired optimism, rode back to Kew to consider the situation. Once at his lodgings, he ordered that his attendants be silent, and asked them to explain his unexpected return to anyone who enquired as being on account of his horses having gone lame. Thus, somewhere round here, it is believed, a king pondered his kingdom to come.

Joggers are commonplace on the towpath near Kew Bridge. The smell of lavender and roses rises from gardens and I pass the Priory Park Tennis Club, where I sometimes play a colleague from work. My route today, via Mortlake (my home), Chelsea and a detour to Limehouse to meet another friend who owns a houseboat in Bermondsey, is probably the longest yet. I have not totted up the entire distance; I just know it is a *very long way*. Have I bitten off more than I can chew?

A tall, blonde, tanned woman strides past wearing a pink vest and leading two small dogs near the blue clapboard boathouse of Putney Town Rowing Club. A sign on the boathouse says, *GOOD LUCK TO TEAM GB*, referring to the ongoing Olympics in Rio; two of the club's members are taking part. Workers in suits and trainers pace along the towpath, some fiddling with smartphones. They're obviously on regular commutes, going at a rigorous arm-swinging four miles an hour.

I pass Mortlake Crematorium, where the riverside is green and pleasant as the path moves onwards beneath Chiswick Bridge. Just afterwards is the purple-painted Ship pub, where the river is so high the water almost blocks the path. It's a short distance from here to my flat on a stretch of the river I know well – and it feels odd to be back. I have never walked for more than, say, five miles in either direction along the River Thames before. Now I've almost crossed the width of the country along the river. I think it's fair to say I have (well and truly) embraced it.

The Ship is in Mortlake, where the annual Boat Race between Oxford and Cambridge universities ends. It is also right by Stag Brewery, which began brewing commercially in 1700, although beer has been produced hereabouts since the fifteenth century. Before being known as Stag Brewery it was a Budweiser Brewery (there is still a big *Budweiser: King of Beers* sign on the wall of the old brick granary building), and before that Watney's Brewery. The Stag Brewery shut down last year and the land was sold to a Singaporean property group that intends to replace the brewery with a 'high-density residential-led' development that will create a 'new riverside quarter'.

The thought of hundreds of designer flats, probably well beyond the pocket of anyone raised in the area, has had many up in arms; myself included. The river seems so gentle and quiet in Mortlake – and the brewery has somehow always defined this bend of the Thames.

Before departing on my Thames walk I wrote a letter to Zac Goldsmith, the local Member of Parliament and son of a billionaire (Goldsmith attended Eton College but was thrown out aged 16 after cannabis was found in his room), asking him what could be done to save the brewery or else keep the land for a similar type of business.

Goldsmith, a member of the Conservative Party who supported Brexit, replied by saying that the reality was that if the council restricted the site to a similar business, the land could be sold to a speculator 'who would then put in a wildly inappropriate application and have it approved by the Planning Inspectorate in Bristol'. I wrote back saying that I had never heard of this Planning Inspectorate in Bristol, and asked what a Planning Inspectorate in Bristol had to do with what went on in Mortlake. Sidestepping this point, Goldsmith replied that 'the Planning Inspectorate frequently approves inappropriate developments. Even where residents, local councillors and elected MPs are united in determined opposition to a given plan, their wishes can be, and often are, simply brushed aside.'

I guess I should have known all about this Planning Inspectorate in Bristol. Goldsmith went on to say that a high-density residential-led development is a better bet than chancing the vagaries of the Planning Inspectorate in Bristol. Who was I to doubt Zac Goldsmith? The high-density residential-led development would be 'in keeping and attractive', he assured me.

Well, I did try.

Mortlake is probably named after a Saxon strongman known as Morta, and the 'lake' ending may refer to a stream entering the river here. The area was for a long time used for farming; asparagus was the most popular crop. A tapestry works employing Flemish master weavers (1619) and a pottery (1743) were built by the river. In the sixteenth and seventeenth centuries, Mortlake was home to John Dee, a scientist, mathematician and magician who claimed to have conversed with angels, and who became an advisor to Elizabeth I. Dee possessed what is believed to have been the world's largest private library and he is buried beneath the chancel at St Mary's Church. Meanwhile, the great nineteenth-century explorer Richard Burton is encased in a strange tomb resembling a Bedouin tent in the close-by grounds of St Mary Magdalen Roman Catholic Church. His and his wife's coffins can be seen through a window reached by a short ladder at the back of this 'tent'. One of Burton's many achievements was a pilgrimage to Mecca disguised as a Muslim; had he, a European infidel, been discovered, he would probably have been lynched. It's a short diversion from the Thames Path to see this unusual grave.

At home, I drop off a few books to lighten my backpack (I have not got round to posting any back, as I had originally planned, but they have proven wonderful company along the way). And, after this pit stop, move on down Cowley Road to the river.

This road, where I live a short distance from the towpath, is named after Abraham Cowley, a seventeenth-century poet who once wrote of a time 'When all the riches of the Globe beside / Flow'd in to Thee with every Tide… When all the liquid World was one extended Thames'.

I rather like those lines.

'Yummy mummies quite often come here on a fine day'
Mortlake to Chelsea

Onwards! Past the metal hoops of Barnes Railway Bridge and a river terrace popular with celebrities, and along a snaking path through trees to the green and gold of Hammersmith Bridge. Mortlake – home – is behind me; the river winds on. I do love Hammersmith Bridge. Bridge aficionados will know that this bridge is no longer the one created in 1827 by William Tierney Clark (the designer of Marlow's suspension bridge). Clark's Hammersmith Bridge was not strong enough. The current version is the 1887 work of Sir Joseph Bazalgette, the civil engineer behind London's life-saving Victorian sewers.

Irish Republicans have three times attempted to blow up Hammersmith Bridge, most recently in 2000, when the Real IRA planted a bomb that caused some damage, and most dramatically in 1939, when a passing hairdresser noticed that smoke and sparks were coming from a suitcase on the walkway. At least, this is the story of hairdresser Maurice Childs, who says he hurled the case into the Thames, where it exploded causing an almighty splash. Another explosion went off elsewhere on the bridge. There is some doubt about Childs's account but he was nevertheless awarded an MBE.

Also of note near here, across the water on a terrace in Hammersmith, is the London home of William Morris; a couple of days' row from Kelmscott. I wonder what it's like over there. But it's closed today and, anyway, I'm in a hurry (one day I'll go and take a look). That's the way it is with a Thames walk: it's impossible to see it all in one go.

Onwards! Past more tanned stick-insect joggers, luxurious-looking apartments and Craven Cottage (home of Fulham Football Club, on the opposite side of the river) are the sailing and rowing clubs of Putney: Imperial College Boathouse, Westminster School Boat Club, Dulwich College Boat Club, King's College School Boathouse. On the embankment by Putney Bridge, two Holsten beer drinkers are arguing about whether it is cold or not.

'It's freezin',' slurs one.

'That's coz youse in the shade,' slurs the other.

'I'm sittin' in the f***** shade coz the bench is in the f***** shade,' slurs the First Drunk.

'Well, get over 'ere then,' slurs the Second Drunk.

The river really does act like a magnet for what seems to be a high proportion of the down-and-outs of southern England.

Beyond the bridge I pop into St Mary's Church. A little room to the side of the main church hall here tells the tale of the Putney Debates. After the Civil War, soldiers and officers of Oliver Cromwell's New Model Army met at the site of St Mary's from 28 October to 9 November 1647 to discuss constitutional matters, such as the role of the king and the question of democracy in the country. It was a moment when the common man could have his say at the highest level; all part of the Leveller movement. At this hearing Colonel Thomas Rainsborough was one of the more prominent of those putting forward the desire for greater equality: 'I think that the poorest he that is in England hath a life to live, as the greatest he; and therefore truly, sir, I think it's clear that every man that is to live under a government ought first by his own consent to put himself under that government.'

Again, as with the Magna Carta in Runnymede, great forward strides in the governance of Britain were being made by the banks of the Thames. I try to put things in perspective. Putney seems to have its place in a string of events by this river that have developed our understanding of how we are ruled: first Shifford (Alfred's get-together in 890), then Runnymede (King John and his showdown with the barons in 1215), then Putney, and of course there's riverside Westminster still going strong: the 'mother of Parliaments'. As it does hoboes and dreamers, the water seems to attract those wishing to exchange opinions. Even recently during the referendum on whether to leave the EU, one of the main leaders of the Out campaign, Nigel Farage, took to the river in a fishing boat commissioned in Ramsgate and yelled slogans encouraging Britain to turn its back on Europe, while another boat with the pop star Bob Geldof in charge, a Remain man, bawled the opposite.

Onwards! In Wandsworth Park a group is practising t'ai chi and a woman with a pram is conducting gymnastics exercises. The river is wide and metallic grey. This is a far cry from the pretty, countrified banks of Castle Eaton, Sonning and Marlow. The Thames has turned big and treacherous-looking: great currents swirl and eddies spin, the muddy water chopping, jerking and oscillating as though possessed by a demon in its depths.

Yet despite the shimmering violence of the waves, four old barges here have been adapted into nesting and roosting sites for herons, cormorants and gulls. Which is lovely to see. I keep going to the end of the park, where the River Wandle joins the Thames. This necessitates an inland detour via the nondescript sorts of plate-glass-and-balcony housing developments I hope are never built in Mortlake. Losing my way near a busy road, I ask a local for directions back to the river.

'I've lived round here for years and can't work out the way,' the fifty-something man says.

He does not seem impressed by all the building work either.

Not quite knowing how, I rediscover the Thames near a 'Solid Waste Transfer Station'. Glass crunches underfoot. Sirens wail. Someone has written, *DON'T VOTE, VOMIT* on a wall. I catch a distant glimpse of the tip of the Shard, Britain's tallest building (309 metres). I cross litter-strewn Wandsworth Bridge, and find the Thames Path blocked by an oil depot and more housing developments. This bit of Thames-side London is a mess. So I move inland before cutting back once again past high-end apartments with imposing smoked-glass facades at Imperial Wharf. Security cameras swivel. Women with personal trainers jog on the spot on a grass verge. Window cleaners abseil from great heights. Sprinklers flicker across little lawns lined with neat box hedges. At Chelsea Harbour I find the path obstructed once more and move north along walkways through apartment blocks coming to the entrance to the Chelsea Harbour Hotel. Outside the hotel a white Lamborghini with a Saudi Arabian number plate bearing the word 'one' is parked; the car surely belongs to royalty. A plummy-voiced woman is looking at the Lamborghini and talking to a hotel doorman wearing a top hat and tails. 'They race up and down in Mayfair, you know…' she says. But I don't catch the rest.

Beyond Lots Road and a community of smart houseboats, a building bears a plaque in honour of the women's rights campaigner Sylvia Pankhurst (1882–1960) and a traffic jam leads to the dainty pink-and-white outline of Albert Bridge. In Cheyne Walk and its environs come more blue plaques: one to William Morris's wife-stealing nemesis Dante Gabriel Rossetti. Many writers have lived in these streets over the years, including – in a single apartment block – Henry James, Somerset Maugham, T. S. Eliot and Ian Fleming. Carlyle Mansions became so well known for authors it was nicknamed Writer's Block. Meanwhile, Bram Stoker (1847–1912) resided at 27 Cheyne Walk. While the creator of Dracula was walking by the Thames one day, he saw a man in the water and pulled him out. Stoker carried the poor fellow, who had attempted suicide, to his house to try to resuscitate him. Unfortunately the man died on his kitchen table.

I watch a white van man shake his fist at a Porsche driver, then I pass a striking and graceful sculpture of a boy hanging on to the dorsal fin of a dolphin on a corner next to a Mercedes Benz showroom, turn up a side road and enter a small doorway in a long brick wall. I have found Chelsea Physic Garden.

Here I have an appointment. A familiar figure waves me forward. This figure is my mother. She has paid my entrance fee and she is with an unfamiliar figure. This figure is Nick Bailey, head gardener at the Chelsea Physic Garden. Somehow my mother, Christine, has unexpectedly arranged an impromptu interview with the man in charge of maintaining one of the most famous gardens in Britain.

Without further ado, I talk to the head gardener of Chelsea Physic Garden, standing next to a statue depicting Sir Hans Sloane, the seventeenth- and eighteenth-century physicist and naturalist who bought the manor of Chelsea and leased four acres to the Worshipful Society of Apothecaries of London for £5 a year in perpetuity.

'That was in 1673. He picked the location because of the access to the river,' says Nick, who seems pretty relaxed about having been hijacked by a backpack-touting Thames hiker. He is wearing aviator shades, jeans and walking boots, looking a little as though he is about to go for a stroll along the river too.

Nick explains that there are precisely 5,003 plant species in the garden and that this figure has held fairly constant for 100 years. Past head gardeners, or curators, have been responsible for all sorts, including the introduction of rubber plants to Malaysia, cotton to southern states in America ('whether that was such a good idea, I don't know') and tea to India. It was the curator Robert Fortune who transported tea seedlings from China to India in new portable glasshouses. Were it not for this garden, British hot-drink habits might be radically different.

The garden remains an important site for educating children and adults about rare plants. 'The magic of the garden is that it's the only place, other than south-west Cornwall, where many of these species will grow,' says Nick. 'See those three people there?' He is pointing to three people sitting on a bench. 'They're sitting under an avocado tree. We've also got the world's most northerly grapefruit tree growing outdoors and the largest fruiting olive tree in Britain.'

'What makes the garden so suited to unusual plants?' I ask.

'It's the *heat island* of London that does it,' Nick says. 'We're south-facing and we get thermals off the river. We're also surrounded by walls.' He pauses for a moment. 'And then there are the millionaires. All around here are the houses of millionaires, who let heat seep out.'

Nick's phone rings and he has to dart off.

My mother and I walk around the Chelsea Physic Garden, inspecting Britain's largest fruiting olive tree as well as species of tulip native to north-eastern Iran, succulent plants from the Canary Islands and Cape Verde, a *Cannabis sativa* plant from central Asia (in a medicinal section) and Dipsacaceae *Pterocephalus* herbs from Greece. I do not think I would ever have known what Dipsacaceae *Pterocephalus* herbs from Greece looked like had I not stopped by on the Thames Path at the Chelsea Physic Garden.

We eat lunch amid well-heeled folk at the Tangerine Dream Cafe, not far from the statue of Sloane in this secret oasis in the heart of London. 'Yummy mummies quite often come here on a fine day,' says the waiter, looking towards thirty-something women not dissimilar to those I've seen with personal trainers on the Thames Path. So do gentlemen drinking sparkling rosé wine and wearing panama hats, blazers, pink trousers and egg-yolk-yellow shirts with polka dots, if the neighbouring table is anything to go by. I feel like asking what some of the folk here do for a living, but I get a sense that what they 'do' is what we are witnessing right now.

We take another turn around the gorgeous, sunny garden.

'I've lost count of the number I've pulled out'
Chelsea to Somerset House

Then I return to the embankment.

After many miles of meadowsweet, cow parsley and nettles in recent days, sometimes walking for an hour or more without encountering another soul, London is sensory overload. Famous sights come and go: the pagoda in Battersea Park, Battersea Power Station (in the midst of restoration for a new office 'campus' for Apple computers), Tate Britain (where I drop in to see the magnificent Thames paintings of J. M. W. Turner and John Constable), the Houses of Parliament (where police eye my backpack suspiciously), Downing Street (where police are even more suspicious and a madman with a piece of old cardboard saying, *END MI5* is walking in circles and muttering: 'Ten thousand fake tourists in London yesterday… MI5, three million pounds harassment, nine years harassment… I'm not leaving here till I get paid!'), the London Eye and Cleopatra's Needle.

This obelisk is from Alexandria in Egypt and dates from 1460 BC. It has a tragic story. When the needle – which, incidentally, has little to do with Cleopatra – was brought to Britain in a specially designed container ship, the vessel almost sank in a storm in the Bay of Biscay during which five lives were lost (the names are listed by the obelisk). For a while the ship was adrift in the bay and many believed it had sunk. But a tugboat discovered it floating without a crew off the north coast of Spain, and the needle, which commemorates Britain's victory over Napoleon, was eventually erected in 1878.

Nearby is another memorial, this one in honour of Sir Joseph Bazalgette, 'creator of the Embankment and London sewerage system' (1819–1891)… and, of course, Hammersmith Bridge. The embankments here and on the other side of the Thames, which widened the land and narrowed the river, thus increasing its depth, were Bazalgette's greatest gift to London. The Victorian sewage pipes beneath them helped improve sanitation and cut outbreaks of diseases such as cholera. It is interesting to note that the Thames would have been 686 metres wide at Westminster Bridge during Celtic times; now it is just 228 metres wide, and Bazalgette's efforts defined the current width.

I pass a large woman, wearing a T-shirt that says, *BRAINS, BEAUTY, BOOTY*, next to Somerset House, up to which the river once lapped, although now the A3211 runs alongside its fine facade. Then I press a buzzer on a gate and am let through on to a ramp by a floating pier swaying on the busy (with clipper ferries and barges), choppy water of the Thames next to Waterloo Bridge.

Here I meet Keith Cima, chief helmsman at the RNLI Tower Lifeboat Station. Keith is aged 65 and has grey hair, though he looks a decade younger. He is tanned and wearing a one-piece drysuit, with the top peeled down, revealing a navy Royal National Lifeboat Institution polo shirt. He is sitting at a paper-strewn desk in an office with a whiteboard on which various figures are listed. These figures show that since 2 January 2002 the RNLI rescue boats from Tower Lifeboat Station, which was opened then, have been on 6,160 call-outs from this main station (there are also stations in Teddington, Chiswick and Gravesend), that the total number of lives saved during this period has been 278, while the number of call-outs this year has been 337 with 14 lives saved. The Tower Lifeboat Station is staffed continuously by a team of ten and its role, Keith says, is to provide first aid and recover bodies. The RNLI's presence on the river, he explains, dates back to the *Marchioness* disaster of 1989 when 51 people died after a dredger ran into the pleasure boat. This tragedy sparked the need for a more effective rescue service.

Keith is a former major-general in the army and was previously governor of the Tower of London. He tells me straight away that the figures for saved lives 'do not reflect the number pulled out of the river'.

I ask about the 14 people saved this year.

'Most were – how can I put this delicately? – people who fell into the river for one reason or another, mostly from the bridges,' Keith says. 'We're non-judgemental: we just go and save lives.'

The RNLI's position here is at the same location that the Thames River Police had 'what they called a "jump boat" permanently stationed from 1877 to 2003'.

'What is the reaction when you fish someone out?' I ask.

'Most are glad to see us,' says Keith, referring to people who have had accidents. Suicides are another matter. 'They'll say: "Just leave me alone. I want to die." I've had more fights in the river than I had in the army.'

How many people has he saved from the Thames?

'I've lost count of the number I've pulled out. I've had five CPRs. Of those, four lived.'

CPR stands for Cardiopulmonary Resuscitation. About 60 per cent of call-outs are for suicides, many of whom are the terminally ill or unemployed, although people are from all social strata and walks of life: all ages, sexes, nationalities, 'a complete cross section'.

Sometimes calls are made when people are still on bridges, about to jump. There are also, of course, accidents; those who have gone for a swim 'for a lark' that has gone wrong. Other mishaps might involve those who have slipped in while, for example, trying to grab sunglasses they have dropped. There are also jumpers who have acted in 'moments of madness', possibly because of 'broken hearts', who immediately regret having leapt in. At night, thermal imagery from helicopters is sometimes used to guide Keith and his team to bodies. The RNLI works alongside the police and the Port of London Authority, which is responsible for navigational safety on the tidal Thames; this role is covered by the Environment Agency on the non-tidal Thames above Teddington.

Keith shows me a video of a jumper from Blackfriars Bridge taken on 22 June 2015. 'He was a chef from Nottingham. He smacked his face on the bridge on the way down. He was like a sack of potatoes.

He'd been drinking. He wanted to die and we pulled him in. We were there before he started hanging from the edge of the bridge. He was in his late thirties.'

'Did he say thank you?' I ask.

'No. They very rarely do that. They have other things on their minds.'

Keith tells me that anyone who jumps from the Queen Elizabeth II Bridge at Dartford has no chance as the bridge is so high 'it's like hitting concrete'.

About 15 per cent of the Tower Lifeboat Station's work involves tow jobs when boats have had engine failure, and other call-outs are to rescue dogs. 'We have to do this as it stops other people trying to rescue them. We'll always rescue dogs. Foxes, too – I've had a couple of those.' Many risk their lives trying to save animals, he explains.

What people do not appreciate is how cold Thames water can be. 'You get cold-water shock in the form of a gasp reflex. Once you have that gasp, you have seventy seconds to drown and anyone who says that drowning is a pleasant way to go doesn't understand it's seventy seconds of terror.

'The Thames is a commercial highway, a tourist highway, a commuter highway, a pleasure-boat highway. There are a lot of snags and dangers in it if you don't respect it properly. There's a lot of debris. The river moves four to five knots here. The mix of salt- and freshwater means the currents are twisting currents. You can lose buoyancy more quickly than you realise.'

We pause for a moment as Keith's office rocks on the Thames as a boat goes by.

'What is it like to work on the Thames?' I ask. Keith is the first person I've met with a floating Thames office.

'The river is a completely different part of London,' he replies. 'Everyone knows everyone – all the people on the commercial boats. It's the river community. It's great. I love it.'

And as we say goodbye on the pier, next to a 40-knot rescue boat named *Hurley Burly*, Keith looks fondly out at the gyrating waves.

'This is the best job I've ever had,' he says softly.

It's certainly a responsible and incredibly demanding one – one that has made me look at the river in a completely different light.

Frost fairs, bear-baiting and Winchester Geese
Somerset House to Borough Market

Beyond Blackfriars Bridge, I cross the river by St Paul's Cathedral, taking the pedestrian Millennium Bridge, aka 'the wobbly bridge' due to its unexpected movement when it first opened (long since fixed). Halfway across I stop to look down at the surface of the Thames. Change into some swimming trunks and, with a jump and a splash, I'd be in. It's a sunny day: a little bit of breaststroke and a touch of crawl, then perhaps some gentle backstrokes to the bank. What could be more pleasant? Not now, though. Perhaps in the past I might have imagined that it would be no big deal to swim in the River Thames. Now I know how unforgiving and deadly it can be.

The bridge brings me to Southwark, home of Shakespeare's reconstructed Globe Theatre and the Tate Modern, built within the shell of the great yellow-brick hulk of Bankside Power Station. I look inside its gigantic turbine hall (half contemplating taking in a Georgia O'Keeffe exhibition) and then go outside and lean against a wall by the river, soaking up the strange centuries-old atmosphere of this part of the River Thames.

There's such a rich history hereabouts, and the former power station provides a link of sorts to what life must have been like in years gone by. From coal merchants in the eighteenth century to gasworks in years that followed, and electricity plants in the nineteenth and twentieth centuries, the riverside here was once very much an industrial place, home to vinegar factories, breweries (including the Anchor Brewery, after which the Anchor pub on the riverfront is named), tanneries, mills and hat factories (the bowler hat was invented in Southwark). It is said that William Blake, who lived in Lambeth and walked through Southwark to cross London Bridge to reach his job in the City, may have been inspired by the tall chimneys and clouds of smoke of Southwark when he referred to 'dark satanic mills' in 'Jerusalem', rather than by new industrial towns elsewhere.

This was once a place of the grit and grime of production, and the riverbank at Southwark used to have a seedy side too. Bankside, the street running along the river, was previously home to a dozen or more brothels, each with big painted signs to attract those passing on boats or on the opposite bank: the Boar's Head, the Cross Keys, the Cardinal's Hat. Women working in these infamous brothels during medieval times came to be known as 'Winchester Geese' as Bankside was under the jurisdiction of the Bishop of Winchester, who indirectly profited from the goings-on and thus allowed activities that were not permitted elsewhere in London. These prominent knocking shops, tolerated by respectable City folk across the river as they served a need and were one step removed by the water, were eventually closed by Henry VIII.

The riverside in Southwark was also where the notoriously harsh Clink Prison was to be found (1144–1780) as well as Marshalsea debtors' prison (1373–1842), described by Dickens in *Little Dorrit*. The streets round here were bustling, edgy and unforgiving; where ducking and diving came naturally. In medieval times bull- and bear-baiting rings drew great crowds. Alehouses lined Borough High Street, including the inn where Chaucer began *The Canterbury Tales* (the Tabard). Rough-and-ready watermen plied their trade with many favouring Southwark as a place to live. Theatres with scrum-like audiences popped up. Traders hawked their wares at Borough Market, crying out to attract customers. For many years this market adjoined London Bridge. During great winter frosts, the more entrepreneurial would set up stalls on the frozen river. The most famous of these 'frost fairs' was during the winter of 1683/84, when fires smoked on the Thames as meats were roasted and boiled, and bull-baiting, puppet plays, skating, and horse- and coach-racing took place. The diarist John Evelyn described this set-up on the river as a 'bacchanalian triumph'.

Which brings me to London Bridge.

In years gone by, the Thames was more likely to freeze as the narrow arches of the old London Bridge slowed the river's flow, making ice more probable (although it did not freeze every year). This old, famous London Bridge, with houses and shops built on top, was torn down in 1760 due to having become so congested that passage by foot was almost impossible unless following directly behind a carriage. The traditional song about London Bridge falling down, however, was not inspired by this demolition. The song is said to originate from much earlier, when Olaf Haraldsen's Norwegian ships assisted Ethelred against the Danish in 1014. The Danish had taken up positions on the bridge and Haraldsen's men are believed to have tied ropes to the support beams and pulled down the structure, causing the Danish to fall in the river.

A song remembering this moment came into being although the words were altered over the years and in a later incarnation 'my fair lady' was added to refer to Henry III's wife, Eleanor of Provence. Eleanor personally benefited from the collection of tolls from the bridge but she did little to maintain its upkeep; hence the fear that the bridge might 'bend and break' and 'wash away'. It is understood that there has been a bridge at this point for as long as London has existed, with the first stone structure dating from 1209 and the most recent from 1973. The days of the possibility of frost fairs ended in 1831 when a new bridge with wider arches was erected, thus increasing the river's flow, as would Bazalgette's embankments a few years later.

I look across at St Paul's Cathedral, standing by a little row of houses that have somehow survived the test of time. Number 49 Bankside is believed to date from as early as 1710. A plaque says that Christopher Wren lived here when he was building the cathedral, although this is known to be untrue; the plaque was put there as a hoax by a former owner and has been kept as a quirk by the current owners, although many guides include the 'fact' in tours.

One way or the other over the years, the riverside here acquired a raucous, licentious, often indecent reputation. Southwark never took on the airs and graces of the likes of Chelsea, Westminster, Richmond or Kew. And until relatively recently, times have been tough. The closure of docks on the River Thames in these parts in the 1960s – with containerisation taking trade downstream to Tilbury, other UK ports and Rotterdam – brought great hardship. However, the reopening of Shakespeare's Globe in 1997 and the opening of the Tate Modern in 2000 have rejuvenated the area, drawing in crowds, while Borough Market has become an epicentre of artisan stalls, attracting foodies from across the world. The completion of the Shard in 2012, with a five-star hotel with an infinity pool and cocktail bar close to its tip, cemented the area's transformation. Now Southwark is one of the most exciting districts in the capital.

Through throngs of tourists I take a look at the new Globe, with its exposed beams and thatched roof, before going a short distance inland to Park Street to see the original location of the Globe.

A plaque says: *Here stood the Globe Playhouse of Shakespeare 1598– 1613*. The site of the former theatre is now modern apartments with a mossy cobbled courtyard with a pick-up truck parked to one side. A bike rack is fixed to the pavement on Park Street and across the way is the smoked-glass office of the *Financial Times*. On the cobbled courtyard the curve of the Globe's original building is marked out. In this space, it is peculiar to imagine, *Hamlet*, *Othello*, *King Lear* and *Macbeth* were performed for the first time. I am the only person here. The theatre, I learn from an information panel, was demolished by the Puritans around 1644 (it had been rebuilt after the fire in 1613).

Shakespeare is depicted in bronze on the plaque, his forehead shiny from where tourists have patted the Bard for good luck. I do the same, before going round the corner to see a lesser-known point of interest in Southwark.

On Redcross Way I come to the Cross Bones Graveyard, where many of the medieval prostitutes who worked as Winchester Geese are buried. Over the centuries this spot, tucked behind an iron fence festooned with flowers and ribbons, became a paupers' burial ground, although it was originally referred to as the Single Women's Churchyard, placed on land well away from the Church of St Saviour, now Southwark Cathedral. 'Single women' was an obvious euphemism.

A half-ripped fly-poster on a brick wall says: *THIS IS STILL THE CROSSBONES GRAVEYARD*. A local group has sprung up to protect the land from development although nothing could be done to stop London Underground building an electricity substation on one part in the 1990s. During excavations for the substation, 148 skeletons were discovered, believed to be less than one per cent of the total buried. One skeleton was tested and found to be of a four-foot seven-inch woman aged about 16, suffering from advanced syphilis. The skeleton was dated as being from the eighteenth century and she was probably a child prostitute. This neighbourhood, known as the Mint, was one of the poorest in London. In reality, the brothel days of Southwark continued long after Henry VIII.

If you want to understand the river in London, head to Bankside and Southwark – and dig about a bit.

'Everyone had their own scam. Criminality was endemic'
Borough Market to Wapping

It is 4 p.m. now. I push on beyond the high-brick atrium of Hay's Wharf, the landscaped gardens of smart accountancy offices and the bulbous bowling ball of the capital's City Hall, crossing Tower Bridge and taking the Thames Path along the north bank as far as the headquarters of the Marine Policing Unit, formerly the Thames River Police.

Standing in the cobbled street by a small heavy wooden door, I find Rob Jeffries.

Rob is the curator of the River Police Museum, which tells the story of the Thames River Police, England's first official police force, formed in 1798 and predating the Metropolitan Police founded in 1829 by Sir Robert Peel. If you go to the museum's website and email a request to make an appointment, as I have, it is possible to be shown round.

Rob leads me through the wooden door into the yard of the working police station. A stack of bulletproof jackets sits in a corner. Next to the jackets are steps leading to the single-room museum in an old carpenter's workshop. This museum has a double door opening to a balcony. From the balcony you can see a pontoon where the Marine Policing Unit's boats are moored.

Before coming, I had also asked if I could go along for a ride on a river patrol but was informed by the Metropolitan Police that 'as the purpose is ultimately commercial, there would be a charge of £319.94 (plus VAT) – this is to cover the cost of the officer's time and the admin for the unit'. As I do not have £319.94 (plus VAT) to spare, I have settled on seeing the museum.

It is a wonderful place. Rob retired from the Metropolitan Police in 2005 after 32 years of service, including 17 with the River Police. He is bald with widely set blue eyes, slightly crooked teeth and a broad frame, wearing chinos and a blue shirt; he looks as though he could still, if called upon, break up a fight on Wapping High Street. Rob tells me that 63 people, including 11 women, work at the Marine Police Unit, operating six boats and reporting to a chief inspector for the Metropolitan Police Task Force, which also covers 'dogs, horses and ANPR'.

I ask Rob what ANPR stands for.

'Automatic Number Plate Reading,' he says, sounding as though he does not much care for acronyms. 'When I joined there was just CID. And that stood for Course In Drinking.'

Rob has the tell-it-straight style and wry humour of a long-serving police constable who has seen plenty in his time and is content with his lot. 'I did study to be a sergeant once, but I got so tired and stressed by it that my wife told me to give up,' he says, explaining his longevity as a PC.

It is clear from the twinkle in his eye as he shows me round the treasure trove of cabinets that Rob has a passion for Thames River Police history. Each object in the cabinets and hanging on the walls (every space taken) tells a story. A strange-looking gun hooked above an old barometer is, I learn, a Schermuly Pistol Rocket Apparatus: a gun designed to fire ropes on to the decks of ships at sea. A wooden staff with a metal tip is an old 'tip stave', used by police to prove that they were not bogus officers in the days before identification cards. A bottle-blue lantern with 'POLICE STATION' inscribed on the glass is the one that used to hang outside on Wapping High Street; this was saved during refurbishments a few years back when a worker was about to 'skip it' and a station officer explained that it had been hanging outside for 200 years. A drawing shows the body of a man being wheeled along nearby streets in 1811; this is the body of John Williams, a notorious murderer who killed seven people in Wapping before committing suicide in jail, or perhaps – Rob says – being bumped off by an inmate paid by an accomplice.

A display cabinet lists the 40 or so river policemen who have lost their lives on duty over the years (the last, in 1989, 'drowned on duty'). Near this, a tattered flag with a red cross and a symbol depicting a spike is the one that hung on the *Princess Alice* paddle steamer when it collided with a collier ship at a bend of the Thames near North Woolwich pier in 1878, resulting in the loss of almost 700 lives; many of those who died were not drowned but poisoned by terrible sewage pollution in the river (prompting calls for sewage to be dumped at sea). The accident remains the worst maritime disaster in British history in British waters.

'This is the house ensign of the London Shipping Company,' he says, looking at the flag. 'The youngest son of the captain William Grimsted took the flag from the river. He had gone out on a police galley to find his father. He was about to join the navy at the time. Instead he joined the River Police and stayed for twenty-five years.'

The Thames River Police, which has always been based here in Wapping, came into being to maintain order in the waters of the Pool of London, a historical location referring to where ships were once moored below London Bridge.

'It was to deal with pilfering on the river,' says Rob. 'About £500,000 a year was being lost, the equivalent of about £40 million now. This was organised theft. All of the criminality of London was in on it: delinquents, mudlarks, rat catchers, watermen, customs men. On West India Quay, where there were ships after dark, they would pay the mate or the watchman. It was accepted practice. Everyone had their own scam. Criminality was endemic. It was just done. First mates would keep the sweepings of the sugar when holes "appeared" in sacks. The same with oil – oil in the bottom of the barge. Some of it might happen to seep out. "Oh, that's in the base," they would say, and it would not go to the merchant. There was no policy on it. It had to be accepted by the merchants. Lumpers, the men unloading the ships, were in on it. If you said that they were thieves they would be most put out.'

In order to create order, the magistrate Patrick Colquhoun, a friend of the economist and philosopher Adam Smith and the social reformist and philosopher Jeremy Bentham, set up the River Police. While the Bow Street Runners had been around since the 1740s, they were detectives – 'the River Police is the oldest force of preventative police, although there had been parish constables since Saxon times,' says Rob, as we look out across the river by the double door at the end of the old carpentry shed.

When the River Police began, Rob continues, 'the middle classes weren't sure. They thought the establishment was taking too strong a role: who are these people?' There was concern that Britain simply was not ready for a police force. 'The French had had police, and look where that got them,' Rob says. The foundation of the River Police was a highly sensitive issue, and seen as a test for whether a wider force could succeed. 'Peel sent two of the original commissioners of the Metropolitan Police down here to see what problems they would face. He decided to keep the River Police and the Bow Street Runners separate from the Metropolitan Police as he was afraid that it might all go wrong, and if it did he did not want to lose what he had originally.' It was only in 1839 that the River Police merged with the Met.

Many of the first river policemen were illiterate. Rob shows me a book in which some had signed their names with an 'X'. Some were watermen who had been pressed into the navy and had returned from the Battle of the Nile in 1798. To join, 'all you had to do is row a boat, use a sword and fire a gun'. Another book shows fines for river policemen who were late for duty: 'Drink was quite often involved.'

Down on the river, the pontoon where the police boats are moored has two blue huts, one of which is for on-duty officers. By the other is a small crane. 'Bodies are lifted in on that and taken to that hut. They need to be pronounced dead by a doctor,' says Rob.

For the second time in the day, I find conversation turning to bodies in the Thames.

'There are no official figures,' says Rob. 'Perhaps fifty a year – about two thousand five hundred in the past fifty years, but probably a great deal more. Although some have said that there is, no book exists in which all the names are written down.'

Rob recently met a mother whose son died in the river and their discussion has led to a development: 'Her son died about six years ago, but she said to me: "The thing is that when you lose someone in the river, there's no focal point for mourning." I said: "Why don't we try to create one?" It's going to happen by All Hallows by the Tower of London. We've got an artist working on it now. We've raised £2,000 and we need double that. There's going to be a tablet in marble with an image of the river – a memorial to all who have lost life in the River Thames.' A quote from the Book of Isaiah is to be inscribed on the memorial: 'When you pass through the waters, I will be with you.'

I ask Rob if he has dealt with dead bodies on the Thames.

'Oh, countless. Loads. I assisted the investigating officer. It's something you do get used to.'

He looks out at the muddy water beyond the police boats. He does not advise that anyone tries swimming in the river in London. 'I remember once there were a couple of Geordies who tried to swim across. Picked out one. Dead. The other managed to swim to the bank. It's an incredibly unforgiving place. It's always cold.'

Policing the river has changed dramatically in recent times, he says. 'When I began, the job was about keeping it safe on the river. After 9/11 everything changed. Not just here – round the world. Every bridge is a risk. If you blew up Hammersmith Bridge you could close down west London. Now there is SO19, the Specialist Crime firearms branch and a rapid response unit. Those boats can go forty-five knots. You could get to Westminster from here in five minutes – though you wouldn't make any friends along the way.'

Rob and I while away an hour or so 'talking river'; Rob is a riverman through and through. We are right by the old Execution Dock, which was located more or less where the Captain Kidd pub is now to be found. 'That was where they switched them off, to use the parlance of the day. It was run by the Admiralty. They'd be taken for a last quart of ale at the Turk's Head. It was always a quart: they didn't want to be stingy. Then they'd be left for three tides on the foreshore. That was the tradition. If they'd gibbet them, they'd be put at a prominent place like Cuckold's Point.' Rob points down the river to Cuckold's Point. 'The last execution was 1832, or something like that. The last public execution in London was 1863, when the Tube was running. It's odd to think of that.'

Rob is a fount of knowledge – and his Thames River Police Museum is a River Thames revelation. Before we part, Rob talks about John 'Joz' Joslin, now aged 86, who put the collection together; the museum opened in its current form in 1974. 'When I retired, no one would take over running it. They're not really interested: younger people.' Rob is referring to younger policemen and women. 'They like the idea of the museum here for the oldest police force in England, but no one is showing any real interest.'

I do hope someone steps forward soon.

A pub crawl
Limehouse, Wapping and Bermondsey

From the museum I walk on past many a warehouse converted into smart apartments, to the Grapes pub in Limehouse, where I am about to meet a *riverwoman* through and through. My friend Laura lives on a houseboat on the Tower Bridge Moorings, also known as the Downings Roads Ancient Moorings in Bermondsey. She has kindly invited me to stay in a spare cabin on her 29-metre Dutch barge named *Ilka*. It will be my first night sleeping on the River Thames.

But before that we have arranged a pub crawl.

The Grapes on Narrow Street is the starting point. This pub was built in the early eighteenth century and is believed to have been the basis for the Six Jolly Fellowship Porters pub in Charles Dickens' novel *Our Mutual Friend*. His description still fits like a glove: 'a tavern of dropsical appearance… long settled down into a state of hale infirmity… it had outlasted, and clearly would yet outlast… many a sprucer public house'. Dickens goes on to describe the pub as being 'impended over the water, but seemed to have got into the condition of a faint-hearted diver who has paused so long on the brink that he will never go in at all'. I enter the narrow, crowded bar with its scuffed wood floor, wine-red walls and pink Victorian lampshades. One of the pub's leaseholders is Ian McKellen, although I cannot see the award-winning actor anywhere. Pictures of Dickens adorn the walls and a leather-bound collection of his works, along with a bust, is in a locked wooden cabinet. Dickens also wrote about this part of the East End in his final, uncompleted novel *The Mystery of Edwin Drood*, in which he vividly describes an opium den used by Chinese immigrants and run by a haggard woman known as ''Er Royal Highness the Princess Puffer'. Sir Arthur Conan Doyle had Sherlock Holmes come to similar dens in search of an opium fix.

I go up creaky stairs and find Laura sitting at a table by a balcony opening on to the sunny river; the part of the pub that feels most as though it might dive into the water, just as Dickens describes in *Our Mutual Friend*.

Laura has lived on *Ilka*, a Dutch barge dating from 1904, for six years and knows the river here well. She has various skippering qualifications, most recently having passed her powerboat licence level two exam. She has fallen in the river between boats at Downings Roads – luckily fished out by a neighbour – and seen river police collect bodies washed up by the moorings: 'It happens about two times a year. One time they thought it was a triad killing. The body had all the tattoos. It came up right by *Ilka*. Another time there was just a hand.'

We switch topics as enormous plates of food we have ordered arrive (the salmon with soy, coriander, ginger and crushed potatoes is the best dish I've eaten so far by the Thames), listen to an affronted blonde waitress amusingly tell an Eastern European customer who has asked whether the fish is fresh that 'We're famous for our fish here. What do you think it is? BirdsEye!', and then make our way to the Prospect of Whitby in Wapping.

Our new pub has a long pewter bar and is where the diarist Samuel Pepys drank in the seventeenth century (as he did in the Grapes). Dickens dropped by in the nineteenth century, of course (without writing about the visit). All pubs have many claims in Limehouse and Wapping. The Grapes is also at the spot where Sir Walter Raleigh is said to have set sail for the New World on his third expedition, while the owners of the Prospect of Whitby, which dates from 1520, say the establishment may be the oldest riverside pub in London. A pamphlet adds that one of its regulars was Judge Jeffreys, the notorious seventeenth-century lawman who had so many people hung at Execution Dock.

We drink glasses of red wine at the long pewter bar and then make our way to the Captain Kidd, overlooking the site of Jeffreys' gallows. Here we sit by the river and contemplate the gruesome goings-on of yesteryear. The sun is setting and a breeze is coming off the Thames. Adopting a slightly mystical 'river person' voice, Laura says: 'Ah yes, the wind gets up as the sun goes down.'

I ask her what she means by this.

'It's to do with diurnal thermal effects,' she says.

I ask her what she means by this.

'Look it up!' she replies.

We continue to Pub Number Three, called the Town of Ramsgate.

Pub Number Three has a long narrow bar and its own claim: that Judge Jeffreys was rounded up here after disguising himself as a sailor and hoping to flee the country in the footsteps of his ally James II. Despite having shaved off his eyebrows, he was recognised by a lawyer's clerk and taken to the Tower of London, where he died of a kidney disease aged 41. The pub is right by Wapping Old Stairs, a stone stairway to the river where fishermen from Ramsgate used to bring their catches, hence the pub's name.

Another red wine to the good, we cross Tower Bridge and go to the Angel in Bermondsey.

This was another Pepys hang-out; the diarist would come to visit his mistress Mrs Bagwell, who lived hereabouts. Judge Jeffreys, who seems to haunt the river in east London, apparently frequented the Angel to watch hangings at Execution Dock; meanwhile, Captain James Cook is said to have stayed before heading Down Under. A man slurring his words at the bar tells Laura: 'I loves youse, I do-es loves youse.' Then the man slurring his words at the bar and declaring his eternal adoration of Laura notices me. He proceeds to look daggers at me. Hatred, pure hatred, burns in his eyes. The man slurring his words appears to be under the impression that I present an obstacle to be dealt with swiftly – and with no shortage of force – if he is to obtain the newly found object of his eternal adoration.

I may be just about to have my first fist fight on the Thames.

'Bermondsey,' says Laura, leading me hastily upstairs, 'it's got a lot of history and character, but not a lot of warmth.'

We have our 'final' drink and Laura waxes lyrical about the Thames: 'It flows through the city. It's taking people on a journey today, as it has been through history. It's the same river Samuel Pepys looked at. The same river. Just different water. So it's a manifestation of time passing, literally passing by.'

With that, we repair to the Downings Roads Moorings, where a party is going on at the 'community barge' and we have another 'final' wine, swaying on the river, watching sodium lights dancing on the water and meeting interior designers, welders, bankers, journalists and IT technicians. Somewhere on the moorings there is an organist from Westminster Cathedral and a zookeeper from London Zoo; but I never do meet the organist from Westminster Cathedral or the zookeeper. Another Laura, a graphic designer, tells me: 'You have to be open-minded to live here.' Then I learn from someone, tongue loosened and pleasingly gossipy, whose name I do not catch, that there are many moorings romances, 'moorings couples' and even one 'moorings baby'. She says: 'Oh yes, there's a lot of love on the moorings.' And we drink more red wine. It has gone one in the morning when I fall asleep in a large spare cabin in a large Dutch barge, listening to the creak of the moorings… an ancient river with many ghosts washing by.

CHAPTER TEN

BERMONDSEY TO GRAVESEND, KENT

TO THE BARRIER, THE BADLANDS AND BEYOND

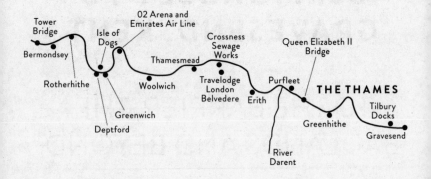

Tower
Bridge

Bermondsey

Rotherhithe

Isle of
Dogs

Deptford

Greenwich

Woolwich

02 Arena and
Emirates Air Line

Thamesmead

Travelodge
London
Belvedere

Crossness
Sewage
Works

Erith

River
Darent

Purfleet

Queen Elizabeth II
Bridge

THE THAMES

Greenhithe

Tilbury
Docks

Gravesend

I wake up wondering where I am. The space in which I find myself has an unlit fireplace, two tropical plants, a retro 1960s-style cabinet and an arty bedside table lamp in the form of an exposed bulb. The room dips and sways, performing minute lurches.

Oh, that's right – I'm on the river.

I walk down a hall with shelves with books by Nelson Mandela, Vivienne Westwood and Michael Frayn, and enter a smart kitchen with a skylight, pistachio-grey walls and a Damien Hirst butterfly print. 'Scandi chic' is, I think, although I may be wrong, the best description. Up steps I find a daybed printed with a bamboo pattern and a little door opening on to a small deck with peeling paint and a coil of rope.

Here I sit with a cup of black coffee – no sign of my hostess, who has yet to rise – and watch the river.

Upstream is Tower Bridge and the erratic skyline of gherkins, cheese graters and walkie-talkies of the City of London. The Shard peeks beyond the expensive apartments and restaurants of Butler's Wharf, which once housed the largest tea warehouse in the world. In the foreground barges are moored in a network connected by walkways. Old tyres hang from fenders with ropes as thick as arms. I cannot see anyone else on deck. It is 8 a.m. on a Saturday morning. The boat owners of the Downings Roads Moorings appear to be having a collective lie-in.

Downstream is the hazy silhouette of the Isle of Dogs. The pyramid-shaped top of Canary Wharf's highest tower pokes into a milky sky. A yacht bearing a French tricolour motors towards Limehouse and, I presume, the open sea.

Meanwhile, straight ahead across the wide, luminous waterway, a row of apartments with high glass windows fills the bank. Docked by these apartments is another assortment of houseboats. This is the Hermitage Moorings in Wapping, former home of the late Jo Cox, the Labour Member of Parliament who was shot dead after being stabbed repeatedly earlier in the year by a neo-Nazi white supremacist in her constituency in West Yorkshire.

Afterwards her boat was covered in flowers and tributes from many mourners. At the time, some believed that her death might swing the vote on whether to leave the European Union towards the Remain camp, due to the widespread condemnation of the attacker, whose 'Britain First' stance aligned with the position of the Brexiteers. That was, of course, not to be.

The Thames is quiet. A gull lands on a neighbouring barge and begins to squawk, but stops as though thinking better of it. Silence resumes.

There is something almost mystical about the river here.

There is also plenty of history – and much of it is grim. The Downings Roads Moorings are right by a bank of the Thames that was, in the first part of the nineteenth century, one of the worst places to live in England. Dosshouses, crumbling mills, tidal ditches into which raw sewage was dropped and rotten animal carcasses could be found… this area, known as Jacob's Island, was the pits. The journalist Henry Mayhew described it as having the 'smell of a graveyard', while his newspaper the *Morning Chronicle* dubbed the neighbourhood the 'capital of cholera' in 1849. This was before Bazalgette's embankments and sewers. Dickens used the slum, which he said was 'surrounded by a muddy ditch, six to eight feet deep', as the setting for Fagin's den in *Oliver Twist*; Bill Sikes comes to a sticky end in the ooze of Folly Ditch. These ditches were filled in the 1850s, meaning that the 'island' disappeared.

This is Dickens' description of Jacob's Island from *Oliver Twist*: 'Crazy wooden galleries common to the backs of half a dozen houses, with holes from which to look upon the slime beneath; windows, broken and patched, with poles thrust out, on which to dry the linen that is never there; rooms so small, so filthy, so confined, that the air would seem too tainted even for the dirt and squalor which they shelter; wooden chambers thrusting themselves out above the mud, and threatening to fall into it – as some have done; dirt-besmeared walls and decaying foundations; every repulsive lineament of poverty, every loathsome indication of filth, rot and garbage; all these ornament the banks of Folly Ditch.'

I finish my coffee and make one for Laura in her Scandi kitchen. She appears and is in a rush to go to an examination for another boat qualification. We leave *Ilka* and take a walkway covered with chicken wire to Jacob's Island, where she departs and I turn my mind to the day ahead.

'Glide gently, thus forever glide'
Bermondsey to Rotherhithe via Tower Bridge

Today's destination is Greenwich, about 11 miles away. I am more than a fortnight into my Thames walk now and 11 miles really does feel like nothing.

I go backwards to Tower Bridge and pay £9 to take a lift to the walkways at the top, 49 metres up, where displays explain how the bridge was constructed in 1894 and show the rather fantastic and fanciful architects' drawings of hoop-shaped versions of Tower Bridge that were not to be. There are magnificent views, including one through a reinforced glass floor to the street across the bridge. The bridge took eight years to build and was designed by Sir Horace Jones, who died before its completion, with subsequent planners adding Victorian Gothic touches so the structure would be in keeping with the Tower of London. I have never been up before, though I have crossed the bridge hundreds of times.

At the top Tower Bridge sways a bit. Looking east, the Downings Roads Moorings by Jacob's Island are, I can see, much more substantial than those across the way at Hermitage Moorings. The sky above east London is now covered in oyster-coloured clouds. Looking west, I can see the HMS *Belfast*, St Paul's and the BT Tower. I learn from a video that despite there being no health and safety laws, only ten people died in the making of Tower Bridge, and that the City of London has 7,800 inhabitants although 300,000 people work there (a potentially handy pub quiz fact, I suppose).

William Wordsworth's poem 'Upon the Thames at Evening' (1790) is quoted on an information panel:

> Glide gently, thus forever glide,
> O Thames! that other bards may see,
> As lovely visions by thy side
> As now, fair river! come to me.
> Oh glide, fair stream! for ever so;
> Thy quiet soul on all bestowing,
> 'Till all our minds forever flow,
> As thy deep waters now are flowing.

Which might be over-egging it just a bit these days with all the nondescript apartments and not-so-lovely visions of walkie-talkie-shaped skyscrapers. Wordsworth really loved the river, and his most famous Thames poem was penned a few years later, in 1802, 'Upon Westminster Bridge':

> Earth has not anything to show more fair:
> Dull would he be of soul who could pass by
> A sight so touching in its majesty:
> This City now doth, like a garment, wear
> The beauty of the morning; silent, bare,
> Ships, towers, domes, theatres, and temples lie,
> Open unto the fields, and to the sky;
> All bright and glittering in the smokeless air.
> Never did sun more beautifully steep
> In his first splendour, valley, rock, or hill;
> Ne'er saw I, never felt, a calm so deep!

> The river glideth at his own sweet will:
> Dear God! the very houses seem asleep;
> And all that mighty heart is lying still!

I glideth back along the Thames Path, past Jacob's Island and a new 'super sewer' being built at Chambers Wharf. This location, along with 23 other sites along the river, is part of the four-billion-pound Thames Tideway Tunnel to update Bazalgette's sewers and prevent sewage spilling into the river (as it still does when there is heavy rain). The concerns over the cleanliness of the Thames and the health of those living beside, or on, the river dating back to the days of Dickens and Mayhew remain; even if the 'capital of cholera' has long gone.

After Chambers Wharf I stop by a mound of grass next to the Angel pub, scene of my near fisticuffs and the Millpond Estate. I did not notice this mound of grass last night.

An elderly man wearing a trilby, who can see I am interested, sidles up and tells me: 'Someone used to live there, you know.'

I thank him for this information.

That 'someone' was Edward III, who built a residence here during his reign (1327–1377). Crumpled cans of Foster's and old paper plates have been tossed on the site of the old manor house, which looks a touch neglected now.

A little further on I get to a place in Rotherhithe where several someones are believed once to have ventured forth on a boat in the direction of the Atlantic Ocean. They were the Pilgrim Fathers, whose journey to the New World in 1620 on the *Mayflower* proved so momentous. Christopher Jones, the ship's captain, is buried in an unmarked grave at St Mary's Church here, and the ship itself was allowed to rot in the river at this spot. A pub by St Mary's that was called either the Shippe Tavern or the Spread Eagle in the seventeenth century is now the Mayflower, at the precise point of the ship's considered embarkation. I say 'considered' as there is some debate about whether the ship officially left from Plymouth.

The pub is open and a Stars and Stripes hangs in the back garden. Inside is an eclectic room with walls crowded with stuffed gulls, ancient documents, pewter mugs and old ship lanterns. Quotes from Dickens ('This is a London particular… A fog, Miss') and Robert Louis Stevenson ('Yo-ho-ho, and a bottle of rum!') are painted in gold on wooden panels. It is proving to be a morning of quotations.

There is one other customer in the pub and I overhear him speaking to the barmaid in an American accent. We get talking and he tells me his name is Anton. He is from New York City but works as a high-flying banker in Frankfurt. He has come to London especially to watch Crystal Palace play West Bromwich Albion at football; I am fairly certain I am meeting the only person in Britain currently fitting this profile. He has paid £179 to watch the game in a corporate box, although he has not told his girlfriend back in Frankfurt that he has spent this much. It is the first weekend of the new football season. Anton, who has come to the Mayflower as a pilgrimage to the pilgrims, offers to buy me a pint.

Anton and I drink our Mayflower Scurvy Ales and discuss presidential hopefuls Donald Trump and Hillary Clinton. Anton cannot stand Trump ('He would be a disaster') and says that most young voters in New York favour Clinton. He is not much in favour of Brexit either. We talk about football and Anton tells me that, like the Pilgrim Fathers, his family are immigrants to the United States. He grew up in the small city of Kherson in southern Ukraine and his father, an anaesthetist, attained a green card to work in America in 1999. His mother is a cardiologist and they now live in Brooklyn. When they first moved to America his parents had to switch jobs: his father initially worked in construction, while his mother was a carer for elderly people. However, they studied and achieved qualifications allowing both to work as 'nuclear technologists'.

Anton sips his ale and continues, sounding thoughtful: 'It is only recently that I started to realise how life-changing the move has really been for my parents. To basically hit a "reset" button on their lives in their forties must have been incredibly difficult.'

It is a classic story of successful immigration – told in the place where immigration to the US began: the American dream still alive and well (for now, at least).

Anton goes off to make the most of his corporate hospitality ticket – 'maybe I can break even on beers' – and the barmaid, who is from Munich, tells me that I can buy American stamps at the Mayflower. Apparently the Mayflower is the only pub in Britain that sells American stamps, should you be passing and require one. Just to say I have done this, I buy an American stamp. Then the barmaid from Munich takes me upstairs to show me a 'Descendents Book'. This book lists all those Americans who have visited the Mayflower pub who are descendents of the Pilgrim Fathers. It has been going for less than a year, so there are not many names in the book yet; just a few Rogers and Hopkins. There were 100 Pilgrim Fathers, Puritans who left England as they felt that the country was in a terribly ungodly state and going from bad to worse (some may wish to draw modern parallels... though now, of course, there are no New Worlds left to discover).

Rotherhithe seems to be full of intrigue if you start poking about.

Across a lane from the Mayflower is the Brunel Museum. This museum celebrates the Thames Tunnel, which runs under the river here at a depth reaching 23 metres. In the early nineteenth century it was a two-mile walk for Rotherhithe dwellers to London Bridge. A way across was needed, but it was too far from bank to bank here for a bridge (about four hundred metres) and an above-water crossing would impede ships.

So a tunnel was planned and the celebrated engineer Marc Isambard Brunel designed and patented a metal-cage device for the digging. The tunnel took 18 years to complete (*The Times* referred to the much-delayed project as 'the Great Bore'), went well over budget at £614,000 and cost ten lives.

That total was almost 11. On 12 January 1828 the Thames burst through the roof of the tunnel, trapping Isambard Kingdom Brunel, the chief engineer (Marc's son, then aged 21), beneath a beam. He managed to break free and was washed to the tunnel's shaft, where Britain's most acclaimed engineer banged on a locked door and was saved by a fellow worker. He was sent to the West Country to recuperate, whereupon he heard about a competition to design the Clifton Suspension Bridge. The Thames Tunnel, when it finally opened in 1843, attracted more than a million people in its first 15 weeks; each paid a penny to pass through. To put this in perspective, the population of London was just over two million at the time. However, despite being dubbed the 'eighth wonder of the world' and being regarded as the world's first tunnel beneath a navigable river, it was not a financial success. Ramps to allow commercial carts through at each end were not built as they would have been too expensive. The tunnel has been used by trains since 1869.

'Ere's your soup, darlin'. Lovely, enjoy'
Rotherhithe to Greenwich

From Rotherhithe I keep going along a soulless stretch with apartments in converted warehouses and a boarded-up pizza restaurant.

Across the way I can see the Grapes pub in Limehouse, where I was drinking about 16 hours ago, and the skyscrapers of Canary Wharf. A little sandy beach with gulls by one of the warehouses faces the financial towers. A breeze sweeps across the water. I come to the Surrey Docks Farm, which is on the site of an old shipyard where more than 100 ships were built between the 1740s and 1820. This small urban farm, tucked between apartment blocks, is home to turkeys, chickens, rabbits, pigs, ducks, donkeys, ponies and sheep. 'Well rotted manure' is available for £2 a bag and a shop sells duck eggs for 50p each alongside kale, spring onions, beetroot, carrots, tomatoes, blueberries, courgettes, beans and parsley. Sausages are in a fridge. 'They're last year's pigs,' says a volunteer. I have a bowl of vegetable soup with toast at a little cafe served by a woman with an East End accent who says, "Ere's your soup, darlin'. Lovely, enjoy', and listen to Otis Redding songs playing on a stereo. Rather a nice place, the Surrey Docks Farm.

The Thames Path is almost empty as it cuts past the Pepys Estate and then, in Deptford, the Trinity Estate, where a couple is having wedding pictures taken on the path and a skinny woman on a bench drinking Strongbow cider asks if I would like to join her. I do seem, increasingly, to attract the waifs and strays of the River Thames.

Not long afterwards, I find myself in Greenwich, walking past the shiny black and gold *Cutty Sark* and continuing beyond the National Maritime Museum and the Royal Observatory to a street with a tarot-card parlour and a shop selling 'all shorts £2.50: get those pins out!' Not far from here is the King William Hotel, where I drop my backpack in a very plain little room with a bed and a shower-room (and that's about it). This very plain little room, with breakfast, cost £66.

The weather has turned sunny; it's a gorgeous Saturday afternoon. I go to the National Maritime Museum, feeling as though I am floating along without the backpack.

Inside, I make a beeline for its brilliant Maritime London room, where an information panel explains the importance of seaborne trade to London over the years, although this business has now transferred to Tilbury and Felixstowe. Despite this, the city 'remains a global centre for ship-brokering, commodity trading, banking and insurance, which are all vital to the modern marine world'. There are glistening watermen's licences from the 1820s, shiny Doggett's badges (from the ancient Thames river race for apprentice watermen), paintings of the

Royal Dockyard at Deptford and old ship figureheads – but the pride of the exhibition is its *Armada Portrait* of Elizabeth I (1590).

Elizabeth I, who was born in Greenwich Palace in 1533, is depicted by an unknown English artist wrapped in great strings of pearls and has a serene expression that suggests both extreme satisfaction (with victory against the Spanish) and disdain (that the Spanish dared to venture towards her shores in the first place). Her right hand rests on a globe, as if to say that the world bows down to the English.

The words of her famous address to the troops gathered by the Thames at Tilbury on 9 August 1588, ahead of the battle against the Spanish, seem to hang in the air: 'I know I have the body but of a weak, feeble woman; but I have the heart and stomach of a king, and a king of England too, and think foul scorn that Parma or Spain, or any prince of Europe, should dare to invade the borders of my realm...' The museum is currently seeking funds to restore this magnificent portrait which is 'in urgent need of conservation work'.

I do two more 'tourist things' in Greenwich.

I go to the *Cutty Sark* and am impressed by the nineteenth-century tea clipper that could once sail at 17.5 knots to Australia in 73 days, but not so impressed by the entrance fee (£13.50). Then I take the Greenwich Foot Tunnel, opened in 1902, across the way to the Isle of Dogs. This tunnel is a damp, chilly place and people are cycling even though there are signs saying cycling is prohibited. On the Isle of Dogs there is a park with a cafe/kiosk run by a scraggly-haired man who is listening to 'Hotel California' by the Eagles and reading *The Guardian* when I visit.

Afterwards I eat an excellent bowl of noodles with prawns and squid at the Tai Won Mein noodle bar near the *Cutty Sark*, before returning to my very plain little room to read the papers.

All sorts of river happenings are afoot. My copy of *The Wharf*, a paper specialising in Canary Wharf and the Docklands, tells me that a 73-metre super-yacht currently moored at West India Quay belongs to the Westfield shopping mall billionaire Frank Lowy and has a helipad, cinema, massage rooms and a gym. It also informs that the MBNA Thames Clipper service will now stop at Westminster Pier, and shows a picture of an armed Metropolitan Police counterterrorism boat speeding along the river. Sir Bernard Hogan-Howe, the Metropolitan Police commissioner, is quoted saying that it is a 'question of when, not if' an attack takes place in London. Meanwhile, the *News Shopper* local paper runs an article on a High Court decision to allow an international cruise terminal on the Thames and a 770-home development at Enderby Wharf (a little downstream of Greenwich); some locals had argued that the plans would cause 'air quality pollution'. The *Southwark News* has a piece headlined *SUPER SEWER WORKS TOO NOISY AND DUSTY*; a resident near Chambers Wharf says construction is making her life 'a misery'. And I learn from an online article from last year in the *East London and West Essex Guardian* that my hotel had its alcohol licence briefly suspended after a St Patrick's Day punch-up in which furniture was used as weapons and a man almost died. At the time of this incident there had been four previous assaults in a period of six months at the hotel, one involving a man who was 'glassed'. Greenwich Licensing Team's PC Jason Coombes describes events at the hotel as having been severe and 'ferocious'.

I decide to get an early night in my very plain little £66 room.

There's a long way to go tomorrow – and a bout of grievous bodily harm is not going to help.

'Riverside living is beautiful'
Greenwich to the Thames Barrier

For much of the London section of the official Thames Path there is the option of going on either the north or the south side of the river. I have taken my pick according to my mood and interest. However, from

Greenwich Foot Tunnel to the Thames Barrier, the end of the official 184-mile trail, the path leads along the south side of the river only.

I consult my map over breakfast in a room with faux-leather banquettes, dance music and one other hotel guest who requests mango juice and is told that there is only apple or orange juice. 'That will do,' he says, without seeming to decide on which. A drinks list on the table shows that a bottle of champagne is on offer for £360. It's a funny sort of hotel, the King William in Greenwich.

Out on the streets, despite my map-reading, I find it hard to locate the Thames Path. Yellow diversion signs send me down Mauritius Road and I walk for some distance past MOT garages, metalworks depots and 'quality used truck' centres. These bring me to noticeboards for the Greenwich Peninsula development. Signs designed to entice customers with a few hundred thousand pounds to spare say: *VISIT OUR MARKETING SUITE… TRADITIONS ARE IMPORTANT IN NEIGHBOURHOODS, SO LET'S INVENT SOME… AMAZINGLY WE'VE FOUND A NEW BIT OF LONDON TO LIVE IN… VIEWS: BRING SOME. FLATS AVAILABLE FOR INTERESTING PEOPLE.*

What happens, I wonder, if a couple of trainspotting accountants with a love of beige clothing, sensible shoes and quiet weekends visits the marketing suite with a suitcase stuffed with banknotes: will they be turned away on account of not being interesting enough?

Pondering this, I continue along what appears to be the A102 in the direction of the Millennium Dome. I know the river is by the Millennium Dome. For the time being, I seem to have lost the River Thames. The scenery is not exactly picturesque in this amazingly new bit of London. Old newspapers and cans of lager are strewn on the street. Weeds grow out of cracks in the pavement. I pass a gasometer. Then I meet a group of birdwatchers.

The twitchers have binoculars and cameras on tripods. They are from the London Natural History Society and they are looking for peregrine falcons, cormorants and kingfishers; there is a close-by ecology park to which they are making their way. I get to know this as I ask a couple of the twitchers what they are hoping to see. One of these twitchers enquires what I do for a living. She is wearing a stripy blouse and a dress, reminding me a little, at first, of Agatha Christie's mild-mannered sleuth Miss Marple. I explain what I'm up to and that I work for a newspaper. Upon hearing this, Miss Marple, whose real name is Ruth, turns on me.

She has strong opinions about the owner of my newspaper. 'I think he has too much power!' she says. 'He owns too much of the media! The media should be spread about! I'm putting that on the table for you! Don't ever speak his name round here!'

I have not spoken anyone's name. I am being savaged by a twitcher who reminds me of Miss Marple on a street near the Thames in north Greenwich. All I have done is ask what birds they are seeking.

'Is Ruth attacking you?' asks a kindly twitcher next to Ruth.

I say that I think Ruth is attacking me.

'Oh, that's just Ruth being Ruth,' says the kindly twitcher.

Ruth gives me a mean stare.

I make my way to the river.

Several unusual sculptures line the shore of the Thames next to the Millennium Dome; one of which appears to consist of a slice of an old ferry. The river is muddy. And I have the path more or less to myself.

It's a slightly desolate stretch on this overcast day. But then I come to the Emirates Air Line cable car, which I decide to take to liven things up a bit. Having gone under the river yesterday, I may as well go way over it (90 metres up) today. This is an awe-inspiring experience in which I have a cable car to myself, travelling the 1,103 metres at a speed of 6 metres a second. A commentary tells me that 'the Romans came and then obviously the Vikings' and that the area around the Royal Victoria Dock is 'invigorating' and 'really very exciting'. The journey takes ten minutes in each direction and I do not get off. From above, the Millennium Dome looks as though it has been struck repeatedly by lightning and that these bolts of lightning, the support beams, now hold up the roof. It really is a quite extraordinary structure.

I return to the riverside after this interlude, following the path by a bench with young marijuana smokers. Two large barges are tied up in the centre of the river here and piled high with rusty containers. Another housing development emerges with more noticeboards and the message *RIVERSIDE LIVING IS BEAUTIFUL*. I pass a yacht club and then walk along an empty stretch of path lined with buddleia on the riverside and a red-brick wall with an enormous pile of sand on the other side. The sand seeps on to the path and metal conveyor belts stretch overhead with chutes for pouring the sand into ships. I soon, however, learn that I am wrong about this 'sand'. It is, in fact, 'marine-dredged aggregate'. A Walk London information board tells me so.

Further on, a wall by the path is topped with razor wire covered in torn plastic sheeting, which is pretty awful though I could see it perhaps doing well in the Turner Prize for contemporary art. After this, I reach the Anchor and Hope pub, where the barmaid makes me a cup of tea. This pub is painted black and has a few picnic tables outside next to a seafood kiosk where I buy a pot of cockles from Mark and Sharon, who are attending the kiosk. Mark is the pub landlord. He tells me that cockles are best with pepper and vinegar. I put pepper and vinegar on the cockles. Then Mark and Sharon watch me eat them. They are very good and I tell them so. 'We wouldn't serve anything we wouldn't eat ourselves,' says Mark.

Not far from the Anchor and Hope is an indoor go-karting centre with thumping music emanating from within. Then I arrive at the shiny gates of the Thames Barrier.

This is, of course, a major place on the official Thames Path. The barrier is where the route either ends or begins for most. I have covered the 184 miles from Trewsbury Mead to here. Beyond the barrier, however, I have 31 further miles to go to cover the river's full 215 miles.

I enter the barrier's visitor centre where I am, on this mid-August day, bang in the middle of the summer holiday season, the sole tourist. It is incredible how few people seem to walk along the Thames. Apart from central London, I have had England's longest river more or less to myself for such long spells.

At the visitor centre I learn a few facts regarding the Thames, some of which I perhaps ought to have picked up by now: that in every tidal cycle the river rises an average of seven metres; that tidal surges happen when a band of low pressure crosses the Atlantic and causes a hump of water to pass to the north of Scotland into the North Sea; that such a surge might cause the sea to rise by over a metre and is particularly likely to cause floods during high spring tides.

A major flood in 1953, which resulted in 58 deaths on Canvey Island in Essex, focused minds about the great danger of sea surges, and the Thames Barrier opened in the early 1980s to combat this threat. As of April 2016, the barrier has been closed to block sea surges on 176 occasions. The structure is designed to be effective until at least 2030, based on a prediction that sea levels will rise by eight millimetres a year, although the current rise is less than this. It is expected that a new barrier may need to be built across the river by 2070 to cope with higher water; a potential site has been earmarked for this downstream at Long Reach. A 2100 Thames Estuary Project has been devised that takes into consideration the likely sea rise caused by melting polar caps; the most this might be by 2100 is 2 metres and 70 centimetres, although experts anticipate a rise of between 20 and 90 centimetres by then. The definition of 'Thames Estuary', I learn, is tricky: it could be said to cover the tidal river all the way to Teddington, although some simply refer to the section of 18 nautical miles beyond Gravesend in Kent.

The woman running the cafe at the visitor centre, Abbie, tells me that the quickest she has ever known anyone do the walk from the source of the Thames to the barrier in one go is 14 days although most people do it over the course of a few years – 'twenty years is the longest'. This would, obviously, have been in stages. I am only the second person this month who she knows to have achieved the feat, which I have managed in 17 days. 'When most people get here, that's it, they've made it,' Abbie says. Not many continue on to Thamesmead and beyond.

Industrial estates, prisons, sewage works and a Travelodge
The Thames Barrier to Belvedere

But stopping here would be a cop-out. The Thames-walking purist – the real Thames walk lover – presses on to the sea.

There is an excitement that comes from walking 'beyond the map': a feeling of stepping into the unknown. Outside, however, there is a sign that says, *Thames Path Extension*. It appears that, although the official path has ended, there is a way forward. I take in the enormous Tate & Lyle sugar refinery on the opposite bank and then cut inland following the extension signs, finding myself weaving through Warspite Road Industrial Estate and passing a boarded-up pub, a McDonald's, some old smoke stacks and a housing estate where a shifty man in a red tracksuit asks: ''Scuse me, mate, have you got a spare eighty pence?'

He has some change in his hand, which he shows me as though this is proof that he is making a legitimate request.

I tell him I do not have a spare 80p and he sighs loudly.

I keep going through the housing estate. A plane is coming in to land at London City Airport when, not far along, I reach the site of the Woolwich Royal Dockyard. This was where Henry VIII's flagship, the *Great Harry*, was constructed. A couple of nineteenth-century cannons face the water here. From around the 1770s to the 1850s great prison hulks floated in the Thames by the banks in Woolwich, prisons with convicts used as dockyard labour. Nearby is land that was once the home of Woolwich Arsenal, the country's main weapon store from the 1670s until the 1960s. Now, like so much of the riverside, it is a building site for expensive new housing.

The partly constructed Royal Arsenal Riverside will be eight minutes from Canary Wharf by train once Crossrail begins in 2018. I go in the marketing suite to look at models of two-million-pound apartments.

The song 'Lovely Day' by Bill Withers is playing. A tall marketing man from Slovakia tells me that the apartments will be 'the best connected development in the outside zone' of London and that they are 'very much pre-sold'. People do love to live by the river – even on old ammunition sites.

I walk down a long bleak pathway with graffiti on a low wall next to another housing estate. I have reached Thamesmead, a town with a population of about 50,000 that was built in the 1960s to solve housing shortages in London. It is also home to HM Prison Belmarsh.

On a whim, I go to the prison. I do not really know what motivates me to do this; I'm just curious, I suppose, to see where some of Britain's most dangerous people are locked away (including many terrorists). It is, as might be expected, an awful-looking place behind high red-brick walls topped with coils of razor wire. I get to the entrance and ask myself: why? Why have I bothered to come here? I go to eat lunch at a McDonald's by the prison, where an assistant looks at my backpack and map and asks: 'What are you doing, going treasure-hunting?'

I'm not sure many tourists make it to these parts.

Back on the river, a piece of graffiti written in yellow capitals declares: *I DON'T CARE ABOUT REAL LIFE.* This seems to set the tone for the next stretch of pathway, which brings me to the site of the dreadful *Princess Alice* disaster in 1878 that I learnt about at the River Police Museum as well as the Crossness Sewage Treatment Works. Tinny pop music floats across the river from a container depot on the other side of the Thames. I enter Crossness Pumping Station, which is the site of an older, now closed sewage treatment works that was originally opened by Sir Joseph Bazalgette in 1865. A little museum here with restored pumping engines has displays on the 'Great Stink' of 1858, during which a combination of high summer temperatures and filthy Thames water forced politicians to hang sacks covered in deodorising chemicals on the windows of the Houses of Parliament.

Having visited a prison and a former sewage works, I walk past the functioning Crossness Sewage Treatment Works to find my hotel for the night: the London Belvedere Travelodge.

This is across a surprisingly picturesque series of fields known as the Crossness Nature Reserve. A noticeboard says that water voles, redshank, reed warblers and peregrine falcons are to be found in the fields next to the gently humming sewage works (which apparently serves two million people and does not, for the record, smell at all when I'm going past). Brown horses are grazing in these fields and it is quite peaceful… if you shut out the sounds of revving motorbikes on a lane leading to the sewage works. Motorcyclists are tearing along and doing wheelies. It's as though they do not have a care in the world and know the police will not come and get them in this hidden place on the edge of Thamesmead.

So I arrive at my Travelodge. It is much more pleasant than expected, although from the outside the hotel resembles a smaller scale Belmarsh, minus the razor wire. For £41, however, I have a large-ish spotless room. Admittedly there is no shower curtain (causing an almighty mess in the bathroom), there is no shower gel in the dispenser (requiring the use of a tiny bar of soap) and I have a dull view of a car park, but the bed is very comfortable. A little piece of folded cardboard tells me all about the bed, which is, I discover, no ordinary bed. It is a 'Dreamer Bed: all the king-sized comfort you'll ever need' with 'more than 900 individual pocketed springs, an extra comfort layer, a hypoallergenic filling, a cosy half-tog duvet and four plump pillows'.

Guests are able to buy their very own Travelodge beds should anyone wish to experience Travelodge slumber in the comfort of their own homes. No price is given for a Travelodge bed. A few hangers dangle in an open wardrobe. There are two comfortable faux-leather chairs and the air conditioning works well. As I said, not bad for £41.

The best thing about the London Belvedere Travelodge, however, is the Morgan pub, which is just across the car park. The sun is out and the picnic tables on its lawn are packed. I sit inside in a room decorated in autumnal colours next to a red-brick fireplace and wait for quite a long time for a hamburger to be delivered.

A man with friends at a table next to me is having a Sunday roast. He says to his companion: 'You don't like black pudding? What are you, racist?' He laughs heartily at his own joke and then discusses Great Britain's efforts in the Olympics. The team is doing well and the man has a theory about this: 'We're good at any sports that involve sitting: rowing, sailing, cycling… we're the best.'

A woman on another table is contemplating the pay for a new job she has just taken: 'It's minimum wage – I've got no experience. It's what you get: fourteen grand. Sally is on seventeen grand. I'm a bit concerned it might all go tits up.'

When you've been walking for long stretches by the Thames in Thamesmead, all on your own, it's good just to hear a bit of chatter. The burger comes and is a decent burger at a reasonable price. This is a far cry from the Thames-side mark-ups of Henley or Clifton Hampden. I have, I realise, stepped well off the traditional holidaymaking trail. I return to my Travelodge room and get another early night.

Lost in the marshes

Belvedere to Gravesend

The Crossness Sewage Treatment Works looks strangely beautiful in the early morning light. The main building has a high curving roof and a blue wave-like pattern painted on one side as well as on a cooling tower. This is only one part of the Crossness Sewage Treatment Works and this building's job is to create energy from waste; the plant can generate 72 megawatts of energy. The rest of the sewage works is somewhere behind Bazalgette's old pumping station.

Down the lane where the motorcyclists had been fooling about yesterday – black tyre marks cover the surface of the road – I reach the Thames.

The river here has an odd beauty too.

The silhouette of a loading pier with cranes and stepladders rises from glistening rivulets that have formed a world of little channels in the thick Thames mud. The tide is out and the sun is bright on the calm water, an avenue of gentle yellow light spreading east. It's going to be a beautiful, hot summer's day. The sky is a delicate blue. The air smells of seaweed. The path by the riverside is empty apart from one other man, who appears to be Eastern European and on his way to work. 'Morning,' he says briskly, with a look suggesting he is amused to see anyone out and about with a backpack.

This is real edge-land. Across the river are power stations and oil depots, while on this south side I am skirting more mini mountains of what appears to be marine-dredged aggregate, yards with stacks of scaffolding and container crate depots. The path ducks beneath conveyor belts. Old wharves with rotted wood come and go. Wild grass and weeds spout from the river wall. The beeping sound of reversing lorries emanates from building sites. I stop to inspect the remains of a motorbike that has been set on fire and left on the path, probably by a joyrider. A Tesco warehouse is followed by a series of silos and heaps of gravel.

More marine-dredged aggregate tumbles from the chute of a conveyor belt into a barge. Beer cans and the remains of a barbecue are strewn by a wall by a dilapidated jetty and a rusting crane. The delicate outline of the Queen Elizabeth II Bridge, also known as the Dartford Crossing, rises in the distance. Bird prints mark the mud near signs that warn of *SOFT MUD, RISK OF DROWNING*. A digger clanks loudly in a demolition yard. A man smoking a joint hustles past, hiding his smoke beneath a copy of *The Sun*. He appears surprised to see me, too.

Long shadows of an old wharf fan out across a mud bank on the outskirts of Erith. A stained information board says that Henry VIII's *Great Harry* was finally fitted out in the docks here and that Alexander Selkirk, on whom Robinson Crusoe was based, returned from his island exile to Erith in the eighteenth century. The board also says that 'it is not unusual to see seals and harbour porpoises in this reach'.

In the centre of Erith, the Playhouse is about to show *Billy Liar*. This is a quiet town in the London borough of Bexley, with a post office, a Paddy Power bookmakers, a Domino's takeaway pizzeria, a Morrisons supermarket and a short nineteenth-century pier that once attracted day trippers from central London. I go down the pier to see if I can spot any harbour porpoises. There are no porpoises about and I ask a couple of old-timer fishermen whether they have seen any today.

'In twenty years of fishing here I've seen porpoises four times,' says Dan, who is wearing braces and jeans, while his mate Bern is in a purple checked shirt. They have a manner that suggests they come most days to sit on this bench on Erith pier.

I ask what fish are to be caught. Dan tells me that he has landed bass, Dover sole, flounder, cod, whiting and sturgeon. Bern once caught a gurnard. Do they eat their catch?

'I wouldn't eat anything out of there,' says Dan, looking down at the water. 'Four or five years ago the fishing was very good here but then there was a storm and about eighty thousand gallons of sewage were released into the river. After that we didn't catch anything for a couple of years. It is cleaner than when I was a kid though. You could never go in the river then. Bloody 'ell, if you did you'd need injections.'

That must have been in the 1950s.

I say goodbye to Dan and Bern and leave Erith, passing a scrap-metal yard and an industrial estate where part-used tyres are available for £10. By now, it has turned into a very hot day; just about the hottest yet. The path on the edge of Erith is littered with broken glass and old cider cans, but this abruptly turns into a glorious salt marsh with reeds by mudflats on the edge of the river. This secretive marshland leads to the River Darent, a tributary to the Thames, where a flood barrier is in place, the Dartford Creek Tidal Barrier (1978).

Looking at the map earlier, I had wondered about this river as it seemed to be both in the way and bridge-less.

This is indeed, I discover, the case.

I read another information panel that tells me there used to be smallpox hospital boats here in the 1880s and that a fireworks factory was once on the banks near the marsh. Then, having no other choice, I head inland along the peaceful river on a path lined with blackberry bushes and purple wild flowers. I seem to have unwittingly joined the Bexley Canal Nature Loop. This takes me for three miles south and slightly westwards, via the Crayford Industrial Estate for a short period, before I find a road crossing of the River Darent and traipse back along the other side for a corresponding three miles.

In order to cross a space about as wide as a tennis court I have walked six extra miles, all in the baking midday sun.

Left somewhat nonplussed by the River Darent, I continue along the Thames, reaching another sewage treatment works and a power station. Across the river in Purfleet in Essex I can see more marine-dredged aggregate depots, an Esso Petroleum plant and a cargo ferry. On this side of the river I pass from Greater London into Kent, walking beneath the Queen Elizabeth II Bridge (1991) and listening to the murmur of vehicles high above on the M25 loop.

London has finally been and gone! It's seven days since I crossed under the M25 just before reaching Staines with my brother.

This section of the river path is peculiar yet rewarding simply for being so. The *Celandine*, a cargo ferry registered in Antwerp, awaits on the other side of the bridge, as does the small town of Greenhithe, not far from the Bluewater Shopping Centre. Feeling tired after my unexpected – and hot – six-mile 'add on', I go to the first place I see in Greenhithe, an Asda, and eat a sandwich at a cafe with a sticky floor and regular announcements requesting that Debbie should go to checkout 15. Then I walk along Greenhithe High Street, where there is a nice-looking riverside pub called the Sir John Franklin that I should have gone to for lunch.

Oh well, I'm thinking, but I don't really care. The route here takes me through Swanscombe Marshes and Broadness Salt Marsh by a bend known as Fiddler's Reach. After the salt marsh, the river has an industrial aspect with various wharves and 'works', according to my Ordnance Survey map, but that's not for too long before the path arrives at Gravesend, where I have a hotel booked by the pier.

I leave behind the graffiti saying *BILLY WAS EAR* and *WEED IS GOOD* on the edge of Greenhithe, and proceed to get thoroughly lost.

The way ahead seems simple, on tracks through the various marshes, but somehow or other, after passing beneath an electricity pylon several times at several points, I just cannot find a way out of Broadness Salt Marsh. Paths have been cut in the grass, but the paths seem to lead nowhere. The map does not appear to make sense. I go down to the edge of the river and contemplate cutting across an industrial plant, but I know that I will probably be shouted at for doing so (and possibly find myself in trouble with the law). So I return to Greenhithe and take a long hilly road into Gravesend. My detour into the marshes probably added an extra four miles to the day. That's ten miles of unexpected walking, in the heat.

I hobble past a tattoo parlour and a slot-machine centre and check into the Clarendon Royal Hotel, where I lie down for quite a long time in a massive room with a window facing the estuary.

Pocahontas, tattoo parlours and a good steak pie
Gravesend

After a while, I go downstairs. The manager is in the reception and he asks where I have come from today. 'You walked from Thamesmead?' he says. He seems genuinely shocked. No guest has ever, he says, walked to the Clarendon Royal Hotel from Thamesmead in the time he has been working here.

On this note, I go out to investigate Gravesend.

At the front of the Clarendon is a small lawn with picnic tables and a few yards away, upstream next to a pontoon, is the yellow-brick headquarters of the Port of London Authority. This point in the river is where coastal pilots hand over to the river pilots of the Port of London, whose job it is to direct large ships along the river. Downstream is a pier that was built in 1834 and lays claim to being the oldest remaining cast-iron pier in the world, while across the river are the Tilbury docks, fort and power station. Somewhere over there, beyond the wide choppy water, Elizabeth I geed up her troops.

The old pier is by a park with a statue of Squadron Leader Mahinder Singh Pujji DFC, who lived locally and who campaigned to have Sikh involvement in the Second World War more widely recognised. Beyond the park is St George's Church, where Pocahontas is believed to have been buried. The Native American – who achieved fame after intervening as a child to prevent the execution of an Englishman in Virginia, later marrying an Englishman (a different one), and travelling to England where she was presented to the court of King James I – was returning home from London in 1617 when her ship stopped at Gravesend. She had succumbed to tuberculosis. There is a statue of Pocahontas in the churchyard.

I go up the narrow high street with its tattoo parlours, Chinese restaurant, clothes shop selling saris, tailors with workers at a row of old-fashioned sewing machines, Afro Queen Hairs and Cosmetics boutique, spiritual cleansing centre, and Brilliant Buffet Worldwide Cuisine restaurant. The latter is sadly closed; I would have liked to have taken a look inside this brilliant worldwide buffet (and perhaps come back later for the cuisine). I go in a little loop around the shops. Gravesend has a subdued, sleepy atmosphere.

Then I return to the Clarendon, where a solitary blowsy woman is requesting a six o'clock Purple Rain vodka and cranberry cocktail at the bar.

Near the solitary blowsy woman is my dad.

My father, Robert, is wearing a lemon-yellow polo shirt, chinos and walking shoes. He has unfurled a map on a table and looks ready for action; he is joining me for the next two days on the final stretch of the walk to the Isle of Grain, staying overnight here in Gravesend and in the village of Cooling on the Hoo Peninsula.

I tell him about getting lost and my unscheduled excursion along the River Darent. He looks at the map more closely. A dark shadow falls across his features as he points to a far northern section of the Hoo Peninsula.

'We don't go to that bit,' he says. He seems, I cannot help detecting, a little concerned about my map-reading. 'My advice is we definitely don't go to that bit. The area north of Cooling.'

There is, I discover, a backstory to this particular concern. My father has been to the area north of Cooling before with a friend; they had been visiting to see the landscape that inspired the gripping beginning of Charles Dickens' novel *Great Expectations*. He and his friend had lost their way. 'So many ditches – it's impossible to get anywhere,' he explains.

I tell him not to worry. The path looks pretty easy to follow compared to today.

'Hmmm,' says my father.

And with that we go for dinner at the Three Daws pub, where I eat a good steak pie but my father is less pleased by his liver and bacon ('you don't usually put all this dark gravy over it'). We listen to pop music playing on a jukebox that has 'every hit since 1952' and look at some of the old photographs on the walls of the ancient inn, which dates back to the fifteenth century. Then we return to the Clarendon, where my father questions the name of his room, the John Silver Suite ('Who is John Silver? Should it not be Long John Silver?'). We say goodnight.

A journey into the marshes lies ahead, to the very end of the River Thames.

CHAPTER ELEVEN

GRAVESEND TO THE ISLE OF GRAIN, KENT

'LOOK, THERE'S ANOTHER ONE OF THOSE USELESS ARROWS'

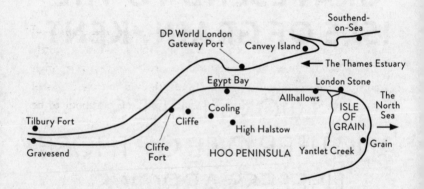

Joseph Conrad describes the Thames Estuary by Gravesend at the beginning of his novella *Heart of Darkness*. His narrator is on a ship anchored on the river, about to tell tales of life on another river, the Congo – and his surroundings establish the atmosphere of the stories to come: 'A haze rested on the low shores that ran out to sea in vanishing flatness. The air was dark above Gravesend, and farther back still seemed condensed into a mournful gloom, brooding motionless over the biggest, and the greatest, town on earth.'

The description captures something about the river as it nears the sea: it is big, bad and quietly dangerous… brooding. The trickle from Trewsbury Mead has taken on a whole new personality.

From my room at the Clarendon I look across the water as the great blue-and-white bulk of the *Cemíl Bayülgen*, a roll-on roll-off cargo vessel registered in Istanbul, glides by. This is followed shortly afterwards by the long, thin, cigarette shape of the *Finnhawk*, another cargo ship – this one from Helsinki. Across the way, on the banks of Tilbury, a warehouse-sized Grimaldi Lines cargo ship is about to be unloaded. Very large boats are out and about, doing things.

'Moses led his people for forty days and nights through the wilderness'
Gravesend to Cooling

My father and I leave Gravesend – named after a local bailiff called Grave or Graff many centuries ago (nothing, apparently, to do with graves) – through a park by the Port of London Authority HQ. Swans bob in the river by this park, quite happy in the salty water. We are uncertain which way to go and ask a courteous man for directions. He points the way ahead.

'You can say that the people of Kent are very friendly people,' says my father,who partly grew up in Kent (and still supports Gillingham Football Club).

The dog walker's directions send us along a path that squeezes between derelict corrugated warehouses.

This is perhaps the least attractive part of the walk to date, with rolls of discarded carpet, rusting fridges, threadbare lorry tyres and mouldy old sofas. The path seems to have turned into a fly-tip. Weeds and larger plants spring out of walls with broken windows and incomprehensible graffiti.

'Look at these derelict buildings. Look at all this rubbish. It will never be cleared up,' says my father, who is given to such statements. 'The thing that makes me sad is all the incredible effort that has gone into this.' He's referring to what once must have been a thriving place of industry. He stops to inspect a smashed air-conditioning unit. 'When Mrs Thatcher came back from Switzerland once, she said it was "time to clean up" Britain. It lasted about two or three weeks – everyone picked up litter from the side of the road. Then it was all forgotten.'

My father is not a fan of the late former Conservative Party prime minister.

Beyond this awful alley we stop by a working wharf with great coils of rusting chains, before coming to the Ship and Lobster pub. Here, the landlady Elizabeth Brown notices us peering through the window and invites us in to have a look even though the premises is closed. Inside is a delightfully old-fashioned boozer with wood-panelled walls, a dartboard, a row of taps for real ales, black-and-white pictures of ships and a few ship models.

'We get a lot of tuggies, watermen and fishermen,' says Elizabeth. 'This building is eighteenth century but there's been a pub here a long time. It's believed to have been in *Great Expectations*. He's meant to have written some of that here.'

A history framed on the wall by the bar explains that the pub was for centuries a meeting place for smugglers. It also quotes the passage from Dickens that is believed to describe the pub:

At length we descried a light and a roof, and presently afterwards ran alongside a little causeway made of stones that had been picked up hard by. Leaving the rest in the boat, I stepped ashore, and found the light to be in the window of a public house. It was a dirty place enough, and I dare say not unknown to smuggling adventurers; but there was a good fire in the kitchen, and there were eggs and bacon to eat, and various liquors to drink… I lay down with the greater part of my clothes on, and slept well for a few hours. When I awoke, the wind had risen, and the sign of the house (the Ship) was creaking and banging about, with noises that startled me.

My father and I thank Elizabeth for showing us around. The Ship and Lobster is a classic Thames pub that feels as though it has strong links to history, partly because it is still mainly frequented by watermen and -women. Nothing too fancy here… just beer and burgers and no messing about.

We keep on along the river, soon passing a yard in which the clanking of metal rings out.

'The old-fashioned term for heavy industry is metal-bashing,' says my father. 'Well, that is certainly going on here.' My father casts his eyes over the yard. 'The term is used in a rather derogatory way these days.' He pauses for a bit. 'Metal-bashing was the sort of thing that Mrs Thatcher despised. She wanted it all high-tech and IT.'

My father really does not like the late former Conservative Party prime minister.

Beyond this yard, the sound of guns comes from within a long, low building that houses the Metropolitan Police Specialist Training Centre. We traverse the stone remains of Shornemead Fort, upon which someone has scrawled: *GO BACK TO YOUR SHITHOLE 2014*. Maybe it's an anti-immigrant thing. We discuss this for a while, as well as recent attacks on immigrants in the UK. Slogans such as 'Leave the

EU – no more Polish vermin' have been bandied about, while a Polish community centre in Hammersmith, a short stroll from the Thames, has just been defaced with racist slurs.

Not the jolliest of topics but then, after Shornemead Fort, the scenery opens up. We have entered the marshland proper and we fall into silence, enjoying the sheer splendour of this little-visited corner of Britain. Ahead, the landscape rolls forth in a flat and intricate no man's land of ditches, wild flowers, brambles, shrubs and tall wispy grass. Late morning light seems to have bleached Kent of colour. We pass the rotting remains of the hull of a wooden ship (an old Finnish schooner from the 1960s). Gulls dive into silver-streaked waves. Sea smells rise from mudbanks. A cargo ship sails towards Gravesend, seeming to float on the grass of the marsh when the trail moves inland. It is a joy for me, after the very interesting but very built-up riverside inside the M25 to be back in the countryside.

Two elderly women emerge on the path.

'Good lord, what are they doing here, trespassing on our solitude?' asks my father. They are the first figures we have encountered since Gravesend, an hour or so back.

We say jolly 'good morning's to the two elderly women.

'I don't think they are long-distance walkers,' comments my father when they are out of earshot.

My father has a wry sense of humour.

And then we reach the fenced-off remains of Cliffe Fort, built to protect the country from foreign invaders in the nineteenth century and once home to a pioneering torpedo defence system. The path by the fort has collapsed into the river. We drop down on to the riverbed for a few steps before returning to the trail, cutting through a gravel yard and entering a large reserve overseen by the Royal Society for the Protection of Birds.

There is a choice of three routes across this reserve on the Ordnance Survey map, although the paths do not appear in reality exactly as they do on the map (at least, they do not seem to). My father asks which way I think we should go. I show him the map and point at the routes.

'I have faith implicitly in your leadership,' he says, leaving the decision to me. 'I have total faith. I put my footsteps where your footsteps fall. I banish the thought that you got lost four times yesterday. Moses led his people for forty days and nights through the wilderness…'

He continues in this fashion for a while. The long and the short of it being: *if we don't make it easily, backtrack-free, through the bird reserve… it's your fault.*

We do get lost in the bird reserve, despite receiving directions from a man (who is not at all clear in what he says). The signposts seem to point in all directions. 'Look, there's another one of those useless arrows,' says my father, who seems to have shed his total faith rather quickly. We do, however, eventually make it out of the bird reserve and climb a hill to the village of Cliffe, or, as my father now calls it, 'Britain's most hidden village'.

In this village we go to the Six Bells pub and eat ham sandwiches in a little garden, after quite a lot of mix-ups over brown and white bread and whether cheese or tomato is to go with our ham sandwiches. 'It's a nice pub,' says my father. 'It's a bit scatty and a bit slow but it's quite nice.'

Rather than risk the notorious 'area north of Cooling' with its many ditches – even locals at the Six Bells are not sure of the way through the area north of Cooling – we take a route along a lane and through a pear orchard to our target for the day. There is only minimal discussion of maps, although my father returns to the subject of the man who gave us directions in the bird reserve, who has become 'that stupid man who suggested cutting up the hill'.

In the village of Cooling we are staying at the Horseshoe and Castle pub, but before we go to the pub we have a couple of sights to see.

First, we stop to look at the grey-stone turreted gateway to Cooling Castle, which was built in the fourteenth century and was once home to Sir John Oldcastle, upon whom Shakespeare based Falstaff. Now the musician and television presenter Jools Holland lives in the castle. Second, we visit St James' Church, where 13 tiny graves are to be found in the churchyard. These poignant graves, belonging to children who died between 1767 and 1854, are referenced in the opening passage of *Great Expectations* when Pip is describing his childhood (in the book they are reduced in number to 'five little stone lozenges'). Inside the church there is an information panel explaining that Dickens visited here with his son Charles, author of *Dickens's Dictionary of the Thames, 1887*, and picnicked in the churchyard. His son said that his father 'loved Cooling Church more than any other'. I pick up a handset and an audio version of the opening passage plays out.

Listening to the words echo across the church is a spine-tingling sensation. The passage seems to freeze in time the scenery at Cooling:

> Ours was the marsh country, down by the river, within, as the river wound, twenty miles of the sea. My first most vivid and broad impression of the identity of things, seems to me to have been gained on a memorable raw afternoon towards evening. At such a time I found out for certain, that this bleak place overgrown with nettles was the churchyard; and that Philip Pirrip, late of this parish, and also Georgiana wife of the above, were dead and buried; and that Alexander, Bartholomew, Abraham, Tobias, and Roger, infant children of the aforesaid, were also dead and buried; and that the dark flat wilderness beyond the churchyard, intersected with dykes and mounds and gates, with scattered cattle feeding on it, was the marshes; and that the low leaden line beyond, was the river; and that the distant savage lair from which the wind was rushing, was the sea; and that the small bundle of shivers growing afraid of it all and beginning to cry, was Pip.

This part of the River Thames, like so many others, is pure Dickens.

'There have been some who were lost on the marshland, mind you'
Cooling

The Horseshoe and Castle is a cream-coloured, pebble-dashed building with gables and hanging plants. There is a pleasant terrace with seats at the front and a vine-covered outhouse at the back with three clean and comfortable bedrooms. The bar is an eclectic space with drawings of Dickens characters on the walls, a collection of miniature bottles, a cricket bat inscribed by the players of Kent County Cricket Club and a signed photograph of Jools Holland.

At the bar we meet Stuart Boyle, son of the landlord Kevin, who gives us our keys and tells us that if we take a path near the castle we will reach the sea wall to continue our walk tomorrow morning. There is a problem, however. 'They are building a bung wall down there,' says Stuart. It is unclear both who 'they' are and what a 'bung wall' is.

Before we get a chance to ask, Nathan, a local carpenter who knows Stuart, cuts in. 'No, no, no,' he says, and he proceeds to tell us no fewer than three ways to find the Thames from Cooling, each subtly different from Stuart's way of locating the river. 'You'll be absolutely fine,' he concludes. 'I've lived here all my life. You really, really won't get lost. It is an enjoyable walk.'

The final route that Nathan seems to have settled upon, the 'best' route across the tricky marsh, involves skirting a farm and another pear orchard.

Stuart nods knowingly and adds: 'There have been some who were lost on the marshland, mind you.'

My father asks Stuart what he means by this.

'Oh,' says Stuart, sounding very casual about this information. 'A guy came for a drink once and said he'd be back in a couple of hours.

Well, he did come back – pretty red-faced, he was – at nine o'clock that night. Many hours later. The map he'd had was out of date as the land had changed so much. They're always cutting new dykes. Luckily a farmer saw him and he jumped in a tractor. It does get unnerving out there. That's why I always give out cards.'

Stuart provides us both with cards with the pub's number.

My father assimilates this briefing and looks at me, wordlessly.

Another local, whose name I do not catch, adds that he believes the sea wall has been bulldozed near Egypt Bay.

His friend adds, rather unhelpfully it must be said: 'I live here but I've never been that way.'

My father assimilates this additional briefing and gives me another look. The eyes say: *Can you make head or tail of any of this?*

I return his look with one of my own that answers: *Your guess is as good as mine.*

It has been a long day. We have covered quite a distance – more than 14 miles, according to the tracking device (and the tracking device never lies).

The terrace at the Horseshoe and Castle is a fine place to while away some time. I do so reading the papers in the sun. The main story in the *Gravesend Messenger* is all about 'rowdy teenagers' going on a 'wrecking rampage' smashing cars for a 'game' in Gravesend. Another concerns a local train hitting a scooter that had been dumped on the tracks. Police have fined a lorry driver for watching television at the wheel, and there are 'safety and hygiene fears' regarding a group of travellers in a park in Gravesend. A columnist in a 'Monday Moan' column, headlined *WE DON'T NEED THIS 'COLOURFUL VIBRANCY'*, says that travellers such as these have been trespassing and 'causing mayhem' involving criminal damage. Officials, he says, are slow to step in as they do not wish to be accused of racism. This is a 'politically correct absurdity'.

Meanwhile the ramifications of Brexit continue to play out. Sterling is at its lowest against the American dollar since 1985, with economists predicting that inflation will rise as a result of more expensive imports. At some bureaux de change a pound is now worth less than a euro. There has also been a sharp increase in immigration. *The Guardian* runs a story highlighting that 110,000 workers have arrived from outside the UK in the second quarter of the year, compared to 58,000 in the first quarter. It is the summer recess of the Houses of Parliament and *The Times* points out that, with Prime Minister Theresa May on holiday, Boris Johnson, the foreign secretary and leading Brexiteer, is in charge of the country. *CRIPES!* says the headline. And in France, Prime Minister Manuel Valls has backed a ban on the wearing of burkinis, full-body swimsuits used by Muslim women at the seaside. Such swimsuits, he says in *The Guardian*, are 'not compatible with the values of the French Republic'.

Oh, what a strange world.

My father and I have an enjoyable dinner at the Horseshoe and Castle, which feels, for the time being at least, far removed from the troubles raging elsewhere on the planet.

'If we get lost, we can always blame Nathan'
Cooling to Allhallows

When I wake, just after six o'clock in the morning, the sun is rising in a ruby orb above a field shrouded in mist. I go outside and watch for a while as the day begins on the Hoo Peninsula.

Over breakfast, Kevin Boyle, who has been landlord at the Horseshoe and Castle for 27 years, regales us with stories about Richard Burton, the nineteenth-century explorer whose grave I saw in Mortlake. Kevin, a large jovial man from Chatham in Kent ('the nut did not fall far from the tree'), is a fan of Burton, who he describes as a 'swashbuckling Victorian hero'.

'The explorers then were the spacemen of their age,' Kevin says. 'He was zonked out on laudanum and brandy every night, you know.

I read a biography. He spoke sixteen languages. He was the first European to translate the *Kama Sutra*. He went to Mecca and to South America too.'

Kevin is a salt-of-the-earth landlord, with many a story (a kind of perfect publican). He hopes one day to do the 'Jerome K. Jerome method' of travelling along the Thames in a skiff. He says that farms near Cooling produce cereals and strawberries ('a big business for them') and some raise sheep. He loves music and has seen Eric Clapton, Amy Winehouse, Smokey Robinson, Paul Weller, Sting and many others play live. He does not like flying to go on holiday: 'I took a cheap flight on a cheap plane once and once only. Who would fly? It's no fun any more.'

Bacon and eggs to the good, we leave the Horseshoe and Castle, and Kevin points in the vague direction of the marshes, wishing us luck. Both my father and I are now firmly of the opinion, correctly or incorrectly held, that no one on the Hoo Peninsula has the faintest idea of the way through the marshes north of Cooling.

We decide to stick to roads away from the river before cutting north through the village of High Halstow to Egypt Bay and then taking what looks like a simple route along a sea wall to the village of Allhallows. This is where we will come to Yantlet Creek, which separates the Hoo Peninsula from the Isle of Grain. From Allhallows we will be able to see the London Stone, which historically marks the official end of the City of London's control of the River Thames. There is another such marker across the river at Leigh-on-Sea in Essex (as well as the corresponding stone way back in Staines). My father intends to take a cab to Rochester train station and return home once we reach Allhallows. I am going to push on to the Isle of Grain, beyond Yantlet Creek, to go as far as I can possibly go along the Thames in Kent.

We set off along a lane with little traffic other than the odd tractor laden with bales of hay. The landscape is hilly on the way to High Halstow and my father comments accurately: 'You could be a million miles from the Thames here, couldn't you?' The village of High Halstow is much larger than Cooling. 'It's actually got a zebra crossing,' says my father.

A 191 bus passes and my father considers whether to take the bus later, rather than call a cab: 'The late Bill Deedes said always travel by bus – you see more of life than in a taxi.'

We walk on through High Halstow, whose population, we have read, suffered terribly from 'marsh fever' (malaria) in centuries gone by; life expectancy was 30 years in the eighteenth century. It is also *Home of the Heron*, says a sign, referring to an RSPB reserve with 200 pairs of herons; a greater concentration than anywhere else in Britain.

We get to another sign. This one simply says, *Footpath*.

'Putting up a sign saying "footpath" doesn't help at all. It's like putting up a sign saying "road",' comments my father, again accurately.

Beyond is a further, green, sign that says, *Saxon Shore Way*. This is next to a purple sign saying, *Curlews, Convicts and Contraband*, which appears to be some sort of themed walk. An additional, yellow, sign says, *Circular Walk*.

'Again, incredibly unhelpful,' says my father, again accurately. We are not really sure where we're going.

'We seem to have gone a long way to the left,' says my father. 'If we get lost, we can always blame Nathan.'

He is on good form this morning.

We continue along a path lined with reeds next to marshland that has been drained to allow cattle to graze. In the distance we can see the giraffe-like cranes of the DP World London Gateway Port and the cooling towers of what looks like a power station on the other side of the river. The path brings us back to the river at Egypt Bay, a former haunt of smugglers, who used the bay to land contraband. A house here has all its windows facing inland so smugglers inside it could see customs officers approaching from the land. Apparently it was once a base of the notorious North Kent Gang.

We join the grassy sea-wall trail, walking alongside channels and ditches. A cockle boat is anchored close to the sea wall, while out in the 'sea' – the Thames no longer feels like a river here – a massive Maersk Line cargo ship topped with containers putters towards DP World London Gateway Port, accompanied by pilot boats. Another ship sails, looking empty, towards the North Sea. 'Returning to China full of fresh air,' comments my father.

Much of the marsh here cannot have changed much for centuries. We are at a wild, isolated spot without a soul in sight. I leap down on to a sandy beach and have my picture taken on the best Thames beach so far. Then we press on beyond St Mary's Bay along the river, buzzed by scarlet dragonflies.

On the horizon the sky fades from metallic blue to shades of lilac, meeting the green-grey line of the sea. We get lost one more time on the edge of Allhallows, having to walk a long way inland up a hill by a wheat field before taking a road into the village, thus bypassing Allhallows Leisure Holiday Park. There were once plans, in the 1930s, to build an amusement park four times the size of Blackpool at Allhallows. But then the war happened and the proposal – which would have included the construction of the largest swimming pool in Britain plus a series of hotels, restaurants and theatres – was dropped, leaving this much more modest park. 'With all the will in the world, I can't see how a latter-day Blackpool would have worked out here' is my father's appraisal. He is tickled by the thought of a latter-day Blackpool, hidden away on the marsh on the edge of the Hoo Peninsula.

In search of a bread sandwich
Allhallows

In Allhallows we are not sure where the centre of the village is. I ask a man with grey hair and glasses, wearing an England football shirt, if there is a pub nearby for lunch. He is loading a van in the driveway of a house in a small terrace.

'You want a pub?' he asks.

I have just told him I want a pub.

'Yes,' I say.

'You've got to go to Stoke for a pub,' he says. He points southwards along a road.

Stoke, another village, looks quite a long way on the map. I ask if there is a pub in Allhallows village instead.

'It's not a village – it's just a place, mate,' he says.

He is with a friend who smirks when he says this.

'Is there a pub in the place?' I ask.

'There's the Pilot,' says the man in the England shirt.

His friend smirks once again, for some reason known only to himself.

'Which way is that?' I ask.

'Down that lane,' he replies.

I thank the man in the England shirt for his assistance.

My father, who has been listening to this, has taken against Allhallows. 'I bet it's a dump,' he says, as we walk down a hill to the British Pilot pub.

A St George's Cross, with *ENGLAND* written in the middle, hangs from a front window of the British Pilot pub. On the door is a picture of two fierce-looking dogs. Accompanying this picture is a message: *WE LIVE HERE. WE CAN GET TO THE GATE IN THREE SECONDS.* I go inside ahead of my father, who pauses outside to look around, entering a dimly lit chamber with a pool table in a corner and one customer drinking lager at the bar. While messing about trying to undo the knot of my backpack, I ask the barmaid, who is wearing a pink top and has Cleopatra-like eyebrows, whether they do any sandwiches.

'You've got the menu,' she says, eyeing a menu I had not noticed on the bar.

Her expression is completely deadpan.

'Oh,' I reply, in a *silly me* way. 'Thanks.'

Her expression remains completely deadpan.

'Have you been having a good day?' I ask, trying to lighten the atmosphere. 'Been busy?'

'No,' says the barmaid in the pink top. She is now holding a pint glass as though waiting for me, finally, to decide what I would like to drink.

I order a lager.

My father enters the British Pilot pub.

He comes up to the bar and enquires of the barmaid in a jovial manner whether she knows the number of a local cab firm.

The man at the bar looks at my father as though he does not know what he is getting himself into.

'Not off the top of my head,' replies the barmaid.

'I'm not asking for it off the top of your head. I just wondered if you had a number written down somewhere here,' says my father.

The barmaid looks momentarily astonished.

'I don't know,' she says. 'There's not one round here, to be honest. Not that I know of.'

Her completely deadpan expression clicks back into place.

The British Pilot offers baguettes. We are about to order a couple of these, having had two lagers plonked on the bar.

My father, however, prefers bread sandwiches to baguettes. He asks the barmaid in the pink top whether he could have his with bread: 'Do you do a bread sandwich?'

The barmaid in the pink top looks momentarily astonished once again.

'What?' asks the barmaid.

'Bread!' says my father. 'A bread sandwich: do you do one?'

'No, we put cement round it,' says the barmaid, taking the encounter to a new level of friendliness. Taken at face value, she seems to be suggesting that the pub makes sandwiches with cement rather than bread.

The barmaid sighs and disappears to the kitchen with our order and the good-natured man at the bar – checking that the barmaid does not notice him do so – whispers the number of a local cab firm. We go to a table outside wondering what we will eat for lunch.

Perhaps a quarter of an hour later, a chef arrives. He is a polite man and he asks what type of bread we would like.

The polite chef departs.

We discuss the barmaid for a while.

'It's not her – it's her brothers that I'm worried about,' says my father. There is a slightly menacing feeling in the air.

Not long after he says this, the barmaid arrives with the well-made sandwiches, which come with side salads.

'Would you like cutlery with that?' she asks.

We say we'll be fine without, thanks, not wishing to upset matters (and then realising it will be tricky eating the salad).

We have no napkins either.

The barmaid in a pink top has departed.

My father has a conversation with a cab firm and books a cab to arrive shortly.

'I thought he was going to say: "I'm not going there, mate. I'll get my tyres slashed,"' he comments.

My father has taken somewhat against Allhallows.

After a while, his taxi for Rochester station comes and we say goodbye. It's been a truly brilliant couple of days, even if getting about in the marshes has been a touch tricky (and despite the threat of 'cement sandwiches' in Allhallows).

On the edge of the river
Allhallows to the Isle of Grain

I remain at the picnic table, where I am joined by an elderly blonde cleaner working at the British Pilot who is having a cigarette break. She is a companionable sort and she tells me that she was under the impression that my father and I were twitchers. Apparently a lot have been in the area recently as a rare red-backed shrike has been spotted. Only a couple of the birdwatchers have visited the pub. Perhaps being regarded as twitchers was the cause of some sort of confusion earlier.

Not sure quite what to make of the British Pilot, I backtrack slightly to investigate Allhallows Leisure Holiday Park. The road to the park is blocked by a barrier attended by a burly man with a Geordie accent. He tells me to 'make sure you stay on the paths', to 'be careful with your camera – there are kids about' and that 'you can't use any of the facilities'. I walk along the path through this could-have-been-Blackpool, with its rows of simple holiday homes, SPAR mini-market, indoor pool and five-a-side football pitch, before regaining the sea wall and covering a short distance to the mouth of Yantlet Creek. It is low tide and across a long expanse of mud and sand I can see the fabled London Stone, an obelisk on a seaweed-black plinth about 30 metres off the edge of the Isle of Grain, beyond the mouth of Yantlet Creek.

For a moment or two, I stand and simply stare at the obelisk. For me this stone – so close, yet so far away across the creek – will mark the end of my Thames walk, from source to sea. Tomorrow morning I'm going to go over to the London Stone from the Isle of Grain, where I'll be staying tonight in the main settlement, the village of Grain.

First, however, I need to cross Yantlet Creek on to the Isle of Grain.

This requires following a long path next to the creek, heading in the direction of the cooling tower of a disused power station and several natural-gas containers poking up at the southern tip of the 'island'. The isle is no longer technically an isle as it is firmly connected to the Hoo Peninsula by landfill and a road. Yantlet Creek was once wider and maintained as such to allow boats to pass from the Medway in the south to the Thames, reducing the journey time around the Nore sandbank at the mouth of the Thames. However, in the mid nineteenth century this passageway ended when a road came for good. In the late nineteenth century the Isle of Grain had a railway connection and a pier at a southern point known as Victoria Port (Queen Victoria herself sailed from there). The pier closed in 1951. Part of the north of the isle is now a Ministry of Defence military firing range and is marked on my Ordnance Survey map as a 'DANGER AREA'; this section is near the London Stone and I am wondering if I'll be able to walk around to see the obelisk up close.

The Isle of Grain – as well as the marshes near Cliffe, where my father and I got lost in the bird reserve – has been suggested as a site for a Thames Estuary airport. The man currently (temporarily) running the country also considered the viability of an airport island, nicknamed 'Boris Island', at a place out at sea known as Shivering Sands, beyond the Isle of Grain and the Isle of Sheppey. Now that the extra runway at Heathrow appears to be going ahead, all of these suggestions seem unlikely to come to fruition. The population of the Isle of Grain is just 1,648 (at the last count). Its name comes from an Old English word for 'gravel'. It is about three and a half miles long and two and a half miles wide, consisting mainly of marshland. There is something intriguing about this unusual isle at the very end of the Thames.

Eventually the path reaches a small bridge across the creek. This does not seem to be the main bridge to the island. It is scorching hot and I am tired from what has turned out to be a long day's walk. Various signs warn of various dangers: *Military Firing Range: do not touch any military debris, it may explode and kill you*; *No access to sea defences – dangerous tidal conditions*; and *This is MoD property. Any persons entering do so at their own risk*. I only spot this last notice after walking up a road past a remote row of houses and turning back to read it.

Shortly afterwards I reach the village of Grain and the Lodge Guest House, which is tucked down a driveway near a church and a Co-operative store. I am met by Henry, the owner, who is wearing a 2012 Olympics T-shirt and has a big smile, gangly limbs and green-grey eyes.

'Oh, bless you! Bless you! Welcome! Bless you!' he says when I arrive and he discovers I have walked from Cooling via Allhallows.

He apologises that I do not have a room in the main part of the guest house and am instead in the family home, with use of a toilet down a hall. He has given me a £20 discount for this inconvenience. 'Bless you!' he says, handing over the note.

I am shown a plain room that looks perfectly comfortable. I drop my backpack here and Henry and I have a chat in the breakfast room.

'We get all sorts here. We did have a couple of Thames walkers – they'd done the whole river over a year and a half,' he says.

I ask him the way to the London Stone.

'That area is run by the Royal Engineers, I think,' he says. 'Twice a year you hear a bang. It's a little bit dangerous, but there's no quicksand. I've never been there. Never done it personally.'

Henry recommends that I go and take a look at a mid-nineteenth-century fort in the sea on the edge of the village. 'It's got an address,' he says. 'The address is: One the Thames. Someone's trying to sell it. Apparently Guy Ritchie was in the pub saying he was going to turn it into a restaurant.'

He pauses for a moment. 'That's just gossip,' he adds. 'It's £500,000 on the Rightmove website.'

As I go back to my room, Henry says: 'Apologies if it's not quite hotel standards.'

I say I like it.

'Oh, bless you! Bless you!' says Henry.

I go to see the old fort on the edge of the Isle of Grain.

It is about 6 p.m. now; it has been an epic day already but it feels as though I'm walking on air without my backpack. I come to a long concrete sea-protection wall that runs along the village, with the Nore stretching beyond in so many shades of grey it is tricky to detect exactly where the sea meets the sky in the bright late afternoon sunlight. The mysterious bulk of the old fort, which may or may not become a restaurant run by Madonna's former husband, lies some way out in the water in the direction of Sheerness. Somewhere beneath the waves here is the wreck of the *SS Richard Montgomery*, an American ship that sank in 1944 with a cargo of 1,400 tonnes of (still unexploded and highly dangerous) explosives.

I walk as far as the cooling tower of the old power station and return to Grain, where I eat a good last supper in the sunny back-room restaurant of the sixteenth-century Hogarth Inn pub.

Afterwards I go to the bar of the pub, with its low beams, dartboards and *No Bloody Swearing* sign. A large man is sitting alone by the window with a bottle of red wine to himself, watching the Olympics on a television. He and a few other regulars are sitting in silence, though my presence has made him curious. Not many outsiders seem to drop by.

The large man asks what brings me here, and when I began my walk. When I tell him, he says: 'I suppose that's an achievement.'

The large man has a droll outlook, and plenty of stories. He seems to be holding court at the Hogarth Inn on this August evening. He tells me that his father was a lighterman on barges and that he himself used to be an engineer on tankers that took oil as far as Mortlake. He says that there was once a tug called *The London Stone* that 'hit a swell and rolled over and all the crew were lost'. He asks if I stayed in Gravesend and says that a pub up the road from the Three Daws, where my father and I ate, 'used to be a knocking shop'.

Get talking to a Thames 'river person', as I long ago discovered, and there are usually many tales waiting to be told.

'There's a lot of history round here,' he says, topping up his wine.

To which a woman who has been quietly listening to us replies: 'There's a lot of history everywhere, you doughnut!'

The large man plays at being offended. 'I'd go and sulk if I wasn't so thick-skinned,' he says.

And so concludes my final evening on the Thames trail.

I go back to the Lodge Guest House, where someone is playing a saxophone in the garage, and fall fast asleep in my plain but perfectly comfortable room.

CHAPTER TWELVE

THE LONDON STONE, ISLE OF GRAIN, KENT

RIVER'S END

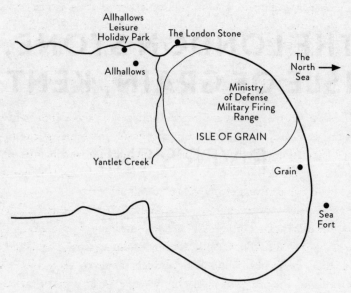

THE THAMES

Allhallows
Leisure
Holiday Park

The London Stone

The
North
Sea →

Allhallows

Ministry
of Defense
Military Firing
Range

ISLE OF GRAIN

Yantlet Creek

Grain

Sea
Fort

THE MEDWAY

Mist hangs over the potentially exploding marshes of the north of the Isle of Grain. It is cool in the early morning. Crickets chirp. Gulls cackle. Rabbits race to burrows. Dew glistens on the sea wall as the sun slowly rises, yolk-like, above the old power station, casting soft yellow light on the surface of Yantlet Creek.

There does indeed seem to be a way forward by the sea wall to the London Stone, avoiding all danger areas.

I walk along the isolated path, hoping not to create a bang.

By chance, the tide is out. At the stone I cross the slippery, rocky surface of the riverbed and pat the granite obelisk for good luck. The stone dates from 1856, and I cannot make out the eroded writing on its side.

So this is it then, I say to myself. From a field in Gloucestershire to the sea in Kent. Job done, you could say.

This journey has, I know and happily admit, been a total indulgence.

There is no great 'why' behind this adventure – no burning reason – just a fascination with the River Thames, an interest that comes simply from living beside the waterway for most of my life and a desire to explore its banks (that so many others seem to share).

Over 21 days covering 368 miles, about 17 miles a day, I have certainly done some exploring. I look across the misty sea thinking of the early days in Cricklade and Lechlade tramping along with Simon and Jamie, the shepherd's hut in Newbridge, the sleepy *Three Men in a Boat* villages, the meadows by Oxford where *Alice in Wonderland* was born, the pretty banks by Marlow, Henley and Cookham, the fantastic sense of history at Runnymede (and so many other spots), the tea room delights of Dorchester, the spirits of the castle at Wallingford, the quads of Eton, the intrigues of the suburbs, the switch to the tidal river, the travellers beneath bridges, the lifeboat-man, the policeman, the pub crawls (the many pubs!), the night on the barge, the tunnels, the cable cars, the edge-lands beyond the barrier, the mysterious industrial zones, the sewage works in a nature reserve, the Thamesmead Travelodge, the tales of Dickens and Conrad, and Chaucer and Shakespeare too… and now here, finally, the marshland.

I have covered a lot of ground. I have seen and done a lot. I have learnt a great deal and met many people. I have lost some weight. My legs are tired. And I have loved (almost) every moment.

A cargo ship forms a faint grey outline on the horizon. From the London Stone, I can hardly make out the opposite bank. Somewhere straight ahead is Southend-on-Sea, or so it says on the map. I take a few deep breaths of salty air, thinking of what a strange summer it has been in so many ways, and return across the riverbed to the Isle of Grain and the Lodge.

A florid-faced man in the breakfast room says he has been staying at the guest house for two months although he is 'just passing through' and 'doing a little business'. 'What business?' I ask.

'The entertainment business,' he replies enigmatically.

Yet another character; the river seems to attract them.

Henry says a final 'Bless you!' upon discovering I have already seen the London Stone this morning.

I read an article in *The Sun on Sunday* about the prime minister and a senior Conservative politician arguing about Brexit. 'The referendum was not a suggestion,' says Iain Duncan Smith. 'It was an order from the British people to Britain's ruling elite to "take back control".' The prime minister should pay attention to the British people, says Iain Duncan Smith.

Then I catch a taxi to Rochester, my first vehicle in three weeks, take my first train in three weeks to London, and my first bus in three weeks across Hammersmith Bridge to Mortlake.

And I am home.

Back by the river.

AFTERWORD

It is fifteen months since I completed my Thames walk, and I write this sitting in my study at my flat in Mortlake, two hundred metres from the river – my subject flowing serenely past the little green by the old electricity depot at the end of my road.

While writing *From Source to Sea* I would frequently pop down to the river to clear my head after a long spell at the keyboard, sometimes strolling towards the source as far as Richmond (about five miles), other times heading towards the sea to Hammersmith (about two miles). I've kept up my river walks since then, always amazed at the quiet that is to be had by these Thames-side banks so close to the centre of London, yet seemingly so far away. Along the towpaths here, even on weekend mornings, you often find yourself alone for long stretches, with just the odd squirrel or heron for company.

My favourite local stroll is to Richmond on a sunny day with the promise of a pint at the White Cross pub at the end; its beer garden must be one of the jolliest on the river. On one such peregrination with my girlfriend, I found the pages of my walk come alive in the form of Graham, the homeless man I encountered on my way in to London for the book. He was in the exact same spot by an arch by Twickenham Bridge. For an instant his jade-green eyes locked on mine with a flicker of recognition. We nodded at one another in the manner of old acquaintances and have done so since; the bridge must be his favourite patch.

I have once returned to the source, again with my girlfriend. We were travelling through the Cotswolds and she was curious to see the beginning of the river. So we made a detour and parked at the Thames Head Inn and walked along the short stretch of the Fosse Way, before crossing fields to the point with the underground spring. Yet again, nobody was around and no water could be seen. Even the hole at Lyd Well was dry on that late summer day. Afterwards, at the Thames Head Inn, it felt like a homecoming. There was the William Tombleson map of the river. There was the bust of Old Father Thames. And there, to my surprise, was *From Source to Sea*, advertised on a board; the landlady had a few copies to sell behind the bar.

That autumn I took to the water itself, along with about sixty others, on *The Hibernia*, a river cruiser with observation windows for tourists. The Henley Literary Festival had invited me to give a talk about the book while floating on the subject; another homecoming of sorts. It turned out that many among the very knowledgeable audience had themselves walked the full length of the river (one couple in a remarkable twelve days), while others were in the midst of completing the feat in sections or contemplating the adventure. What struck me, as we puttered to Temple Island and back, was just how fondly the river was held in the hearts of those there. For them, as for me, the Thames clearly had – and has – a very special allure.

Why is that? Well the more I consider this, having learnt so much about the river on my long walk, the more I believe that the Thames possesses a kind of magic that comes simply from having witnessed so much over the centuries. The lure is in its timelessness, its wisdom… and its ghosts.

The office of *The Times*, where I work, is close to the river in Southwark. During lunch breaks, it is curious to consider the days of the Winchester Geese who once plied their trade by London Bridge. Where the ladies of the night once walked, millennials now buy artisan bread, Singaporean noodles and kangaroo burgers. Fine wines from New Zealand are to be had alongside the best French cheeses and cured hams from Spain. After work, I sometimes go with colleagues for a drink at the George Inn. It's a lovely old place in an alley just off Borough High Street beyond a Ryman stationery shop. Dickens came here. Shakespeare probably enjoyed a tipple or two (in the pub's earlier incarnation). Chaucer would have known its old courtyard.

Then there is the story of Olaf Haraldsen and the defeat of the Danish at London Bridge. Then there are memories of river frost fairs. Then there is the legend of Eleanor of Provence collecting her London Bridge tolls (while letting the structure fall into disrepair). Then there are the tales of the dastardly goings-on downstream at the Tower.

This is just near my office. The point is that the river has seen a lot and will see much more. It is, if you like, a constant, offering a form of reassurance in our mad, bad world. It has its course. It follows its bends. The tide flows in and out.

And there has, of late, been plenty of madness. The summer of 2016, looking back, feels somehow like a gentler age. Now, the tortuous and often bitter process of enacting Brexit continues to be played out, dragged onwards by politicians (some of whom do not even believe in the project). A snap general election has resulted in a weakened prime minister. The British economy falters. Donald Trump's victory – inconceivable as I ambled along England's longest river – sends worrying ripples across the globe; nuclear war with North Korea (prone to firing test missiles over Japan) is a real possibility, say some.

Leaders trade insults via Twitter. Journalists are accused of 'false news' (so regularly that real news is disbelieved). Authoritarian leaders rise in Europe. Far right groups gain members. It seems as though the world wobbles almost every day. It may just have been fifteen months ago that I checked in to the Thames Head Inn, but it feels a whole lot longer than that.

The Thames has also witnessed Islamic terrorist attacks. As this book was going to press in hardback in March 2017, Khalid Masood, aged 52, drove a car onto the pavement of Westminster Bridge, mowing down pedestrians and injuring 50 people – four of them fatally. He then stabbed to death PC Keith Palmer at the Houses of Parliament before being shot by armed guards and dying. One of those killed included Andreea Cristea, a 31-year-old tourist from Romania, who fell into the Thames as the deadly car swerved by.

The former Metropolitan Police commissioner Sir Bernard Hogan-Howe's prediction – that 'it is a question of when, not if' an attack would occur by the river – has proven tragically accurate. A bridge so loved by Wordsworth and Turner has seen a bloodbath – and it was not long afterwards, in June 2017, that a van driven by three Islamic terrorists struck pedestrians on London Bridge before careering to a halt on the south side. The attackers then began stabbing people near restaurants and pubs in Borough Market, some of which I frequent. Eight people were killed and 48 injured. The attackers were shot dead by police. For days afterwards while the police investigated the crime scene, the office of *The Times* was cordoned off and closed.

*

I have kept in touch with some of those I met by the river. Simon wrote to tell me that he and his son Jamie made it from the source of the Thames as far as Hampton Court, covering 170 miles in 16 days. His 'random thoughts from the path' were wide and varied. 'Who put the Himalayas between Goring and Pangbourne?' he asked. 'When did the English forget what a real pub should be? Why aren't boat-hire companies fined for boats capable of more than four knots? Who needs a three-storey cabin cruiser on the Thames? Hikers seem to be clean and day trippers filthy. The richer the area, the more unfriendly the inhabitants; ditto, the bigger the boat. The river, when visible, is the highlight: always sedate. One mile it is very English, the next like a steamy Louisiana bayou or maybe the Amazon.'

Karen, the human resources officer for Peterborough City Council, whom I met as deer frolicked in a wheat field near Newbridge, emailed to say that she and her friend Toni got as far as Castle Eaton on their walk from Oxford. They had hoped to reach Cricklade but found it 'quite difficult as the signage was less effective than on other parts of the walk.' They intend to complete the final section soon.

Jan, with whom I shared a pizza in Pangbourne, reached Rotherhithe on the latest stage of her walk from the source to the Thames Barrier. She had a 'wonderful afternoon in the sunset,' she said, 'tramping through Bermondsey to Rotherhithe, occasionally looking back across the cluster of buildings around Whitechapel and Tower Hamlets with windows lit up in gold.' She is considering going beyond the barrier all the way to the Isle of Grain.

Anton, whom I met at the Mayflower pub in Rotherhithe before he went to watch Crystal Palace versus West Bromwich Albion, has also written. He was devastated by Donald Trump's presidential win. 'The election result caught everyone in New York by surprise,' he said. 'The city voted overwhelmingly for Hillary, so needless to say everyone was quite shocked the morning after.' But despite the election disappointment, we continue to build bridges and not walls. Anton and I are planning to watch a Premier League match together one day.

Walking the Thames can be very social. People do seem simply to like the river, often opening up to others as though this is just a natural thing to do.

I don't have far to go to take another look. Perhaps a pint at the White Hart is in order – won't take me long to get there.

Cheers! And, happy walking.

January, 2018

ACKNOWLEDGEMENTS

Many people I met on the trail gave their time and their stories; some are mentioned within the text and there were many others (apologies to anyone I have missed out). Special thanks go to my parents, Robert Chesshyre and Christine Doyle, my brother Edward Chesshyre, my sister Kate Chesshyre, John Kiddle and Laura Ivill, each of whom proved to be great company on sections of the long walk. I would also like to thank Kate Quill, Lysbeth Fox, Zsuzsa Simko, Alasdair MacTavish, Danny Kelly, Damian Whitworth, Ben Clatworthy, Jamie Fox, Luisa Uruena and Clare Buckler for their encouragement. Thanks also to David Smith (for his information about river illustrations); Sophie Lucas, Colin Boag and Peter Woodward (for information on Doggett's Coat and Badge Race, which I was unfortunately unable to squeeze in); Melanie Wright (for information about Cooling); John Fielding (for his wild flower expertise); Helena Caletta of the Open Book in Richmond (for her advice on books about the river); the team at Stanfords in Covent Garden (for their ongoing support); and Denise Kelly and Michael Hartley (for their help with the Tombleson cover). Special thanks must go to Jane Knight, travel editor of *The Times*, and to Lesley Thomas, *Weekend* editor of *The Times*. I am also grateful to Christopher Somerville, *The Times* walks correspondent, Christina Hardyment and Harry Bucknall for kindly casting their eyes over the proofs.

The enthusiasm of Claire Plimmer, editorial director at Summersdale, gave me the boost needed to get this book off the ground, for which I am very grateful. I would also like to especially thank Debbie Chapman for her astute line edit, Madeleine Stevens for her excellent copy-edit, Robert Drew for diligently overseeing the project, Hamish Braid for the maps, Lizzie Curtin for her energetic publicity, Derek Donnelly for his proofread and Joanne Phillips for the index.

DISTANCE COVERED

Day 1 – Around Thames Head: 30,543 steps, 21.93 kilometres (13.70 miles), 3,392 calories, 251 active minutes

Day 2 – Thames Head to Cricklade: 39,106 steps, 28.08 kilometres (17.55 miles), 3,706 calories, 338 active minutes

Day 3 – Cricklade to Lechlade: 41,247 steps, 29.62 kilometres (18.51 miles), 3,998 calories, 345 active minutes

Day 4 – Lechlade to Newbridge: 43,485 steps, 31.22 kilometres (19.51 miles), 3,994 calories, 363 active minutes

Day 5 – Newbridge to Oxford: 45,714 steps, 32.82 kilometres (20.51 miles), 4,089 calories, 406 active minutes

Day 6 – Oxford to Abingdon: 31,053 steps, 22.30 kilometres (13.93 miles), 3,333 calories, 245 active minutes

Day 7 – Abingdon to Wallingford: 46,123 steps, 33.12 kilometres (20.70 miles), 4,600 calories, 402 active minutes

Day 8 – Wallingford to Pangbourne: 30,823 steps, 21.25 kilometres (13.28 miles), 3,215 calories, 222 active minutes

Day 9 – Pangbourne to Henley: 46,357 steps, 33.83 kilometres (21.14 miles), 4,323 calories, 371 active minutes

Day 10 – Henley to Marlow: 35,239 steps, 25.30 kilometres (15.81 miles), 3,660 calories, 313 active minutes

Day 11 – Marlow to Eton: 47,734 steps, 34.27 kilometres (21.41 miles), 4,356 calories, 408 active minutes

Day 12 – Eton to Staines: 41,234 steps, 29.61 kilometres (18.50 miles), 4,041 calories, 343 active minutes

Day 13 – Staines to Hampton Court: 41,639 steps, 29.90 kilometres (18.68 miles), 4,004 calories, 363 active minutes

Day 14 – Hampton Court to Kew: 35,907 steps, 25.78 kilometres (16.11 miles), 3,555 calories, 315 active minutes

Day 15 – Kew to Bermondsey: 53,615 steps, 38.87 kilometres (24.29 miles), 4,779 calories, 468 active minutes

Day 16 – Bermondsey to Greenwich: 31,912 steps, 22.91 kilometres (14.32 miles), 3,520 calories, 290 active minutes

Day 17 – Greenwich to Thamesmead: 31,866 steps, 22.88 kilometres (14.30 miles), 3,200 calories, 273 active minutes

Day 18 – Thamesmead to Gravesend: 54,742 steps, 39.30 kilometres (24.56 miles), 4,734 calories, 480 active minutes

Day 19 – Gravesend to Cooling: 33,057 steps, 23.74 kilometres (14.83 miles), 3,527 calories, 323 active minutes

Day 20 – Cooling to the Isle of Grain: 47,206 steps, 33.92 kilometres (21.20 miles), 4,292 calories, 462 active minutes

Day 21 – The Isle of Grain: 13,120 steps, 9.42 kilometres (5.88 miles), 1,305 calories, 119 active minutes

Total distance covered: 590.07 kilometres (368.72 miles)

Average daily distance covered: 28.09 kilometres (17.56 miles), about par for the course for a soldier marching in the Roman army (which is rather strange to think of, although my backpack did not weigh as much as a Roman legionnaire's kit)

Total number of steps: 821,722

Total calories burnt: 79,623

Total 'active minutes': 7,100 (118.33 hours or 4.93 sets of 24 hours)

OVERNIGHT STAYS

- The Thames Head Inn, near Kemble, Gloucestershire
  www.thamesheadinn.co.uk

- The White Hart, Cricklade, Wiltshire:
  www.thewhitehartcricklade.co.uk

- The Riverside, Lechlade, Gloucestershire
  www.riverside-lechlade.com

- The Shepherd's Hut, Newbridge, Oxfordshire
  www.themaybush.com

- The Head of the River, Oxford
  www.headoftheriveroxford.co.uk

- Susie Howard B & B, Abingdon, Oxfordshire
  www.abingdonbedandbreakfast.com

- The Coachmakers Arms, Wallingford, Oxfordshire
  www.coachmakersarmswallingford.co.uk

- The George Hotel, Pangbourne, Berkshire
  www.georgehotelpangbourne.com

- Nicola's Airbnb, Henley-upon-Thames, Oxfordshire
  www.airbnb.co.uk

- The Prince of Wales, Marlow, Buckinghamshire
  www.the-prince-of-wales.co.uk

- The Crown and Cushion, Eton, Berkshire
  www.thecrownandcushioneton.co.uk

- The Swan Hotel, Staines, Surrey
  www.swanstaines.co.uk

- The Mitre Hotel, Hampton Court
  www.mitrehamptoncourt.com (under new ownership since my
  visit and it has changed its name from the Carlton Mitre Hotel)

- The Coach and Horses, Kew
  www.coachhotelkew.co.uk

- The King William Hotel, Greenwich
  www.thekingwilliamhotel.co.uk

- London Belvedere – Travelodge, Belvedere
  www.travelodge.co.uk

- The Clarendon Royal, Gravesend, Kent
  www.clarendonroyalhotel.co.uk

- The Horseshoe and Castle, Cooling, Kent
  www.horseshoeand castle.com

- The Lodge Guest House, Isle of Grain, Kent
  www.thelodgeisleofgrain.com

No hospitality was taken.

PUBS VISITED

- The Thames Head Inn, near Kemble, Gloucestershire
  www.thamesheadinn.co.uk

- The White Hart, Cricklade, Wiltshire
  www.thewhitehartcricklade.co.uk

- The Red Lion, Cricklade, Wiltshire
  www.theredlioncricklade.co.uk

- The Red Lion, Castle Eaton, Wiltshire
  www.red-lion.co.uk

- The Riverside, Lechlade, Gloucestershire
  www.riverside-lechlade.com

- The New Inn Hotel, Lechlade, Gloucestershire
  www.thenewinnhotel.co.uk

- The Plough Inn, Kelmscott, Oxfordshire
  www.theploughinnkelmscott.com

- The Trout at Tadpole Bridge, Buckland Marsh, Oxfordshire
  www.troutinn.co.uk

- The Rose Revived, Newbridge, Oxfordshire
  www.oldenglishinns.co.uk

- The Perch, Binsey, Oxfordshire
  www.the-perch.co.uk

- The Head of the River, Oxford
  www.headoftheriveroxford.co.uk

- Kings Arms, Sandford, Oxfordshire
  www.chefandbrewer.com

- The Barley Mow, Clifton Hampden, Oxfordshire
  www.chefandbrewer.com

- The Coachmakers Arms, Wallingford, Oxfordshire
  www.coachmakersarmswallingford.co.uk

- The Beetle and Wedge, Moulsford, Oxfordshire
  www.beetleandwedge.co.uk

- The Bull, Streatley, Berkshire
  www.bullinnpub.co.uk

- The Swan, Pangbourne, Berkshire
  www.swanpangbourne.co.uk

- The Bull Inn, Sonning, Berkshire
  www.bullinnsonning.co.uk

- The Angel on the Bridge, Henley, Oxfordshire
  www.theangelhenley.com

- The Flower Pot, Aston, Oxfordshire
  www.brakspear.co.uk

- The Olde Bell, Hurley, Berkshire
  www.theoldebell.co.uk

- The Prince of Wales, Marlow, Buckinghamshire
  www.the-prince-of-wales.co.uk

- The Hand and Flowers, Marlow, Buckinghamshire
  www.thehandandflowers.co.uk

- The Hinds Head, Bray, Berkshire
  www.hindsheadbray.com

- The Crown and Cushion, Eton, Berkshire
  www.thecrownandcushioneton.co.uk

- The Swan, Staines, Surrey
  www.swanstaines.co.uk

- The George, Staines, Surrey
  www.jdwetherspoon.com

- The Anglers, Walton-on-Thames, Surrey
  www.anglerswalton.com

- The Weir, Walton-on-Thames, Surrey
  www.weirhotel.co.uk

- The London Apprentice, Isleworth
  www.taylor-walker.co.uk

- The Coach and Horses, Kew
  www.coachhotelkew.co.uk

- The Grapes, Limehouse
  www.thegrapes.co.uk

- The Prospect of Whitby, Wapping
  www.taylor-walker.co.uk

- The Captain Kidd, Wapping
  no website, so see www.londonist.com

- Town of Ramsgate, Wapping
  www.townoframsgate.pub

- The Angel, Rotherhithe
  no website, so see www.londonist.com

- The Mayflower, Rotherhithe
  www.mayflowerpub.co.uk

- Anchor and Hope, Charlton
  www.anchorandhope.co.uk

- The Morgan, Belvedere
  www.themorganpubbelvedere.co.uk

- Three Daws, Gravesend, Kent
  www.threedaws.co.uk

- The Ship and Lobster, Gravesend, Kent
  no website, so see entry in www.pubshistory.com

- The Six Bells, Cliffe, Kent
  www.sixbellscliffe.co.uk

- The Horseshoe and Castle, Cooling, Kent
  www.horseshoeandcastle.com

- The British Pilot, Allhallows, Kent
  no website, so see www.whatpub.com

- The Hogarth Inn, Isle of Grain, Kent
  see www.beerintheevening.com

- The White Hart, Barnes
  www.whitehartbarnes.co.uk

No hospitality was taken. All prices mentioned at both pubs and hotels may have changed.

NOTES ON WILD FLOWERS

I am no botanist but walking along the river I came across many interesting wild flowers. As I did, I wished I knew what they were as there were so many unusual varieties. In order to identify them later, I took pictures. I believed it would be a simple matter of looking on the internet at home and matching what I saw with the images. I was wrong to think this. I asked my mother, Christine Doyle, who is both a keen gardener and a journalist, whether she could help. She put her hands up and said that these wild flowers were beyond her. So she took my pictures to the botanist John Fielding, who is the author of the cult book *Flowers of Crete* and lives on the same street as my parents. He managed to identify all of the wild flowers, and a few of what turned out to be weeds-with-flowers. Here, using his expertise and my mother's words, is a quick rundown. To match the descriptions to the images I took, go to www.tomchesshyre.co.uk and look for the 'Thames wild flowers' in the Gallery section.

- **The Great Willowherb (or Hairy Willowherb, because it is covered in fine hairy down) –** *Epilobium hirsutum*: very tall with deep pink/purple flowers. Common in damp habitats.

- **Himalayan Balsam –** *Impatiens glandulifera*: one of the tallest wild plants, it can reach 2.5 metres. Deep pink. It is a spreading wild plant, especially by rivers, and is said to be changing wild flower ecology. It is poisonous to horses and cattle. It is more of a 'weed' that should be controlled.

- **Hollyhock –** *Alcea rosea*: very widespread, an attractive wild flower found in a range of habitats. Deep pink.

- **Field Bindweed – *Convolvulus arvensis*:** pretty and merrily rampant, as is the white form in gardens and allotments. Pink and white.

- **Comfrey – *Symphytum officinale*:** also known as Common Comfrey. A plant with tubular purple, pink or cream flowers. It is used in herbal medicine and is said to ease pain and stimulate healing. Many gardeners grow comfrey to make a rich green manure.

- **Sweet Pea – *Lathyrus odoratus*:** unlike the garden sweet pea, they come back year after year. They are, though, increasingly rare. A delicate range of pink tinged with white and purplish pink.

- **Hemp-Agrimony – *Eupatorium cannabinum*:** a tall plant with tiny clusters of small pink-white flowers and long-toothed leaflets. Some call it the 'raspberries and cream plant'. The name comes from its likeness to Hemp Cannabis, but it is not related!

- **Brown Knapweed – *Centaurea nemoralis*:** a thistle-like weed often found in damp areas. It is one of a group of knapweeds which can poison horses and is hated by farmers.

- **Marjoram – *Origanum vulgare*:** produces pink flowers, and very like the Mediterranean version used in cooking. The scent of the wild British marjoram is a little different, but the leaves are still an excellent walkers' find for the kitchen.

- **Woody Nightshade or Poisonberry – *Solanum dulcamara*:** this has clusters of purple flowers and red berries that are poisonous. The plant scrambles across shrubs and up trees. It is called 'bittersweet' because the red berries have a sweet taste at first which rapidly becomes increasingly bitter, so 'accidents' through overeating it are rare.

- **Evening Primrose – *Oenothera biennis*:** a wild flower 'tar' with prolific yellow flowers that open at dusk and fade by noon the following day. Studies suggest that evening primrose oils and creams help to ease a wide range of conditions, such as asthma, migraines, rheumatoid arthritis and heart disease.

- **Yellow Ragwort** – *Senecio jacobaea*: bright yellow flower heads and straggly growth. This plant is best described as a pernicious weed rather than a charming wild flower. Farmers dread this plant appearing in their fields because leaves contain toxic chemicals that are deadly to horses and cattle.

- **St John's Wort** – *Hypericum perforatum*: it has yellow flowers and is widely held by alternative-health therapists to relieve the symptoms of depression. Clinical studies, though, are mixed.

BIBLIOGRAPHY

Ackroyd, Peter *Thames: Sacred River* (2008, Vintage)

Belloc, Hilaire *The Historic Thames: A Portrait of England's Greatest River* (1988, Webb & Bower; first published in 1907)

Carroll, Lewis *Alice's Adventures in Wonderland* (1994, Penguin; first published in 1865)

Chaucer, Geoffrey *The Riverside Chaucer* (2008, Oxford University Press)

Clapham, Phoebe *Thames Path in London: From Hampton Court to Crayford Ness: 50 Miles of Historic Riverside Walk* (2012, Aurum Press)

Conrad, Joseph *Heart of Darkness and the Secret Sharer* (1950, Signet Classics; first published in 1910)

Cowley, Abraham *Selected Poems* (1994, Fyfield Books; first published in the seventeenth century)

Dickens, Charles *Great Expectations* (1985, Penguin; first published in 1860–1861)

Dickens, Charles *Our Mutual Friend* (1997, Wordsworth Classics; first published in 1865)

Dickens, Charles *The Mystery of Edwin Drood* (1896, Chapman & Hall; first published in 1870)

Dickens, Charles Jr *Dickens's Dictionary of the Thames, 1887: An Unconventional Handbook* (1994, Old House Books)

Fathers, David *The London Thames Path: A Guide to the Thames Path from Putney Bridge to the Barrier* (2015, Frances Lincoln)

Goldsack, Paul *River Thames: In the Footsteps of the Famous* (2003, Bradt)

Grahame, Kenneth *The Wind in the Willows* (1993, Wordsworth Editions; first published in 1908)

Hall, Mr S. C. and Mrs A. M. *The Book of the Thames: From Its Rise to Its Fall* (1983, Charlotte James Publishers; first published in 1859)

Hampson, Tim *London's Riverside Pubs: A Guide to the Best of London's Riverside Watering Holes* (2011, New Holland Publishers)

Hardyment, Christina *Writing the Thames* (2016, the Bodleian Library)

Huw Davies, Gareth *A Walk Along the Thames Path* (1990, Michael Joseph)

Jerome, Jerome K. *Three Men in a Boat* (1994, Penguin; first published in 1889)

Kneale, Matthew *Sweet Thames* (2001, Penguin; first published in 1992)

Lambe, Stephen *The 'Three Men in a Boat' Companion: The Thames of Jerome K. Jerome* (2013, Amberley Publishing)

Lichtenstein, Rachel *Estuary: Out from London to the Sea* (2016, Hamish Hamilton)

Long, Roger *Historic Inns Along the River Thames* (2006, Sutton Publishing)

McDowall, David *The Walker's Guide: The Thames: Hampton to Richmond Bridge* (2002, David McDowall)

McDowall, David *The Walker's Guide: The Thames: Richmond to Putney Bridge* (2005, David McDowall)

Morris, William *News from Nowhere* (1993, Penguin; first published in 1890)

Morton, H. V. *H. V. Morton's London* (1949, Methuen & Co.; first published in 1940)

Newton, Joel *Thames Path: Thames Head to the Thames Barrier* (2015, Trailblazer Publications); this was my favourite guidebook

Sharp, David and Gowers, Tony *Thames Path in the Country* (2012, Aurum Press)

Tindall, Gillian *The House by the Thames and the People Who Lived There* (2007, Pimlico)

Tomalin, Claire *Charles Dickens: A Life* (2011, Viking)

Winn, Christopher *I Never Knew That About the River Thames* (2010, Ebury Press)

INDEX

Have you enjoyed this book?
If so, why not write a review on your favourite website?

If you're interested in finding out more about our books,
find us on Facebook at **Summersdale Publishers**
and follow us on Twitter at **@Summersdale**.

Thanks very much for buying this Summersdale book.

www.summersdale.com